Transnational Management and Globalised Workers

There are 60 million health care workers globally and most of this workforce consists of nurses, as they are key providers of primary health care. Historically, the global nurse occupation has been predominately female and segregated along gendered, racialised and classed hierarchies. In the last decade, new actors have emerged in the management of health care human resources, specifically from the corporate sector, which has created new interactions, networks, and organisational practices.

This book urgently calls for the reconceptualisation in the theoretical framing of the globalised nurse occupation from International Human Resource Management (IHRM) to Transnational Human Resource Management (THRM). Specifically, the book draws on critical human resource management literature and transnational feminist theories to frame the strategies and practices used to manage nurses across geographical sites of knowledge production and power, which centralise on how and by whom nurses are managed. In its current managerial form, the author argues that the nurses are constructed and produced as resources to be packaged for clients in public and private organisations.

Transnational Management of Globalised Workers strives to broaden the theoretical and empirical examination of migrating nurses to encompass the transnational management of private and public organisational representatives engaging in recruitment and placement practices. Furthermore, the book is critical of international human resource management as a discipline and practice, and discursively analyses structural and societal issues of control and compliance of the historically gendered and racialised occupation of nursing. To illustrate this argument, the author provides what she calls 'a situation' to place transnational management of nurses in a Nordic welfare state, Finland, by recanting the practices of Finnish private and public representatives producing care by recruiting registered nurses from the Philippines to work in Finnish elderly care services and hospitals.

This book will be of interest to researchers, academics, policymakers, and students in the fields of health care systems and management, migration studies, sociology, gender and race studies, and critical management and organisational studies.

Tricia Cleland Silva is a Lecturer and Post Doctoral Researcher at Hanken School of Economics, Finland. She is the co-founder of Metaphora International, a consultancy that works with finding meaning in management and strategy through stories and metaphors.

Routledge Studies in Employment and Work Relations in Context

Edited by Tony Elger and Peter Fairbrother

The aim of the *Employment and Work Relations in Context Series* is to address questions relating to the evolving patterns and politics of work, employment, management and industrial relations. There is a concern to trace out the ways in which wider policy-making, especially by national governments and transnational corporations, impinges upon specific workplaces, occupations, labour markets, localities and regions. This invites attention to developments at an international level, marking out patterns of globalization, state policy and practices in the context of globalization and the impact of these processes on labour. A particular feature of the series is the consideration of forms of worker and citizen organization and mobilization. The studies address major analytical and policy issues through case study and comparative research.

Rediscovering Collective Bargaining
Australia's Fair Work Act in International Perspective
Edited by Breen Creighton and Anthony Forsyth

Transnational Trade Unionism
Building Union Power
Peter Fairbrother, Marc-Antonin Hennebert, and Christian Lévesque

Temporary Work, Agencies and Unfree Labour
Insecurity in the New World of Work
Edited by Judy Fudge and Kendra Strauss

Human Resource Management in Emerging Economies
Piotr Zientara

The Origins of Worker Mobilisation
Australia 1788–1850
Michael Quinlan

Transnational Management of Globalised Workers
Nurses Beyond Human Resources
Tricia Cleland Silva

Transnational Management and Globalised Workers

Nurses Beyond Human Resources

Tricia Cleland Silva

Routledge
Taylor & Francis Group
LONDON AND NEW YORK

First published 2019 by Routledge

2 Park Square, Milton Park, Abingdon, Oxon, OX14 4RN
605 Third Avenue, New York, NY 10017

Routledge is an imprint of the Taylor & Francis Group, an informa business

First issued in paperback 2020

Library of Congress Cataloging-in-Publication Data
Names: Cleland Silva, Tricia, author.
Title: Transnational management and globalised workers : nurses beyond human resources / Tricia Cleland Silva.
Other titles: Routledge studies in employment and work relations in context.
Description: New York, NY : Routledge, 2018. | Series: Routledge studies in employment and work relations in context | Includes bibliographical references.
Identifiers: LCCN 2018016447 | ISBN 9781138614017 (hardback) | ISBN 9780429464256 (ebook)
Subjects: | MESH: Nursing—manpower | Nurses, International—supply & distribution | Personnel Selection | Internationality | Socioeconomic Factors | Finland | Philippines
Classification: LCC HD5724 | NLM WY 16 GF5 | DDC 331.13/602461073—dc23
LC record available at https://lccn.loc.gov/2018016447

ISBN: 978-1-138-61401-7 (hbk)
ISBN: 978-0-367-73400-8 (pbk)

Typeset in Sabon
by Apex CoVantage, LLC

To Paulo and the roots we nurture together in our transnational life

Contents

Figures

Tables

Context Boxes

Preface

Human beings are social. Social, in the sense, that, as humans, we construct our realities through socialised values and symbols that we receive as children through our families, schools, peers, and communities.

For social constructionists, who had a strong influence on this book, taken-for-granted realities are formed through our social interactions. Through these social interactions, multiple realities compete for truth and legitimacy, and the way we speak about objects and people may not mirror reality but rather create it.

In this spirit, I would like to propose that we reflect for a moment on what it is to be a nurse. What are your reflections when asked these questions?

> When you think of a nurse, what first comes to mind? What does this person look like? What does this person do? Now, think about when you are sick, what type of care would you like or expect? And if your parents were sick or not capable of taking care themselves due to age? Or your children? Who would you expect to provide this care? And, where would you go?

In my research journey for this book, these questions were continuously in my mind. During my research, I had many discussions and debates on what it is to be a nurse and what does nurse work entail, especially when it comes to something as intimate as care for oneself or loved ones. Who has the authority to define what it is to be a nurse or what is care? How does the way the nurse occupation is spoken about affect who is chosen to work as a hired nurse? How does talk affect the day-to-day working conditions of a nurse? And, what happens when a nurse is hired from outside a country in which the employers, thousands of kilometres away, have decided on what it is to be a nurse and what nurse work entails in the employers' country?

In the situated story of this book, these questions were the essence of what I wanted to investigate. Who is claiming authority of how nurses should be transnationally recruited and placed into Finnish organisations? What type of talk and text are being used to socially construct the non-Finnish-educated nurse, and in this particular case, the Filipino nurse? How does talk and text influence practices of hiring and placement or future policies and practices on how to create and maintain a workforce?

This book, through maps of organisational social worlds, which are based on work commitments and actions, wants to metaphorically explain how nurses are produced for particular care networks in Finland. What I want to illustrate with the maps to the reader is that individual representatives and their associated organisations emerge onto the maps with particular organisational commitments such as providing care workers for paying clients, which made certain claims more dominant and others silent.

Finland is, in recent times at least, a relatively new destination for internationally educated nurses in particular and work-related immigration in general. Until the late 1990s, Finland was mainly sending nurses abroad, particularly to other Nordic and European countries like the UK, and the country continues to be a 'source' for nurses. Today, there are an estimated 9,000 Finnish-educated nurses living abroad.

Finland is a welfare state in which accessible, equal health care is constitutionally a guaranteed right to all its residents. The legislative aim is a socially sustainable society in which everyone is treated fairly, where social inclusion and participation are encouraged, and everyone's health is promoted and supported through services equally available to all its citizens. In the Finnish health care sector, there is hardly any unemployment, rather a lack of workforce, especially in rural regions. It is estimated that, by 2025, 20,000 health care professionals will be needed but the figure might be as high as 59,000.

And yet, some scholars have argued that fewer people are being attracted or retained in the nursing occupation. For instance, over 38,000 Finnish-educated nurses are not working in the health care field. Similar to Finland, in both developed and developing countries, careers in health care are also becoming less attractive unless it is a means to migrate. With this in mind, however, research has also shown that many migrant nurses are unable to use all their existing skills, and that much of nurse migration has largely been associated with deskilling. In addition, although many nurses are able to transfer their qualifications across borders, they generally do not advance in their careers and experience downward mobility in terms of occupational seniority and overall financial status. Furthermore, contractual work permits in nursing, which are based on employers' needs and nationalised standards of qualifications of the nursing profession, have created both female migratory tracks towards lower-status professional segments and new intra-professional divisions that reflect the status of citizenship and the place of graduation for migrant nurse workers.

Migrant and domestic nurses also struggle with a common assumption that a *nurse is a nurse is a nurse*, which entails that all nurses are the same in qualifications, education, and experience and that a nurse can be 'substituted' for another position. This leads to nurses being offered positions that do not suit their qualifications and masks the established hierarchy of global nurses that create experiences for migrating nurses based on their skin colour, ethnic origin, or language skills. Historically, nursing, an occupation that requires advanced education, skill building and experience, continuously struggles to identify its worth among traditionally male-dominated health care fields, such as medicine, dentistry, and public health in tangible ways: salary, prestige, and work conditions.

Today, the amount of internationally educated nurses living and working in Finland remains low, at 1.4% of the total personnel, of which 86% are women. Nonetheless, there has been a growing interest in foreign recruitment of nurses in Finland, especially since 2006 when immigration was adopted as a means to alleviate shortages in the Finnish labour market. In fact, since 2007, there has been a number of recruitment projects that have developed models for the international recruitment of social and health care personnel. The majority of foreign nurses in Finland come from the neighbouring and EU countries, but Asian and African countries are also significant source countries, including the Philippines.

Recent political and economic practices within the global health care industry have created a competitive market amongst countries that equates to big business. Parallel reforms within Nordic welfare regimes have shifted employer's responsibilities from permanent, stable, unionised labour to more flexible and inexpensive labour.

However, some scholars have argued that although the private investment of recruitment, training and placement is extremely expensive, the profit may not be as high as the employers had hoped. It has been documented that some migrating nurses use countries as 'stepping stones' to acquire skills and experience in order to move to another country where the working conditions are deemed as better. This recognises the agency of the migrant nurse but also raises the question of the need to understand and change the local work conditions to better suit nurses in order to retain the nurses to sustain a future workforce, which is much needed in all countries.

In this book, I want to dig deeper into organisational practices of recruitment and placement that serve to construct internationally educated nurses and their day-to-day work. I also want to know who in these Finnish organisations, either directly involved or not, were claiming to be experts on how nurses should be selected and recruited and how the nurses should be managed once in the workplace. In general, I want to understand how the Finnish nursing occupation and the recruited nurses from the Philippines were being constructed through talk and text, and what implications would this have for inclusion of the recruited nurse in the workforce but also the type of care expected for the so-called Finnish clients.

I argue in this book that language does matter. Talk influences our local surroundings and expectations of each other and our institutions of democracy, as well as national and local security such as policing, education, and health and social services, to name a few.

In the case of public health care, there is not one individual who decides on the provision of care. Public health care materialises out of a historical evolution of institutionalised practices and constructed work roles of health care occupations that are legitimised through legislation and expectations for its presence and relevance. In Finland, the practice of accessible, equal health care for all its residents is constitutionally guaranteed and continues to serve as political and social issues within peoples' homes, the media, and the public domain. When it comes to care, the issues are close to people as, in human nature, we all get sick. That is one thing about being human. Everyone gets sick. And, if life allows, most of us will get old and eventually our bodies will need care.

As pointed out in this book, nursing as an occupation is dominated by females all over the world. Care has also often been historically associated with women's work, and these assumptions have served to legitimise and reproduce the structuring of care within the home and public organisations. The assumptions have also materialised in the form of global care chains that not only reflect the dominance of women but also hierarchies of race, nationalities, and classes in an unequal economy of trade and resource distribution.

Taken-for-granted assumptions should be problematised both within the practices of how nurses are selected and placed but also in the academic discipline of examining and discussing these practices. This reflective approach means going beyond what is considered the 'normal' expectations of care and the occupation and dig deeper in understanding the social and material implications of talk, texts, and interactions that promote either inclusion or exclusion. In order to have a workforce, we need to care about the workers and their work. This means valuing the worker's time, their identities, and work but also striving for various ways of management that include workers that, in turn, retain and sustain the workforce. In other words, moving beyond human resources with a central focus on the nurses.

1 Transnational Management of Globalised Workers

Nurses Beyond Human Resources

Introduction

The recruitment and placement of nurse labour from economically poor countries to more affluent countries are not new phenomena. Private nursing schools in the Philippines have been training a large number of nurses for the economically rich labour markets, particularly the United States, since the 1950s (see Choy, 2003). The current patterns of transnational health-labour migration from poor to more affluent countries represent a new phenomenon, however. Even though large numbers of third-world nurses migrated transnationally before the 1990s, they moved along established migration pathways that existed between countries with long-term historical ties and legacies of imperialism and colonialism. Traditional destinations for nurses from third-world countries included the United States, Canada, Australia, New Zealand, France, Germany, and the United Kingdom, all of which benefited from their ties to specific 'donor' countries (Brush et al., 2004).

Since the 1980s, however, newly affluent destination countries and poor donor countries have emerged, with different trajectories explaining their entry into the global health care labour market. In some new destinations, countries' increasing demand for migrant nurses results from rising affluence; in others, structural labour shortages related to the diversification of women's employment and demographic developments such as an ageing population serve as an explanation (for instance in Saudi Arabia, Southern Europe, and Ireland; Yeates, 2009). In other new country destinations, changes in the organisation of welfare services provide a central explanation for the rising interest in recruiting nurses transnationally (Dahl and Eriksen, 2005; Dahl, 2012).

This book explores emerging human resource practices in a Nordic welfare state, internationally renowned for universal health and social care as well as gender equality. Traditionally, the affluent Nordic countries recruited nurses mainly within the Nordic region, where cultural ties are comparatively close and all of the countries have extensive welfare states (Wrede et al., 2008; Isaksen, 2010). In the Nordic context, the new practice of managing a labour market through transnational recruitment and placing activities is related to welfare state reforms aimed at increasing labour flexibility (Wrede, 2010; Näre and Wrede, 2013). This book examines how nursing work is transnationally managed as a resource through interactions of representatives, both private and public, working to acquire quantities of predetermined 'human resources'. This reflects a broader, historical management pattern of the nursing occupation.

To illustrate this phenomenon, the book describes the emerging human resource management practices of nurse work in Finland by private and public representatives of nurses from the Philippines. The analysis identifies private and public representatives that are managing the transnationalisation of nurse labour in terms of which representatives and organisations are asserting authority over how nurse labour is transnationally produced and relocated to Finland.

A central argument of this book is that even though the nursing labour market remains anchored in the Finnish welfare state, the emerging recruitment and placement practices globalise the demands associated with nursing work with the aim of increasing labour flexibility. For the private actors, imported nurses are a source of making and saving money. For that purpose, they compete on global markets for suitable nurses and seek to manage their human resources for their clients. The book further argues that the process of managing nurses as marketable 'products' for possible clients reproduces not only traditional social hierarchies within nursing at the organisational level, but also within national and transnational levels, impacting the lives of both migrant and domestic nurses in tangible ways (wages, job security, occupational mobility, work/family balance). Historically, nurse work and its workforce have been segregated along gendered, racialised, and classed hierarchies. The social categories constituted around gender, race, and class have essentially designated certain groups of workers into specific divisions of labour within the health care market (Apesoa-Varano and Varano, 2004; Chang, 2000).

Transnational Human Resource Management of Nurse Labour

Nursing, as an occupation, has increased in demand over the last decade and recruitment by organisations in developed countries from less developed countries has intensified. Many scholars, policymakers, and human resource (HR) practitioners argue that this increase in demand is due to 'push' and 'pull' factors such as better pay and working conditions in recipient countries than sending countries (push) and changing demographics worldwide that place strain on health care systems due to an ageing population (pull).

However, the scope and magnitude of the current process of migration has created a 'carousel' of international nurse mobility (Kingma, 2006), causing the dichotomous nature of 'push' and 'pull' to be limited in its explanation.

What was once a one-way exchange among a number of developed and developing countries has become a more complicated and circuitous stream of nurses flowing in new directions and patterns (Brush, 2008). As such, greater competition and demand for these nurse migrants among recruiting countries has created a market demand that is translated into big business (Brush et al., 2004) and encompasses not only micro explanations of push/pull but also a macro context of trade and uneven development.

Demands for nursing from areas such as the Middle East (Saudi Arabia, Kuwait, Libya, Iran, Bahrain, and Iraq), Asia (Japan), the UK, North America (Canada and the United States), and Australia have amplified the importation and exportation process of these skilled workers (Brush and Vaspuram, 2006; Buchan et al., 2003). In response, countries such as the Philippines and India are producing nurses in greater numbers than required to satisfy domestic demand to send abroad (Choy, 2003; George, 2005). Simultaneously, countries such as China and South Korea are also following the Philippines and India as an example to export their own human resources (George, 2005; Percot, 2006). In addition, other professionals such as doctors and lawyers in the Philippines are being driven into the nursing profession in order to be exported abroad (Galvez-Tan et al., 2004).

Although there is an increase in demand for active recruitment of nurses in all countries worldwide, in many countries, fewer people are being attracted to the health care profession domestically. For example, while nursing is an occupation requiring advanced education and skill building, it continually struggles to identify its worth among more traditionally male-dominated health care fields such as medicine, dentistry, and public health in tangible ways: salary, prestige, and work conditions (Apesoa-Varano and Varano, 2004; Melchior, 2004). Subsequently, in both developed and developing countries, careers in health care are becoming less attractive unless it is a means to migrate (Connell, 2008: 24). With this in mind, however, research has shown that migrant workers are unable to use all their existing skills and migration has largely been associated with deskilling (Ribeiro, 2008; Kingma, 2006). In addition, although many nurses are able to transfer their qualifications across borders, they generally do not advance in their careers and experience downward mobility in terms of occupational seniority and overall financial status (Ho, 2008; McNeil-Walsh, 2008). Furthermore, as pointed out by Ribeiro's study (2008), the institutional conditions and regulatory mechanisms of the nursing profession creates both female migratory tracks towards low-status professional segments and new intra-professional divisions alongside the status of citizenship and the place of graduation for migrant workers.

In 1995, Davies notes that nursing is highly gendered, and management—as well as the nursing work itself—requires the re-examination of nursing as an occupation in which gendered processes and relations are re-enacted on a daily basis in organisations and power dynamics. Davies also argues that, through specific management practices, nursing has been correlated with 'disposable labour'. Subsequently, nursing labour and its human resources are flexible, complaint, replaceable, and, in the end, disposable.

These circuitous and transnational patterns of nurse migration and the transfer of care from one health care system to another—which are embedded in gendered and racial social divisions—denotes the importance of understanding further the management and organisation of migrating nurses.

Within the discipline of international human resource management (IHRM), the conceptualisation of transnational has been used to explain corporate HR systems in terms of practices and strategic processes (Festing and Eidems, 2011: 162), but the actual term 'international' has not been subjected to analytical criticism or replaced with a deeper understanding of what transnational means. The discipline of IHRM, within management and organisation studies, continues to view the processes and practices of managing people across borders in terms of a duality between centralisation (or global integration) versus decentralisation (or local responsiveness) or 'international' as in 'between nation-states' (Ståhl et al., 2012). This analytical understanding of the geographical (or locational) management of human resources, I argue, has narrowed the empirical focus within IHRM to multinational corporations (MNCs) by focusing solely on headquarters and subsidiaries as well as expatriates, specifically from the West. As raised by management and organisation scholars, 'transnational' as a concept is critical to the function of national borders, but also the concept of 'international' encapsulates the organisation and management of migrating people, either paid or unpaid workers, or the movement of people for various other reasons (Hearn et al., 2008). Hearn conceptualises 'transnational' as the nation and its borders being affirmed and deconstructed simultaneously (2004: 278). More specifically, Hearn defines 'trans' as

> moving across something or between two or more somethings, in this case, across national boundaries or between nations; metamorphosing, problematizing, blurring, transgressing, breaking down, even dissolving something(s), in the case, nations or national boundaries-in the most extreme case, leading to the demise of nation or national boundaries.

'Trans' and its subsequent associations such as transmigration, trans-organisation, and transcommunities stress the shift from a monolithic, centralised conceptualisation of management and the operations of organisation and management. As a result, transnational organisation, management and processes can be understood in the context of the global, political economy, and its associated social divisions and inequalities around class, gender, ethniciti-sation/racialisation, etc. (Locke Swarr and Nagar, 2010; Hearn, 2004: 285; Cleland Silva, 2010: 106).

In this book, I strive to reconceptualise IHRM as a discipline to transnational human resource management (THRM). This reconceptualisation,

I argue, broadens not only the theorisation beyond the national borders and the enterprise, but provides a space for health care sectors and human services in terms of empirical exploration into the management of people in a transnational context. Henry Mintzberg recently wrote that he 'can think of no other field that is more global in its professional practices yet more parochial in its administrative ones than health care' (2017: 6). I would argue that the need for nursing is a global demand, and yet, the management of the occupation is systematically practiced within the unequal notions of gender and ethnicity, which are both, simultaneously, localised and globalised.

In the following chapters, this book situates a study that focuses on how, in the years 2007 to 2010, five groups of nurses from the Philippines were recruited and transnationally managed and organised to live and work in Finland for both private elderly care facilities and surgical wards in Finnish municipal hospitals. Through the case, the work is critical of IHRM as a discipline and practice and discursively analyses structural and societal issues of control and compliance of the historically gendered and racialised occupation of nursing. Furthermore, the transnational processes and movement of human capital from the Philippines to Finland is discussed in terms of (re) producing the managerial practices of nurse work, which create barriers to equality in the workplace but also construct life patterns that conflict with the situated life patterns of the nurses.

Aim of the Book

I argue in this book that to understand transnational management of nurses, we need to explore organisations and representatives whose work is to manage the nurses within their associated 'social worlds' (Strauss, 1978, 1979, 1982a, 1982b). Social worlds are structurally situated, interactive units of analysis that consist of representatives making collective meaning of and acting from at least one primary activity (e.g. management of nurses). Social worlds are structured in society so much so that, 'we can bet with relative safety[,] will remain basically "in place" and predictable over some time' (Clarke, 1991: 129). The difference between social worlds, therefore, is the degree of structuration. In other words, the social world's 'staying power' (see Giddens (1979) on structuration).

Social worlds interact in an arena. An arena is 'a field of action and interaction among a potentially wide variety of collective entities. It is a meso/macro level, voluntaristically oriented, collective-action approach' (Clarke, 1991: 128). Social worlds function in a field of action through the representatives negotiating, maintaining boundaries, and gaining social legitimisation of the social world itself through the representatives' work practices and discourses. An arena of a field of study can be metaphorically perceived as a 'battle field' (Clarke, 1991) of competing commitments and actions that are believed to be meaningful to representatives of the associated social world. As such, social world/arena theory 'aims at capturing, describing, and thus rendering susceptible to analysis the multiple simultaneous organized actions of individuals, groups of various sorts, and formal organizations' (Clarke, 1991: 131).

To develop this understanding of social interactions and associated social worlds, the book uses mapping and maps suggested in the method of situational analysis (Clarke, 2005). Through the analysis of interviews, the book creates and illustrates maps of social worlds in which representatives and organisations transnationally manage nurses through practices and discourses. The maps are considered products of the analysis of spatial representation, and mapping is considered a byproduct of storytelling and the retelling of a journey made. In this case, the story is about the transnational management of nurses framed by the question 'who cares about the recruitment and placement of Filipino nurses into Finnish institutions and what do they want to do about it?' Through this situated question, the representatives and the discourses are discussed around the expected work commitments of the identified social worlds in the arena or battle field.

The managerial practices constituting the human resource management of foreign nurses in Finland did not emerge in a vacuum. In the era of economic globalisation, the HRM practices of any country are created and implemented in a wider socio-economic context of trade and development. For Finnish companies, this involves, in addition to influences from countries with a history of recruiting and placing foreign nurses and neighbouring countries, institutional input from international organisations and the European Union.

The Structure of the Book

This book is divided into three parts to discuss transnational management of nurses and moving beyond international human resource management: (1) framing, (2) situating, and (3) a situation.

The first part entitled 'Framing' starts with an overview on the transnationalisation of care and nurse labour market as conceptualised through macro, meso, and micro understandings of the circuits and processes of migrants moving for work in the health care industry or private and public actors and organisations producing, recruiting, and relocating nurse labour transnationally. Empirical documentation of the nursing occupation through historical and organisational analyses reveals gendered, racialised, and classed hierarchies that create barriers to equality for the nurses in tangible ways.

Through the theoretical framework of transnational feminism in Chapter 3, I critique international human resource management (IHRM) as a discipline and practice. Using the transnational feminist lens both theoretically and empirically signals attention to uneven and privileging circuits of nonhuman and human capital elements such as financial currency and human resources (or people's labour) and problematises the concept of 'international'. The concept 'international' implies nation-states as being fixed and sovereign entities with boundaries that can include and exclude political, economic, and social elements, taking for granted that these boundaries are established through a system of inequality and exploitation. Furthermore, Western and/or Eurocentric discourses of entitlement and the superiority of one country over others institutionally creates hierarchies of people and their labour in material forms (for instance, wages, where people live, whether or not family members are separated geographically). The term 'international' revolves around cultural differences or, in some instances, a nationalistic discourse of 'us versus them', allowing actors in various networks to legitimise uneven circuits of labour and capital based on socially constructed ideas of particular nationalities and cultures.

The transnational feminist lens is considered critical to IHRM as a discipline and practice as I argue that the term 'international HRM' should be reconceptualised to 'transnational HRM' to not only reflect the current political economy, but also to move 'beyond the enterprise' or MNCs of particular sectors. This means considering other sectors that manage human capital across borders such as nurses. This broadens the scope of research but also questions taken-for-granted issues of race and gender in the practice and theorisation of IHRM in management and organisational studies.

The second part of this book is entitled 'Situating'. To examine the transnational management of nurses, in Chapter 4, I discuss the methodology of situational analysis: a grounded analysis that navigates the data with the use of maps. The 'situational maps' (Clarke, 2005), constructed by the researcher, revolve around the central work activity of recruitment and placement of nurses. Various 'social worlds' and their representatives related to the work activity emerge into the 'arena' to claim authority, and 'produce' human resources of nurses.

In Chapter 5, I define discourse(s) and situational analysis and explain how I use these methods of analysis. The goal of these methods is to situate the actors, organisations, and institutions in their respective social worlds and discuss various discursive positions that emerge in the produced talk and text collected. In this way, the unit of analysis is the organisational or meso level and not the individuals.

In the final part, 'A Situation', I illustrate transnational management of nurses through a situated story about the recruitment and placement of Filipino registered nurses into Finnish private and public health care organisations. Focusing on the transnational management of 75 Filipino nurses recruited and placed in Finland from 2007 to 2010 (the first recruitment of non-European nurses by businesses), I discuss which representatives are claiming authority in the recruitment and placement practices of Filipino nurses in Finland and which social worlds are associated with the representatives. I aim to illustrate the emergence of these representatives and their respective social worlds and arenas through social world maps, and I analyse the various discursive resources used by the representatives to gain social legitimation. In Chapter 7, I look at the discursive positions of the dominating representatives in the recruitment and placement of Filipino nurses and at the structuring and material implications of these discursive positions.

References

Apesoa-Varano, E. C. & Varano, C. S. (2004) Nurse and labour activism in the United States: The role of class, gender, and ideology. *Social Justice*, 31(3), pp. 77–104.

Brush, B. L. (2008) Global nurse migration today (world health). *Journal of Nursing Scholarship*, 40(1), pp. 20–25.

Brush, B. L., Kingma, M. & Lorenzo, F. M. (2005) Imported care: Recruiting foreign nurses to US health care facilities. *Health Affairs*, 23, pp. 78–87.

Brush, B. L., Sochalski, J. & Berger, A. M. (2004) Imported care: Recruiting foreign nurses to US health care facilities. *Health Affairs*, 23(3), pp. 78–87.

Brush, B. L. & Vaspuram, R. (2006) Nurses, nannies, and caring work: Importation, visibility, and marketability. *Nursing Inquiry*, 13(3), pp. 181–185.

Buchan, J., Parkin, T. & Sochalski, J. (2003) *International nurse mobility: Trends and policy implications*. Geneva: World Health Organisation (WHO).

Chang, G. (2000) *Disposable domestics: Immigrant women workers in the global economy*. Cambridge: South End Press.

Choy, C. (2003) *Empire of care: Nursing and migration in Filipino American history*. Durham: Duke University Press.

Clarke, A. (1991) Social worlds/arena theory as organizational theory. In D. R. Maines (ed.) *Social organization and social process*. New York: Aldine de Gruyter, pp. 119–158.

Clarke, A. (2005) *Situational analysis: Grounded theory after the postmodern turn*. Thousand Oaks: Sage.

Cleland Silva, T. (2010) Gender globalized skilled work and new challenges: A transnational perspective on international human resource management of Filipino nurse to Finland. In M. Iwatake (ed.) *Gender, mobility, and citizenship in Asia*. Helsinki: University of Helsinki Press, pp. 102–117.

Connell, J. (ed.) (2008) *The international migration of health workers*. London: Routledge.

Dahl, H. M. & Eriksen, T. R. (2005) *Dilemmas of care in the Nordic welfare state: Continuity and change*. Aldershot: Ashgate.

Dahl, H. M. & Rasmussen, B. (2012) Paradoxes of elderly care: The Nordic model. In A. Kamp & H. Hviid (eds.) *Elderly care in transition—management, meaning and identity at work: A Scandinavian perspective*. Copenhagen: Copenhagen Business School Press, pp. 29–49.

Davies, C. (1995) *Gender and the professional predicament in nursing*. London: McGraw-Hill Education.

Festing, M. & Eidems, J. (2011) A process perspective on transnational HRM systems—A dynamic capability-based analysis. *Human Resource Management Review*, 21(3), pp. 162–173.

Galvez-Tan, J. (2004, October). The national nursing crisis: seven strategic solutions. In International Conference on the Medical Workforce sponsored by the United States Educational Commission for Foreign Medical Graduates (ECFMG), UP Diliman, Quezon City (pp. 4–7).

George, S. (2005). *When women come first: Gender and class in transnational migration*. California: University of California Press.

Giddens, A. (1979) *Central problems in social theory: Action, structure, and contradiction in social analysis*. Berkley: University of California Press.

Hearn, J. (2004) Tracking "the transnational": Studying transnational organizations and managements, and the management of cohesion. *Culture and Organization*, 10(4), pp. 273–290.

Hearn, J., Jyrkinen, M., Piekkari, R., & Oinonen, E. (2008) "Women home and away": Transnational managerial work and gender relations. *Journal of Business Ethics*, 83(1), pp. 41–54.

Ho, C. (2008) Chinese nurses in Australia: Migration, work, and identity. In J. Connell (ed.) *The international migration of health workers*. New York: Routledge, pp. 147–163.

Isaksen, L. W. (ed.) (2010) *Global care work: Gender and migration in Nordic societies*. Lund: Nordic Academic Press.

Kingma, M. (2006) *Nurses on the move: Migration and the global health care economy*. London: ILR Press.

Locke Swarr, A. & Nagar, R. (2010) *Critical transnational feminist praxis*. Albany: State University of New York.

McNeil-Walsh, C. (2008) Migrant nurses and the experiences of skill: South Africa nurses in UK health care sector. In J. Connell (ed.) *International migration of health care workers*. New York: Routledge, pp. 129–146.

Melchior, F. (2004) Feminist approaches to nursing history. *Western Journal of Nursing Research*, 26(3), pp. 340–355.

Mintzberg, H. (2017) *Managing the myths of health care: Bridging the separations between care, cure, control, and community*. Oakland: Berrett-Koehler Publishers, Inc.

Näre, L. & Wrede, S. (2013) Glocalising care in the Nordic countries: An introduction to the special issue. *Nordic Journal of Migration Research*, 3(2), pp. 57–62.

Percot, M. (2006). Indian nurses in the Gulf: Two generations of female migration. *South Asia Research*, 26(1), pp. 41–62.

Ribeiro, J. Sousa (2008) Gendering migration flows: Physicians and nurses in Portugal. *Equal Opportunities International*, 27(1), pp. 77–87.

Ståhl, G. B., Björkman, I. & Morris, S. (eds.) (2012) *Handbook of research in international human resource management*. Cheltenhuam: Edward Elgar Publishing.

Strauss, A. L. (1978) A social worlds perspective. *Studies in Symbolic Interaction*, 1, pp. 119–128.

Strauss, A. L. (1979) *Negotiations: Varieties, contexts, processes and social order*. San Francisco: Jossey-Bass.

Strauss, A. L. (1982a) Interorganizational negotiation. *Urban Life*, 11(3), pp. 350–367.

Strauss, A. L. (1982b) Social worlds and legitimation processes. In N. Denzin (ed.) *Studies in symbolic interactions*, 4. Greenwich: JAI Press, pp. 171–190.

Wrede, S. (2010) Nursing: Globalization of a female-gendered profession. In *The Palgrave handbook of gender and healthcare*. London: Palgrave Macmillan, pp. 437–453.

Wrede, S., Henriksson, L., Høst, H., Johansson, S. & Dybbroe, B. (eds.) (2008) *Care work in crisis: Reclaiming the Nordic ethos of care*. Lund: Studentlitteratur.

Yeates, N. (2009) *Globalising care economies and migrant workers: Explorations in global care chains*. Basingstoke: Palgrave Macmillan.

Part 1

Framing

2 Perspectives on the Transnationalisation of Care and the Nurse Labour Market

The body of research concerning the care labour market ranges from the traditional macro understanding of flows and patterns generated from statistical information by nation-states (e.g. OECD and WHO) as well as bringing gender into the analysis of labour migration patterns (ILO, UN, and IOM). At a micro/familial level, analysis of global dynamics in the provision of care and the economic restructuring of the domestic sphere is conceptualised through Hochschild's concept of 'global care chains' (Hochschild, 2000).[1] In her analysis, the concept of 'global care chains' reveals a reconfiguring of care roles and links migrant carers (read: women) into social networks of transnational families/caring in which migrant women leave their families in order to care for their employer's families abroad. In 2009, Yeates explores the 'global care chains' by expanding its conceptualisation to skilled, paid labour migrants such as nurses and coins the term 'global nurse care chains' in global care economies. This term denotes a shift from focusing on the micro familial level of domestic care workers to meso and macro levels in which various actors become involved in the chains of supply and demand of skilled professionals in nursing. The nursing occupation, as understood in this overview, is gendered and racialised both structurally and discursively but also through managerial practices that normalise the devaluation of nurse work, reinforcing what Davies (1992) coins as 'coping management' and what Acker terms as 'inequality barriers'.

The transnationalisation of care, nonetheless, includes not only the migrants' provision of care labour, but also other complex networks that promulgate ideas and practices of care. These transnational networks include epistemic communities, transnational advocacy, transnational social movements, ethnic diasporas, transnational families, transnational consumers, transnational corporations, transnational criminals, transnational professions, and transnational and cross-borders spheres of governance (Khagram & Levitt, 2004; Yeates, 2011). As this book details a situated story of the corporate pursuit of economic gain and profit through the recruitment of Filipino nurses by Finnish businesses, this chapter revolves around nurse migration and the transnational labour market of nurses. It also introduces concepts of 'global care chains' and 'global nurses care chains' to emphasise not only the commodification and capital invested into nurse labour recruitment, but also to highlight that the concept of these chains draw from global commodity (GCC) analysis which is grounded in network methodology (Dicken et al., 2001: 91) and global social network analysis (Holton, 2008: 43).

Transnational Nurse Labour Migration: A Macro Overview of Regional and Global Flows of Transnational Nurse Migration

Various countries can both import and export nursing labour. For instance, in an OECD study on doctor and nurse migration, the primary 'donor' countries were Philippines, the United Kingdom, Germany, Jamaica, India, Canada, and Ireland. Comparatively, the primary 'receiving' countries were Australia, Canada, Ireland, Denmark, the United Kingdom, New Zealand, and the United States (OECD, 2007; see Tables 2.1 and 2.2).[2]

Table 2.1 Number of foreign-trained nurses in receiving countries

	2000		*2005*		*2007/2008*	
Foreign-Trained Nurses	*Number (N)*	*Share % (S)*	*N*	*S*	*N*	*S*
Australia	..	..	31 472	*12.1*	*34 866*	*16.4*
Canada	14 910	*6.4*	19 230	*7.6*	*20 319*	*7.9*
Denmark	4 618	*6.0*	5 109	*6.2*	..	..
Finland	122	*0.2*	274	*0.3*	*530*	*0.5*
Ireland	..	..	8 758	*14.0*	*37 892*	*47.1*
Netherlands	..	..	3 479	*1.4*		
New Zealand	6 317	*19.3*	9 334	*24.3*	*9 895*	*22.1*
Medea	2 517	*2.5*	2 878	*2.7*	*2 585*	*2.6*
United Kingdom	50 564	*8.0*	..	..	..	..
United States	..	..	101 791	*3.5*		

(source: OECD 2007, 2010)

Table 2.2 Number of nurses sent by donor countries to OECD countries, circa 2000

Donor Country or main country of origin	*Number of foreign born nurses in OECD countries by main countries of origin*
Philippines	11 0774
United Kingdom	45 638
Germany	31 623
Jamaica	31 186
Canada	24 620
India	22 786
Ireland	20 166

(source: OECD, 2007)

These flows of nurses mark not only global territory but also regional territory. Even though most migration is from 'periphery' to 'core' countries, there are also regional processes and divisions of labour that are characterised by movements from weak core countries to strong core countries, and from weak peripheries to strong peripheries (Ishi, 1987). For example, within the core countries, there is large migration of nurses from Canada to the United States, and from the UK and Ireland to the United States (Wickramasekara, 2002). Outside these core countries, one popular destination area is the Middle East, specifically to the states of the Arabian Gulf, whose health services draw migrants from, for example, the Philippines, Egypt, Bangladesh, and India. Within regional migration, South Africa is an example of drawing migrants from Swaziland (Buchan et al., 2003: 11).

Some scholars have considered the general characteristics of nurse migration with the analogy of 'chains' (Hochschild, 2000; Yeates, 2009a). These chains correspond with the status of the countries where the migrants flow both away from and into the national borders. Countries at the top of the chain are provided with human capital from the bottom or lower down the chain. As Yeates (2009a: 80) explains:

> [T]he United States draws nurses from Canada; Canada draws nurses from England to make up for its losses to United States; England draws from South Africa to fill its vacancies; South Africa draws on Swaziland. Countries at the bottom end of nursing chain may supply international markets but not replenish their stocks by importing health workers from other countries: the Philippines is a major example of this. The problem for such countries is that they have no further countries from which they may recruit to make up for the losses of their own nurses.

The metaphor of chains highlights how countries are linked as potential 'stepping stones' by the migrant nurses, in which nurses work in some countries to acquire skills and experience before moving on to a more 'desirable' country (Kingma, 2006). Some reasons why a country may be at the top of the chain include tangible incentives and the regulatory practices of the destination country. For instance, nurses migrate to the United States because of its high wages and standard of living, together with opportunities to pursue additional education (Aiken and Cooper, 2007: 1301). Conversely, if the United States restricts the flow of nurse migration and recruitment, the migrants deploy to other destination countries. Indeed, this means that government policies and agreements are important in explaining how countries attain nurses transnationally.

Traditional Nurse Migration Patterns

Historical and colonial ties explain the territorial spread of nurses both globally and regionally. Examples of colonial ties from where the traditional supply of nurses derive are Australia, Canada, and India to the United Kingdom; from Mozambique to Portugal; from Suriname and South Africa to the Netherlands; and from the Philippines to the United States (Bach, 2003). Colonial ties provide understandings as to why some countries become exporters and others importers within the nursing market (Choy, 2003). Choy exemplifies this supply and demand relationship by exploring the historical foundations of Filipino nurses' international mobility. This mobility can be traced to the establishment of US-orientated health and nursing education system, in which both missionary and military influences were important. Another influence of colonial ties between the United States and the Philippines is the spread of US-American or, more generally, Western ideologies and practices of medicine and nursing (Albrecht, 2003: 17–23).

The choice of destination countries is also related to colonial historical legacies that have created common cultural ties and languages. As Buchan et al. note (2003: 84):

> It is possible to map out English speaking, Spanish speaking, French speaking and Portuguese speaking 'zones' within which much of the mobility of nurses between 'source' and destination country exists.

Nordic countries do not share common languages with other countries, and the countries have become importers of migrants, albeit in small numbers (see Table 2.1). In the past, nurses moved within the Nordic region to look for better salaries and in situations when domestic labour markets offered little opportunities for permanent employment. For instance, Finnish nurses have migrated to Sweden and Norway in times of high domestic unemployment. Smaller numbers of Finnish nurses have moved to countries such as the United Kingdom and the United States, but this mobility is better understood in terms of mobility as a life choice rather than as a reaction to the conditions of the Finnish health care labour market (Wrede et al., 2008). For nurses from affluent countries, labour migration is likely to offer the choice of a mobile life.

For nurses from poorer countries, and for nurses from first-world countries experiencing economic crisis, however, historical and associated cultural ties may be lessening in importance as factors of migration routes, 'as destination countries become more utilitarian in encouraging migration primarily on the basis of economic requirements rather than historical or family connections' (Bach, 2003: 9).

Gendered Migration of Labour

In the global economy, third-world country poverty is impacting women in new ways, as there is a global demand for cheap and flexible labour particularly in the service sectors. In the affluent countries, in particular, different kinds of labour-intensive services are growing rapidly as other labour market sectors are declining in some parts of the world (Glucksman and Nolan, 2007). Worldwide, there is an estimated 214 million skilled and unskilled migrants; 49% are women (INSTRAW, 2007; Zlotnik, 2003). Women from poorer countries are important new labour pools for care work, domestic work, cleaning, and hospitality services (Kofman, 2004; Vertovec, 2002). This increasing demand for women workers is an indication of the new, feminised migration patterns, and women migrants are becoming agents of economic change for many countries as they continue to enter the international labour market.[3]

Increased awareness of female migration in migration research has led to the development of the concept of the 'feminization of migration' (INSTRAW, 2007). Yet, this concept may be deceptive in regards to the increasing numbers of migrant women. In the 1960s, women made up nearly 47% of all international migrants, which is only a two-point difference from present numbers (Paiewonsky, 2007). The real change of the last decade has occurred in (1) the way women move and (2) where they move. In regards to the way they move, more women are now migrating independently in search of jobs, rather than as family dependents travelling with their husbands or joining them abroad (Chammartin, 2004).

Regional migration flows reflect where the female migrants are moving. Females currently represent over half of all international migrants in more developed areas and slightly less than half in the less developed and least developed areas of the world. These regional variations reflect preferences regarding male and female labour, as well as different wages (IOM, 2006).

Gender differences in migration flows often reflect the way in which gender divisions of labour are incorporated into uneven economic development processes, leading to differences in the movement and opportunities available to women and men (Sassen, 2000). This has created a level of awareness of female migration by migration and feminist scholars and other stakeholders, particularly in regards to the importance of women as remittance senders (Brown, 1997: 208), women's working conditions within domestic and caregiving jobs (Lutz, 2008, 2011; Anderson, 2000; Hondagneu-Sotelo, 2001), the changing role of women in the family and the community (Parreñas, 2001, 2012), and the vulnerability and exposure of migrant women to different kinds of risks, including trafficking (Ehrenreich and Hochschild, 2002, 2003).

Transnational processes and practices that facilitate the gendered flows of women workers and nurses are remittances payments that are revered in home countries and expected. Governments such as the Philippines establish schools (Bach, 2003) and the deployment of sophisticated governmental systems (Ball, 2004) in order to send migrant workers abroad. Today, it is estimated that over 250,000 nurses from the Philippines are employed throughout the world (Ball, 2004). This labour exportation is also mainly of women, and the government has started to rely on exported labour as a means for servicing Philippine indebtedness (Barber, 2000: 399). These linkages between countries will be discussed more in the next section, global care economies, but illustrate that global labour systems begin before the nurses leave their country of origin (Kelly, 2007, 2010, 2012a, 2012b; Kelly and D'Addario, 2008; Kelly and Olds, 2007).

Because care work and nursing remain predominately female occupations, openings to migration for women have led to precarious situations in which these jobs are typically affected by low wages, instability, deskilling, lack of recognition, absence of benefits, and poor working conditions (Ribeiro, 2008; Smith and Mackintosh, 2007). As such, even if women are migrating legally, they are still slotted into employment in which they can easily be discriminated against or face arbitrary employment terms and abuses (Dicicco-Bloom, 2004). The reproductive care sectors such as education, as well as the health and social work sectors, are also heavily regulated by states and corporate bodies (Bauder, 2003; Raghuram and Kofman, 2002). These bodies are more likely to lead migrants into social and health service professions (Le Espiritu, 2002) as welfare is seen, at least in part, as a state responsibility. For instance, the migration of skilled women operates, in practice, within a complex intersection of immigration regulation and regulations around accreditation of foreign credentials by corporatist professional bodies (Groutsis, 2003; Kelly, 2010; Kelly and D'Addario, 2008). Furthermore, it has been argued that the use of internationally educated nurses (IENs) has helped the overcommoditisation of care (Folbre, 2005), resulting in the devaluing of nurse and patient care (Gordon, 2005) and further marginalising the relative power the nurses hold within the health care systems (Smith and Mackintosh, 2007).

Gender differences are also reflected in the very moment that either a female or a male decides to migrate; this migration can no longer be considered a 'gender-neutral' phenomenon. Men and women differently experience the risks and challenges that might be presented during migration such as different employment opportunities, vulnerability to human rights abuses, exploitation, discrimination, and specific health risks (UNFPA, 2006). These differences are highlighted when the woman enters the destination country on the basis of her labour market skills as occupational categories that are often opened to women and are limited to the service or 'pink collar' industry. Except for nursing, the migration of highly skilled women is relatively invisible as many women migrants with an education and professional skills work in jobs for which they are overqualified due to entry restriction to the country (e.g. work permits/visas) and the domestic labour market (Castles and Miller, 2009).

The global migration patterns of nurses—as well as their transnational demand as a policy response to structural changes in the welfare state—can act as a reflection but also as a perpetuation of the structural deficiencies in health systems globally (Connell, 2008; Stilwell et al., 2004). Indeed, the global health care labour market and its demand for human capital can facilitate creating a 'quick fix' to the gaps in care of the domestic health care systems (Brush et al., 2004; Kingma, 2006). Subsequently, not fully acknowledging the gendered and the racialised aspects of nurse work that marginalises the workers' power through managerial practices and processes becomes not only detached from the historical and social underpinnings of the occupation itself but also silenced.

Global Care Economies

The provisions of care in domestic and global economies have changed as described in the previous sections. Women have entered the paid domestic and global workforces, but the provision of paid and unpaid care still remains defined as women's work. The concepts of global care chains and global nurse care chains open the discussion to the global networking of care provision and demand, which links women transnationally through service and other care occupations such as nursing.[4]

Global Care Chains

Hochschild (2000) first coined the term 'global care chains' (GCCs) to refer to a series of personal links between people across the globe based on paid and unpaid work of care. These 'chains' create networks of transnational dimensions that are formed for the purpose of maintaining social life and transfer caregiving tasks from one household to the next on the basis of power axes. For example, the chain is based on 'motherly labour' and is driven by a woman in a rich country with dependent children who relies on another woman from a less rich country to provide care for her children. The children of the latter woman are connected to this process or 'chain' as they are cared for by other family members or a woman from a poorer household in the caregiver's home of origin. In other words, global networks of families are established and create transnational households, as well as links between different families through the employment nexus. The concept of global care chains helps to clarify the broader social processes that create the transnational transfer of domestic labour and care, which assists in the conceptualisation of the distributive features of this transfer. (Re)distributive features can be the social divisions of gender, the absence of men in the distributive process, the racial hierarchies, and the intersections of social division of class, 'race', ethnicity, and gender (Yeates, 2009a). As a result, GCCs create links between service-providers and service-recipients (and their families):

> links that are textured by wider socio-economic inequalities resulting from hierarchies of states, classes (and castes), genders and ethnic groups.
> (Yeates, 2009a: 42)

Influenced by global value chain theory, a theory that focuses on the production and consumption of manufactured goods and their corresponding networks of agents, GCCs inject new dimensions into feminist analysis of the globalisation of social reproduction. As stated by:

> In particular, it calls for a supplementary focus on: the geographically interlocking, extensive mechanisms of production (in its widest sense) and exchange; the creation of value and the distribution of surplus among agents in these global care networks; and the non-material (emotional) as well as material inputs into, and costs of, this globalization of care, or love.
>
> Yeates (2009a: 48)

Global Nurse Care Chains

Yeates argues that the concept of Global Care Chains (GCCs) needs to broaden its focus to include migrant women workers of different skills and occupations; family status, obligations, and expectations; types of care provided; care settings; and historical context such as colonial ties. These broadened chains encompass a more complex range of care services including

> services as diverse as domestic cleaning, family care, health care, sexual care, educational care and religious/spiritual care, provided in a wide range of settings such as home, hospitals, hospices, churches, schools, and brothels and in a wider range of contexts such as individualised private settings and institutionalise state and non-state settings.
>
> (Yeates, 2005: 8)

This broadened understanding of GCCs aims to capture why richer countries are able to acquire skilled workers from poorer countries, but also illustrates the complex nature, and unequal operation, of citizenship regimes, particularly since skill and occupation levels are correlated with a range of employment and settlement related rights (see Fudge and MacPhail, 2009, for a discussion on citizenship regimes and inequalities).

Global Nurse Care Chains (GNCCs), as coined by Yeates, expands the concept of GCCs and helps to understand the properties and dynamics of global nursing. The chains conceptualise nurses as highly skilled or specialised workers that can be regulated in institutional settings by a variety of public and private agents, provisions and interests. Focusing on nursing chains can permit an elaborated contextualisation of social divisions of labour within the global care economy of a highly prized human resource for social development (Yeates, 2009b). GNCCs can consist of many actors and institutions such as nursing institutions (whether hospitals or nursing homes), educational institutions in the source and host countries, recruitment agencies, training companies, governance (state immigration services and nursing licensing authorities), and international agreements. Other groups that can influence these chains are trade unions, NGOs, and advocacy groups as well as family, friends, and colleagues that provide financial entry to the market or assist in the decisions to emigrate and the choices of destination countries. These actors and institutions are considered, like global commodity analysis, to be producers, services, and consumers moving along a chain of different links and nodes that are regulated, governed, and yet murky in their far-from-linear directional force. GNCCs also highlight the complexity of migrating nurses and their subsequent management and can shed light on 'the ways and institutions through which unequal resources are distributed globally' (Hassim, 2008: 397). Yeates further notes that GNCCs can critically explore how GCCs may reinforce care work as women's work, privilege some aspects of care transnationalisation over others, and renaturalise the nation-state (Yeates, 2004). With this in mind, the expansion of analysis of GCCs to GNCCs as concepts can guide empirical data sources to make intersectional dimensions of migration and transnationalisation processes and practices more visible (Yeates, 2012).

Transnationalisation of Care and Producer-Based Care Networks

A dominant feature of contemporary social life has become the increase of transnational flows of multiple kinds: people, money, ideas, and images. These flows are not limited to linear directions, but multiple directions of back-and-forth interconnections of people, practices, and processes.

Multidirectional flows of transnational health care workers such as nurses bring people from different nations, classes, races, ethnicities, genders, and ages together, which can create new relationships and alter existing ones. With this mixture of people and other transnational flows comes unequal power relations that, in turn, reflect global relations that are systematically divided and historically (re)produced (Rafferty and Solano, 2007). Complicities to these transnational unequal flows of power relations recast national patriarchies (Hearn, 2015; Connell, 2008) that (re)produce gendered and racialised negotiations, which are institutionally embedded in regulatory practices, normative expectations, and rules and behaviours (McDowell, 2008: 504).

According to Yeates, the transnationalisation of care (Yeates, 2011: 1112) can be defined as 'the processes of heightened connectivity revolving around consciousness, identities, ideas, relations and practices of care which link people, institutions and places across state borders' (Yeates, 2011: 1112). Different conceptual premises (Vertovec, 1999) can be distinguished as underpinning different articulations of care transnationalisation such as

> border spanning social morphologies (e.g. migrants networks ethnic diasporas, transnational families); a type of consciousness (e.g. awareness and concern for the well being of one or more 'distant' others; dual/multiple identities of belonging); a conduit for capital flows (e.g. remittances of goods and money, transnational care corporations); a site of

> political engagement (e.g. global public fora and cross border spheres of governance through which claim making is directed and care policies are constructed), and the reconstruction of place or locality (e.g. care identities, orientations and practices that connect and position actors in more than one country).
>
> (Yeates, 2011: 1114)

To examine the transnationalisation of care, Yeates suggests an analytical concept that she calls 'producer-based care networks'. Producer-based care networks are global nurse care chains containing public and private actors that produce, recruit, relocate, and settle labour abroad. The analysis, instead of being on the familial or individual migration of care labour, focuses on private and public actors that interact to produce human capital for local and national health and social care institutions. With the transnationalisation of care, Yeates argues that these networks are likely for economic exchanges (e.g. capital investment and gains) that link other institutions such as education and training organisations to produce health care labour (Yeates, 2011: 1119). The transnational production of health care labour from these networks generates significant (often negative) externalities for public health and welfare institutions in the sending countries of the human capital (Yeates, 2011: 1120).

Various private and public actors collaborate in diverse ways in the recruitment and placement of nurses, formulating producer-based care networks. These actors create gates that regulate which workers can enter, work, and stay in a nation-state through particular practices and processes that are both managerial and legal.

Corporate recruiting agencies often operate in partnership with state actors as state ministries are largely involved in the facilitation of visas and nursing applications, relocation and housing, and continuous education opportunities. The relationship between the corporate and state actors, in turn, can create power asymmetries between those actors and the migrants in the sense that either the state and/or the recruiters can change the conditions of migrant entry at will.

As stated by Bakan and Stasiulis:

> [G]atekeepers to citizenship serve to regulate the entry into and exit from nation-states and labour markets as well as access to citizenship rights. All gatekeepers accomplish this work in part through the construction, articulation and reproduction of stereotypes about who is, or is not, an appropriate candidate for citizenship with a given nation-state.
>
> (2003: 317)

The state actors' collaboration with private corporate recruiters to fill human resources of the health care sector can allow the recruiters to define who the ideal candidate is, the conditions of the workers' visa, and where the migrant workers live and are employed. One major concern of this is that it leads to gendered and racialised institutional processes in the form of state and private policies and practices that prevent migrant nurses from working in areas in which the nurses are skilled due to the non-recognition of qualification, lack of experience in the local system, and closure of public sector employment to noncitizens (Kofman, 2007: 159). Deskilling can also occur even when the migrants are allowed to practice their profession in the destination country. Various reports have shown that migrant nurses are channelled into the lower non-promotional grades or unpopular specialties through the practices of private and public actors (Kofman and Raghuram, 2006: 293).

Nurse Work as Gendered and Racialised Labour in Work Organisations

Organisations and work are gendered (Witz and Savage, 1992; Kurma et al., 2014). Examining organisations and work through a gendered lens requires the breaking down of organisations in terms of structure, processes, relations, power, and discourses within a wider historical and social context. Organisations are considered sites of contest and negotiations that the actors navigate and the organisations are formed (Clegg, 1989: 198).

The development of large organisations at the turn of the 20th century was directly associated with what is now called the 'white blouse revolution' (Witz and Savage, 1992; Anderson, 1989). The modern organisation was formed through the dependency of cheap female labour, and, in turn, helped define women as subordinate workers to men within emergent white collar labour markets (Witz and Savage, 1992).

In 1989, although gender was not the focus of her study, Mackay described gender as the recurrent theme of nurse work, something that 'fundamentally affects the way that nurses are seen and see themselves' (Davies, 1991: 235). Mackay (1989) argues that the system perpetuates gender relations through a 'disposable ethos', use one and throw away, that is demeaning to the women who choose to take up nursing as a profession. Mackay concludes that

> [T]he disposable workforce ethos-use-once-and-throw-away-is demeaning to the women who choose to take up nursing as a career. It also serves to reduce the prestige and status of nurses, nursing, and women. Thus nursing can easily be seen as a job at which women are only playing. At the same time the work of nurses can be trivialized if it is done by a perpetual stream of young learners. How then, can nursing be viewed as having a real contribution to make to the improvement of the health of patients? The past ease of replacement has meant that attempts to develop the skills and potential of the workforce are not made. What a waste!
>
> (1989: 92–93)

This 'ethos' is reflected in the perpetual use of young learners (ease of replacement), and the failure to provide facilities for daycare to balance work and motherhood. Davies (1995) echoes this claim of 'disposable labour' by arguing that high turnover among nurses is accepted as an inevitable aspect of a predominantly female workforce, leading to the perception that nurses are disposable. Davies notes that

> neither the student labour system, nor the perpetuation of a set of terms and conditions that favour men rather than women are new observations, yet it is new to point to the way in which they make it impossible for nurses, as women, specifically to demonstrate and enhance the value of their work.
>
> (1995: 235)

With this in mind, Davies reexamines gender and the organisation of paid work and tries to build a theoretical synthesis. She aims to transcend the uneasy 'gender talk' that surrounds nursing and advocates to examine gendered processes of inclusion more directly (1991: 230). She argues that this can be done by (1) starting from the premise that social life in all its forms is deeply gendered and that this gendering operates at different levels and in different ways. (She is convinced that we should stop regarding gender as an 'unwanted import' and acknowledge that it is built into the very design and functioning of organisation, and it is important to demonstrate in concrete terms what this means). And (2) she states that we must abandon the concept of gender attributes and talk instead about gender relations and power, as enacted through daily organisational practice and processes.

Coping Management of Nurse Work

'Nursing must always be accomplished with a variable and transient workforce' notes Davies (1995: 102). Moving from gender attributes of the nurses to gender relations, Davies defines a management of nurses that derives from highly gendered structures and processes found within the nursing profession. Reflecting on Acker's work (1990), Davies defines the management of nurses as 'coping'. Coping is a style of management that allows the gender division of labour in health care to continue as managers of the nurses 'cope' with a structure of paid work done by women that is a time and life pattern that is very male-orientated.

As Davies indicates:

> since it is not only jobs, but the very terms and conditions of paid work itself that render participation convenient for men and problematic for women, it seems preferable to refer to this phenomenon as the gender division of paid work.
>
> (1995: 141)

As paid work done by women, nursing simply cannot be managed on the conventional, full-time, life-time pattern but must rather adjust to that pattern. The current management (coping) of nurses is full of necessary adjustments to the impossibility of delivering work on the male pattern. Through this management, Davies points to a wider theoretical model, the processes of the trivialisation of work and the devaluation of women that Mackay identified. These managerial 'solutions' are deeply problematic as they reinforce the unimportance of the work and the workers and trivialise the nurses.

Through gendered division of labour in health care that devalue the occupation of nursing, Davies notes that nursing is a pattern of education and service that seems intertwined to the detriment of both. She writes:

> We find a workforce that appears to be stretched beyond the limits of what is tolerable; we find management that apparently cannot cope and a leadership that is accused of being out of touch. All this before we even begin to look at the questions of opportunity, access and discrimination and at the position of specialist groups within nursing, and the arguments of those midwifery and in health visiting and district nursing who feel that it would be better if they were not associated with nursing at all. Nurses frequently display the dedication to their work that is the stuff of public image, but they combine this with an uneasy sense of their own oppression and a seeming belief in their own inability to tackle some of the fundamentals that would enable nurses to practise as they would wish.
>
> (1995: 12–13)

Subsequently, the support for the development and growth of the nursing occupation is not granted in the same way as other medical occupations such as doctors. As Davies points out that nursing is seen, from the outset, as a fairly homogenous activity which solely requires a pair of hand, and qualities such as dedication, sympathy, and altruism (Davies, 1995: 6). This demarcation of the nursing occupation perpetuates the management to 'cope' within this familiar mindset.

Inequality Regimes in Work Organisations

As discussed previously, gender and race are embedded in work organisations: their processes, practices, and discourses. The construction of a social reality that perceives nurses as a homogenous activity that can be done by any nurse that encompasses particular attributes maintains inequalities in work organisations of care or what Acker terms 'inequality regimes'.

Acker (2006: 443) defines inequality regimes as 'loosely interrelated practices, processes, actions, and meanings that result in and maintain class, gender, and racial inequalities in particular organisations'. She distinguishes between six barriers to equality. These are (1) the bases of inequality, (2) the shape and degree of inequality, (3) the organising processes, (4) the invisibility of inequality, (5) the legitimacy of inequality, and (6) the degree of control and compliance. These six barriers serve as an analytical organisational approach to local, ongoing practical activities of organising work in which complex inequalities are reproduced (2006: 442). The bases of inequality, according to Acker, can vary but usually class, gender, and race are present. She states that although other differences are important (e.g. religion, sexuality, age, physical inabilities) 'they are not, at this time, as thoroughly embedded in organising processes as are gender, race, and class' (2006: 445). Gender, race, and class, to Acker, are socially constructed in the work organisation. For the term 'class', Acker views the concept as systematic differences in access to and control over resources for provisioning and survival (Acker, 2006). 'Gender', to Acker, is the socially constructed difference between men and women and the beliefs and identities that support difference and inequality in work organisation. And, lastly, 'race' refers to socially defined difference based on physical characteristics, culture, and historical domination and oppression, justified by entrenched beliefs (444). For Acker, ethnicity can also be accompanied by race, or stand alone, as a basis for inequality.

The second barrier to equality is the shape and degree of inequality. Acker (2006: 445) argues that 'the steepness of hierarchy is one dimension of variation in the shape and degree of inequality'. She illustrates, through traditional flat organisations with team structures, that the steepness of the hierarchy determines the degree of control and the decision making among the participants in the organisation. She argues that hierarchies in organisations are usually racialised and gendered, with top management being predominately white, middle-class men as in the United States and European countries. Another degree and pattern of the second barrier is race and gender. Acker notes that the degree and pattern of this inequality is complicated as segregation is

> hierarchical across jobs at different class levels of an organisation, across jobs at the same level, and within jobs. This means that sex segregation may not be found in the occupation, but persists in the different jobs or tasks assigned to the employee.
>
> (446)

In addition, Acker emphasises that wages can be different in organisations that impact the degree of hierarchy as well as power differences amongst those dominating the top levels of the organisations.

The third barrier to equality is ongoing processes used to achieve organisational goals that produce inequality in terms of class, gender, and race. Acker acknowledges that a considerable amount of research exists in exploring class or gender inequalities which are produced, both formally and informally, as work processes are carried out (Acker, 1990, 1994, 2004). She argues that these practices are often guided by textual materials supplied by consultants or developed by managers influenced by information and/or demands from outside the organisation.

She goes on to divide up the different work processes: the general requirements of work, class hierarchies, recruitment and hiring, wage setting and supervisory practices, and the informal interactions of 'doing the work' (448–451). She states that recruitment, hiring, supervision and the work itself are processes of selecting a particular person suitable for the job from the perspective of the employer. She indicates that

> Images of appropriate gendered and racialized bodies influence perceptions and hiring. White bodies are often preferred, as a great deal of research shows. Female bodies are appropriate for some jobs; male bodies for other jobs.
>
> (2006: 449)

However, other groups that do not embody these characteristics, such as women of colour as well as immigrant women, can be considered the most desirable worker for many jobs as the employer may believe that the employee is compliant and willing to accept orders and low wages (2006: 450). Acker concludes that

> Gender and race as a basis for hiring or a basis for exclusion have not been eliminated in many organizations, as continuing patterns of segregation attest.
>
> (450)

The final three barriers that Acker looks at are the invisibility of inequalities, the legitimacy of inequalities, and control and compliance. The invisibility of inequalities stems from those in privileged positions that do not see themselves as privileged. She argues that people in dominant groups generally see inequality as existing somewhere else, not where they are. Gender, race, and class become invisible to those in power or denied. Other researchers have noted that in discussing work practices and processes with managers, gender disappears or is consider not important (Ely and Meyerson, 2000). The fifth barrier is the process and practice of legitimising inequalities. Legitimacy of inequalities varies between organisations and can be high or low. Legitimacy is high when the process is legal, socially entrenched, and put into practice. The legitimacy is low when the inequalities are challenged and spurs actions for change. For instance, Acker discusses the legitimisation of certain low wages and statuses for particular occupations, which reinforces gender, race, and class inequalities as the practice is taken for granted. The practice becomes more legitimate and visible as some deem the visible inequalities are 'deserved':

> Gender and race processes are more legitimate when embedded in legitimate class processes. For example, the low pay and low status of

> clerical work is historically and currently produced as both a class and a gender inequality. Most people take this for granted as just part of the way in which work is organized. Legitimacy, along with visibility, may vary with the situation of the observer: some clerical workers do not see the status and pay of their jobs as fair, while their advantage is richly deserved. They see visible inequalities as perfectly legitimate.
>
> (2006: 453)

Lastly, Acker argues that inequalities are reinforced through control and compliance. According to Acker, foundational to organisational controls are class controls 'directed at maintaining the power of managers, ensuring that employees act to further the organisation's goals, and getting workers to accept the system of inequality' (454). She notes that controls are enforced through hierarchical organisational power (e.g. managerial control), but also can draw power from hierarchies embedded in gender and race relations.

Mechanisms for exerting organisational control can vary amongst organisation, but Acker identifies three types: (1) direct controls (e.g. wages, bureaucratic rules, various punishments for breaking the rules, rewards), (2) unobtrusive or indirect controls (e.g. control of technology or selective recruitment of relatively powerless workers), and (3) internationalised control. This last control includes the 'belief in the legitimacy of bureaucratic structures and rules as well as belief in the legitimacy of male and white privilege' (2006: 454).

Acker points out that there persists a belief related to internalised control within organisations that there is no point in challenging the fundamental gender, race, and class nature of things, which can be considered a form of control. The internalised controls are invisible as they become natural and normal. Pleasure can be an internalised control as well as fear and self-interest. Self-interest can be categorised in terms of economics, status, and identity, all of which can be produced as organising takes place (Acker, 2006: 454).

Neoliberalism Governance Within the Transnationalisation of Care

Since the 1970s, neoliberalism has dominated the shaping of economic and social policies worldwide (Harvey, 2007). Neoliberalism is described as a market-driven approach that prioritises private enterprise, liberalised trade, and relatively open markets (Harvey, 2010: 2). This ideology seeks to blur the roles of the state and private sectors by contracting out services and using private sector techniques and values such as efficiency and emphasis on results rather than processes (Hood, 1991; Pollitt, 1990, 1995).

Neoliberalism affects the international division of care by influencing the contexts and policies of countries both sending and receiving immigrant care workers. Through the withdrawal of the state support for care and subsequent restructuring, care work has been passed back into the private sphere, where women are expected to subsidise the economy with their caring work (Sparr, 1994; Wichterich, 2000). Transnationally, economic restructuring has placed greater pressure on women to meet the family's care needs, while absolving the state of responsibility for playing a large role in meeting care needs (Michel and Mahon, 2002). Neoliberal restructuring has also lead to an intensification of work that has impacted on the working conditions for women, in particular, and their experiences of care work (Selberg, 2013).

Although neoliberal ideologies have not completely eroded the social welfare policies of wealthier nations, the ideology itself has encouraged and promoted market-based solutions and a decreased role of the state in care provision (Morgan, 2002; Mahon and Phillips, 2002). Mattingly (2001: 372) emphasises this smaller role of the state rather than a complete erosion of care provisions by arguing that 'social welfare programs around the world have been reduced. The lessened ability of national governments to tax corporations, coupled with the often-enforced ideology of neo-liberalism, has contributed to the reduction of state support for social reproduction'. Restructuring of the welfare states has also led to rearranging services that are decentralised and privatised (sending care provision to private, non-profit, and voluntary sectors) (Daly and Lewis, 1998) as well as contracting out services and care provision that were formerly provided by the state (Knijn, 2000).

Instead of providing services through the public sector, the state is now encouraging the development of low-wage private sector services, which leads to higher levels of wage inequality (Pierson, 2001). As pointed out by an United Nations report:

> [M]igrant women thus fill expanded needs for care in advanced economies, enabling their growth to take place under neoliberal conditions of welfare restriction and flexible labour forces. The role of the migrant woman in providing care for the elderly, children, the disabled in paid, unpaid, formal, and informal capacities is a factor too little addressed in the context changes in the care economy and the welfare state.
>
> (2005: 119–120)

By relying, and subsequently encouraging, flexible and cheap labour of immigrant women workers, reproductive care in wealthy countries is then carried out despite the declining state provision of social service (Momsen, 1999). As a welfare state's support for care declines and families of different nations struggle economically, there becomes a strong demand for low-wage immigrant care workers, who may have few other employment opportunities due to their immigration status (Hondagneu-Sotelo, 2001; Momsen, 1999; Anderson, 2000; Parreñas, 2001). As stated by Heyzer and Wee:

> The shifting division of responsibility between the State and the family for social reproduction of everyday life has, thereby, been transformed

> into a transnational division of labour between middle class and working class women . . . this results in hidden savings for the governments of the receiving countries, because the need for adequate state investments in child care, care of the handicapped, care of the elderly and other social services is instead provided for by the income subsidy of middle class professional women and by the labour subsidy of relatively low-paid migrant workers.
>
> (1994: 44–45)

In the Nordic welfare regimes, neoliberal policies started to emerge from the 1980s onwards as political debates began to critique welfare policies that were facilitating an ongoing expansion of the public sector and to the strong position of professional power (Wrede and Näre, 2013). These debates and an orientation towards market-based discourse that problematised the state-centre systems coincided with a global paradigm shift to neoliberal politics and reforms on the decentralisation of the state and services. As such, discourses critiquing state centralisation promoted market-based ideas such as efficiency, flexibility, and cost effectiveness, which impacted the way services were provided and managed. Although unintentionally (Wrede et.al, 2008), these critiques created a demand for a more flexible workforce, particularly in low-skill occupations of care such as services to the elderly (Wrede, 2010).

Summary and Concluding Thoughts

This chapter provides an overview of the transnationalisation of care and the market of nurse human capital. The analytical concept of global care chains (GCCs) is applied to the examination of managing and organising global care labour at the familial and micro level of unskilled labour migrants such as nannies. Yeates' introduction of Global Nurses Care Chains (GNCCs) broadens the concept of GCCs to include skilled workers such as nurses.

To move the analysis to the meso-institutional and organisational levels in the transnationalisation of care, Yeates recommends the analytical concept of 'producer-based care networks'. These networks include private and public actors that, mostly through economic gain, are producing, recruiting, relocating, and settling nurse labour transnationally. This network of actors interacts with various public and private organisations to produce nurse labour through various negotiations of practices and processes that influence state regulations, normative expectations, and rules and behaviours.

As pointed out in the overview, the nurse occupation and its organisation are historically gendered and racialised. Complicities by actors and organisations to gender, race, and class inequalities in the transnationalisation of care (re)produce inequality barriers within the various processes of recruitment and placement in the domestic nursing workforce.

Moreover, interactions between state and private actors have increased in the Nordic welfare states due to the ideologies of neoliberalism. Within this paradigm of governance, market-based ideas of efficiency, cost effectiveness, and flexibility begin to dominate managerial and policy practices and agendas, giving space to the economic interests in the recruitment of care workers for state organisations.

Notes

1 Parreñas uses global care chains to examine reproductive care labour from the Philippines (2001, 2005).

2 Data from Australia, Canada, and Sweden, 2007. Data from Finland, New Zealand, and Ireland, 2008. Share (%) refers to 'labour share', which means the overall percentage of foreign-trained nurses employed in the nurse labour market of the country.

3 Migration is not limited to skilled workers. There are other migrants who are skilled and non-skilled that are forced into migration, such as refugees and illegally trafficked people. However, for the purpose of this research, the focus will be on skilled workers who migrate legally and voluntarily.

4 For a discussion on the 'glocalisation' of care that illustrates global linkages between the 'local' and the 'global' provision of care, see Wrede and Näre (2013). In this journal issue, the authors examine the globalising capitalist economy's impact on reproductive labour and care regimes in Nordic welfare states. They argue that the 'glocalization' of care is creating domestic health care markets that are characterised by efficiency, productivity, and flexible workforce policies that seek large labour forces to perform predefined low-skilled occupations such as elderly care.

References

Acker, J. (1990) Hierarchies, jobs, bodies: A theory of gendered organizations. *Gender and Society*, 4(2), pp. 139–158.

Acker, J. (1994) The gender regime of Swedish banks. *Scandinavian Journal of Management*, 10(2), pp. 117–130.

Acker, J. (2004) Gender, capitalism, and globalization. *Critical Sociology*, 30(1), pp. 17–41.

Acker, J. (2006) Inequality regimes: Gender, class, and race in organizations. *Gender and Society*, 20(4), pp. 441–464.

Aiken, L. & Cooper, R. (2007) Nurse staffing impact on organizational outcomes. In D. Mason, J. Leavitt & M. Chaffee (eds.) *Policy and politics in nursing and health care*. St. Louis: Elsevier, pp. 550–559.

Albrecht, G. L., Fitzpatrick, R. & Scrimshaw, S. (eds.) (2003) *The handbook of social sciences in health and medicine*. London: Sage.

Anderson, G. (Ed.). (1988). *The white-blouse revolution: female office workers since 1870*. Manchester: Manchester University Press.

Anderson, B. (2000) *Doing the dirty work? The global politics of domestic labour*. New York: Zed Books.

Bach, S. (2003) *International migration of health workers: Labour and social issues*. Geneva: International Labour Office.

Bakan, A. B. & Stasiulis, D. K. (2005) *Negotiating citizenship: Migrant women in Canada and the global system*. Toronto: University of Toronto Press.

Ball, R. (June–July 2004) Divergent development, racialised rights: Globalised labour markets and the trade of nurses—The case of the Philippines. *Women's Studies International Forum*, 27(2), pp. 119–133.

Barber, P. (2000) Agency in Philippine women's labour migration and provisional diaspora. *Women's Studies International Forum*, 23(4), pp. 399–411.
Bauder, H. (2003) Brain abuse or the devaluation of immigrant labour in Canada. *Antipode*, 35(4), pp. 698–717.
Brown, D. (1997) Workforce losses and return to migration to the Carribbean: A case study of Jamacian nurses. In P. Pessar (ed.) *Carribbean circuits: New directions in the study of Carribbean migration*. New York: Centre of Migration Studies, pp. 197–223.
Brush, B. L., Kingma, M. & Lorenzo, F. M. (2004) Imported care: Recruiting foreign nurses to US health care facilities. *Health Affairs*, 23, pp. 78–87.
Buchan, J., Parkin, T. & Sochalski, J. (2003) *International nurse mobility: Trends and policy implications*. Geneva: Royal College of Nursing, World Health Organisation and International Council of Nurses.
Castles, S. A. & Miller, M. (2009) *The age of migration: International population movements in the modern world*. Hampshire: Palgrave Macmillan.
Chammartin, G. (2004) *The feminisation of international migration*. Geneva: International Migration Programme.
Choy, C. (2003) *Empire of care: Nursing and migration in Filipino American history*. Durham: Duke University Press.
Clegg, S. R. (1989) Radical revisions: Power, discipline, and organizations. *Organization Studies*, 10(1), pp. 97–115.
Connell, J. (2008) Towards a global health care system? In J. Connell (ed.) *The international migration of health care workers*. New York: Routledge, pp. 1–29.
Daly, M. & Lewis, J. (1998) Introduction: Conceptualizing social care in the context of welfare state restructuring. In J. Lewis (ed.) *Gender, social care, and welfare state restructuring*. Aldershot: Ashgate, pp. 1–24.
Davies, C. (1991) Gender, history, and management style in nursing: Towards a theoretical systhesis. *The Sociological Review*, 39(1), pp. 229–252.
Davies, C. (1995) *Gender and the professional predicament in nursing*. Buckingham, UK: Open University Press.
Dicicco-Bloom, B. (2004) The racial and gendered experiences of immigrant nurses from Kerala, India. *Journal of Transcultural Nursing*, 15(1), pp. 26–33.
Dicken, P., Kelly, P. F., Olds, K. & Wai-Chung Yeung, H. (2001) Chains and networks, territories and scales: Towards a relational framework for analyzing the global economy. *Global Networks*, 1(2), pp. 89–112.
Ehrenreich, B. & Hochschild, A. (2002) *Global woman: Nannies, maids and sex-workers in the new economy*. New York: Metropolitan Books.
Ehrenreich, B., & Hochschild, A. R. (2003) *Global woman: Nannies, maids, and sex workers in the new economy*. New York: Macmillan.
Ely, R. J., & Meyerson, D. E. (2000) Theories of gender in organizations: A new approach to organizational analysis and change. *Research in Organizational Behavior*, 22, pp. 103–151.
Folbre, N. (2005) Nursebots to the rescue? Immigration, automation, and care. *Globalizations*, 3(3), pp. 349–360.
Fudge, J. & MacPhail, F. (2009) The temporary foreign worker program in Canada: Low-skilled workers as an extreme form of flexible labour. *Comparative Labour Law and Policy Journal*, pp. 101–141.
Glucksman, M. & Nolan, J. (2007) New technologies and the transformations of women's labour at home and work. *Equal Opportunities International*, 26(2), pp. 96–113.

Gordon, S. (2005) *Nursing against the odds: How healthcare cost cutting, media stereotypes, and medical hubris undermine nurses and patient care.* Ithaca: Cornell.
Groutsis, D. (2003) The state, immigration policy and labour market practices: The case of overseas-trained doctors. *The Journal of Industrial Relations*, 45(10), pp. 67–86.
Harvey, D. (2007) *A brief history of neoliberalism.* Oxford: Oxford University Press.
Harvey, D. (2010) *The enigma of capital and the crises of capitalism.* Oxford: Oxford University Press.
Hassim, S. (2008) Global constraints on gender equality in care work. *Politics and Society*, 36(3), pp. 388–402.
Hearn, J. (2015) *Men of the world: Gender, globalizations, transnational times.* London: Sage.
Heyzer, N. & Wee, V. (1994) Domestic workers in transient overseas employment: Who benefits, who profits. *The Trade in Domestic Workers: Causes, Mechanisms and Consequences of International Migration*, 1, pp. 31–102.
Hochschild, A. (2000) Global care chains and emotional surplus value. In W. Hutton & A. Giddens (eds.) *On the edge: Living with global capitalism.* London: Jonathan Cape, pp. 130–146.
Holton, R. J. (2008) *Global networks.* London: Palgrave Macmillan.
Hondagneu-Sotelo, P. (2001) *Domestica: Immigrant workers cleaning and caring in the shadows of affluence.* Berkeley: University of California Press.
Hood, C. (1991) A public management for all seasons? *Public Administration*, 69(1), pp. 3–19.
International Organisation for Migration (2006) *Female migrants: Bridging the gap throughout life cycle.* Geneva: International Organization of Migration.
International Organisation for Migration (IOM) and United Nations Reseach and Training Institute for the Advacement of Women (UN-INSTRAW) (2007) Survey on remittances 2007: Gender perspectives. *Working books on migration 24.* Geneva: United Nations.
Ishi, T. (1987) Class conflict, the state, and linkage: Migration of nurses from the Philippines. *Berkley Journal of Sociology*, 37(1), pp. 281–312.
Kelly, P. F. (2007) *Filipino migration, transnationalism, and class identity.* Working paper series 90. Signapore: Asia Research Institute, National University of Singapore.
Kelly, P. F. (2010) Filipino migration and the spatialities of labour market subordination. In S. McGrath-Champ, A. Herod & A. Rainnie (eds.) *Handbook of employment and society: Working space.* London: Routledge, pp. 159–176.
Kelly, P. F. (2012a) Labor, movement: Migration, mobility, geographies of work. In T. Barnes, J. Peck & E. Sheppard (eds.) *The new companion to economic geography.* Oxford: Wiley-Blackwell, pp. 431–443.
Kelly, P. F. (2012b) Migration, transnationalism, and the spaces of class identity. *Philippine Studies: Historical and Ethnographic Viewpoints*, 60(2), pp. 153–185.
Kelly, P. F. & D' Addario, S. (2008) Filipinos are very strongly into medical stuff: Labour market segmentation in Toronto, Canada. In J. Connell (ed.) *The international migration of health workers.* London: Routledge, pp. 77–98.
Kelly, P. F. & Olds, K. (2007) Researching transnational networks in economic geography. In T. Barnes, J. Peck, E. Sheppard & A. Tickell (eds.) *Politics and practices in economic geography.* London: Sage, pp. 255–266.
Khagram, S. & Levitt, P. (2004) *Towards a field of transnational studies and a sociological transnationalism research program.* Working paper No. 24. Cambridge:

Hauser Center for Non-Profit Organizations at Harvard University. http://ssrn.com/abstract=556993 (accessed June 12th, 2009)

Kingma, M. (2006) *Nurses on the move: Migration and the global health care economy*. London: ILR Press.

Knijn, T. (2000) Marketization and the struggling logics of (home) care in the Netherlands. In M. Harrington Meyer (ed.) *Care work: Gender, labour, and the welfare state*. New York: Routledge, pp. 232–248.

Kofman, E. (2004) Gendered global migrations. *International Feminist Journal of Politics*, 6(4), pp. 643–665.

Kofman, E. (2007). The knowledge economy, gender and stratified migrations. *Studies in Social Justice*, 1(2), pp. 122–135.

Kofman, E. & Raghuram, P. (2006). Gender and global labour migrations: Incorporating skilled workers. *Antipode*, 38(2), pp. 282–303.

Kurma, S., Simpson, R. & Burke, R. J. (2014) *The handbook of gender in organizations*. London: Sage.

Le Espiritu, Y. (2002) Filipino navy stewards and Filipina health care professionals: Immigration, work, and family relations. *Asian and Pacific Migration Journal*, 11(2), pp. 47–66.

Lutz, H. (2008) *Migration and domestic work: A European perspective on a global theme*. Aldershot: Ashgate.

Lutz, H. (2011) *The new maids: Transnational women and the care economy*. London: Zed Books.

Mackay, L. (1989) *Nursing a problem*. New York: McGraw-Hill.

Mahon, R. & Phillips, S. (2002) Dual-earner families caught in a liberal welfare regime? The politics of child care policy in Canada. *Child Care Policy at the Crossroads: Gender and Welfare State Restructuring*, pp. 191–218.

Mattingly, D. (1999) *Making maids: United States immigration policy and immigrant domestic workers*. New York: Routledge.

McDowell, L. (2008) Thinking through work: Complex inequalities, constructions of differences, and trans-national migrants. *Progress in Human Geography*, pp. 491–507.

Michel, S. & Mahon, R. (eds.) (2002) *Child care policy at the crossroads: Gender and welfare state restructuring*. New York: Routledge.

Momsen, J. (ed.) (1999) *Gender, migration, and domestic service*. New York: Routledge.

Morgan, K. (2002) Does anyone have a 'Libre Choix'? Subversive liberalism and the politics of French child care policy. In S. Michel & R. Mahon (eds.) *Child care policy at the crossroads: Gender and welfare state restructuring*. New York: Routledge, pp. 143–167.

Organisation for economic cooperation and development (OECD) (2007) *Immigrant health workers in OECD countries in the broader context of highly skilled migration*. Geneva: Sopemi, pp. 161–228.

Organisation for economic cooperation and development (OECD) (2010) *International migration outlook*. Geneva: Sopemi, pp. 27–28.

Paiewonsky, D. (2007) *Feminization of migration*. Geneva: United Nations International Research and Training Institute for the Advancement of Women.

Parreñas, R. S. (2001) *Servants of globalization*. Stanford: Stanford University Press.

Parreñas, R. S. (2005). The gender paradox in the transnational families of Filipino migrant women. *Asian and Pacific Migration Journal*, 14(3), pp. 243–268.

Parreñas, R. S. (2012) The reproductive labour of migrant workers. *Global Networks*, 12(2), pp. 269–275.
Pierson, P. (2001) Post-industrial pressures on mature welfare states. In P. Pierson (ed.) *The new politics of the welfare state*. New York: Oxford, pp. 80–104.
Pollitt, C. (1990) *Managerialism and the public services*. London: Blackwell.
Pollitt, C. (1995) Justification by works or by faith evaluating new public management. *Evaluation*, 1(2), pp. 133–154.
Rafferty, A. M. & Solano, D. (2007) The rise and demise of the colonial nursing service: British nurses in the colonies, 1896–1966. *Nursing History Review*, 15, p. 147.
Raghuram, P. & Kofman, E. (2002) State, labour markets and immigration: Overseas doctors in UK. *Environment and Planning A*, pp. 2071–2089.
Ribeiro, J. Sousa (2008) Gendering migration flows: Physicians and nurses in Portugal. *Equal Opportunities International*, 27(1), pp. 77–87.
Sassen, S. (2000) Women's burden: Counter-geographies of globalization and the feminization of survival. *Journal of International Affairs*, 53(2), pp. 503–524.
Selberg, R. (May 2013) Nursing in times of neoliberal change: An ethnographic study of nurses' experiences of work intensification. *Nordic Journal of Working Life Studies*, 3(2), pp. 9–35.
Smith, P. & Mackintosh, M. (2007) Profession, market and class: Nurse migration and the remaking of division and disadvantage. *Journal of Clinical Nursing*, 16(12), pp. 2213–2220.
Sparr, P. (1994) *Mortgaging women's lives: Feminist critiques of structural adjustment*. London: Zed Books.
Stilwell, B., Diallo, K., Zurn, P., Vujicic, M., Adams, O. & Dal Poz, M. (2004) Migration of health-care workers from developing countries: Strategic approaches to its management. *Bulletin of the World Health Organization*, 82(8), pp. 595–600.
United Nations Research and Training Institute for the Advancement of Women (UN-INSTRAW) (2005) *Crossing borders: Remittances, gender, and development*. Geneva: United Nations.
Vertovec, S. (1999) Conceiving and researching transnationalism. *Ethnic and Racial Studies*, 22(2), pp. 447–462.
Vertovec, S. (2002) *Transnational networks and skilled labour migration*. Oxford: University of Oxford. Transnational Communities Programme, pp. 1–15.
Wichterich, C. (2002) *The globalized woman*. New York: Zed Books.
Wickramasekara, P. (2000) *Policy response to skilled migration: Retention, return, and circulation*. Geneva: International migration programme, ILO.
Wickramasekara, P. (2002). *Asian labour migration: Issues and challenges in an era of globalization*. Geneva: ILO.
Witz, A. & Savage, M. (eds.) (1992) *Gender and bureaucracy*. Oxford: Oxford University Press.
World Health Organization. UNFPA. (2006) *Mental health aspects of women's reproductive health: A global review of the literature*. Geneva: World Health Organization.
Wrede, S. (2010) How country matters: Studying health policy in a comparative perspective. In I. D. Bourgeault (ed.) *The Sage handbook of qualitative methods in health research*. London: Sage, pp. 88–105.
Wrede, S., Henriksson, L., Høst, H., Johansson, S. & Dybbroe, B. (eds.) (2008) *Care work in crisis: Reclaiming the Nordic ethos of care*. Lund: Studentlitteratur.
Wrede, S. & Näre, L. (2013) Glocalising care in the Nordic countries: An introduction to the special issue. *Nordic Journal of Migration Research*, 3(2), pp. 57–62.

Yeates, N. (2004). Global care chains. *International Feminist Journal of Politics*, 6(3), pp. 369–391.

Yeates, N. (2005). Global migration perspectives. Global Commission on International Migration, pp. 1–20.

Yeates, N. (2009a) *Globalising care economies and migrant workers: Explorations in global care chains*. Basingstoke: Palgrave Macmillan.

Yeates, N. (2009b) Production for export: The role of the state in the development and operation of global care chains. *Population, Space and Place*, 15(2), pp. 205–228.

Yeates, N. (2011) Going global: The transnationalization of care. *Development and Change*, 42(4), pp. 1109–1130.

Yeates, N. (2012) Global care chains: A state-of-the-art review and future directions in care transnationalization research. *Global Networks*, 12(2), pp. 135–154.

Zlotnik, H. (2003) *The global dimensions of female migration*. Washington, DC: Migration Information Source, Migration Policy Institute (MPI).

3 Framing Transnational Human Resource Management of Nurse Labour

This chapter theoretically challenges the 'international' in the discipline and practice of international human resource management (IHRM) by replacing 'international' with the term 'transnational'. Through this new conceptualisation, the chapter argues to move the analysis of IHRM practices to include more organisations that manage health care provisions and nurse labour, either for private profit or publically funded. The management of human capital within the industry of nurse labour has become big business and competition for firms recruiting and placing health care professionals from one country to the next (Brush et al., 2004), but also involves other actors from various levels of management and organisation: local, regional, national, and transnational. These levels are both intertwined but also situated in terms of structures, economies, and societal and ideological histories. The taken-for-granted idea that the management of people across borders/levels can be generally prescribed marginalises voices and ignores the complexity of how various actors are situated within networks, structures, and discourses that socially construct how people are organised within their occupation and subsequent workplace. This chapter is divided into four sections: (1) an overview of critical approaches towards IHRM in management and organisation studies, (2) framing transnational feminism as a lens to analyse empirical data in situated human resource management practices, (3) conceptualising transnational human resource management (THRM), and (4) the use of producer-based care networks as an analytical focal point to situate the production of knowledge of the management of people within the transnational health care industry.

An Overview of Critical Approaches Towards IHRM in Management and Organisation Studies

Critical Engagement Within International Human Resource Management

The theoretical development and practice of international human resource management (IHRM) is highly embedded and influenced by the field of international management. This interdependence of the two fields lays claims that the development of international management, particularly within businesses, extends from an interest of achieving a better understanding of HRM in international contexts from both a managerialist and performance-based understanding (De Cieri et al., 2007: 283; Jack et al., 2008; Boxall et al., 2007).

Although the linkage between HRM and a managerialist agenda raises concerns amongst mainstream IHRM and IM scholars, critical scholars vocalise the narrowness and conservatism of this mainstream outlook. Critical scholars of IHRM argue that the fields of international management and IHRM lack in critical engagement in their metatheoretical assumptions which has led research in both fields 'to be firmly rooted in traditional functionalist-positivism, with little reflexivity about the claims and consequences of such an epistemological stance' (Jack et al., 2008: 5). Scholars contend that the narrow focus prompts an inefficient examination of the research's inclusions, exclusions, and its effects, such as the reproduction of universalist assumptions that have marginalised voices (Westwood, 2006; Nkomo, 1992) and decontexualises practices (Cooke et al., 2017). Furthermore, the current mainstream approach limits the scope of engaging with important social and structural questions such as the production of knowledge and power amongst various actors through negotiations and networks, the situatedness of managing people, and the economic and political institutions, networks, and structures that regulate borders in which practices and people cross (Delbridge et al, 2011: 484).

The focal point of theory and analysis in IHRM mostly revolves around multinational corporations (MNCs) that manage production or deliver services in more than one country, all of which is largely shaped by global capital(ism). As the global economy changes, IHRM scholars take heed. IHRM considers the changes in the global workforce and the growing management of human capital in global services. And yet, a significant change in the production of global services, that of human services, has not been considered. The global human capital that is now being produced and used transnationally to fulfill the lack of health care services has been viewed to be a concern for migration studies not IHRM.

This book aims to critique IHRM by suggesting a transnational feminist (gendering/racialising) lens, but also by bringing the health care sector into the analytical conversation on the management of people in the current global, capitalist economy. The intention is to go beyond positivist, managerial understandings of HRM practices by not only situating the practices in terms of geography, structures, economies, and societal and ideological histories, but also considering the industrialisation of health care and its human capital as a part of IHRM as a discipline within management and organisation studies.

Critical engagement with management and organisation studies, and here with IHRM, is not only about approaching the research from the periphery of the field but also challenging the epistemological and methodological underpinnings of the fields by situating the critical researcher's own understandings. As argued by Delbridge et al.:

> [W]hile there has been a major push for studies to open the 'black box' to explain how and why HR practices may lead to better performance (Wall and Wood, 2005), few studies have been able to illustrate convincingly causal and mediating mechanisms.
>
> (2011: 487)

This is due, according to Delbridge et al. (2011), to theoretical and epistemological weakness that centralises around micro-level theories of organisational behaviour and individual motivation, cognition or effect, and theories of human capital and a resource-based view of the firm (Delbridge et al., 2011; Batt and Banerjee, 2009).

In the next section, I discuss both the critical engagement with international management and IHRM as both fields have been developed together in mainstream research as if IHRM is an extension of understanding management internationally. These last implications may shed light on why MNCs and expatriates are the main focal point of analysis in IM and IHRM.

Critical Theorists in HRM and IHRM

In 1993, Townley (1993, 1994) critically challenged the concept of HRM's practices and discourse by using the work of Foucault to illustrate how these practices manage, through a number of disciplinary techniques, to create the individual 'as [an] analyzable, describable subject to be assessed, judged, measured, and compared with others' (1993: 535). She states that research on HRM should involve a discursive analysis of situations that provoke the discourse of HRM, the consequences to which it gives rise, the practical field in which it is deployed, who is accorded the right to speak, the institutional sites from which the discourse derived its legitimisation, the position in which it places its subjects, what is recognised as valid, and who has access to discourse (Townley, 1993: 540).

By using Foucault's work, Townley associates herself epistemologically with poststructuralism by not only viewing HRM practices and discourse as socially constructed but also intertwined with power implications (in terms of subordination of subjects through discourse) which institutionalises hierarchies of people, their labour, and physical bodies as well as taken-for-granted practices of how to organise employees.

In the 1990s, other organisation and management studies increasingly became interested in issues related to knowledge, power, discourse, and identity (Alvesson and Willmott, 2012; Fournier and Grey, 2000; du Gay, 1996; Clegg, 1989; Clegg and Hardy, 2006). Calás and Smircich (1999) have argued that the introduction of postmodern and poststructuralist approaches have influenced the conduct of sociological research on management. In particular, there has been a focus on situated reflexivity toward common sense categories and knowledge claims prevalent in the authorial articulations on the nature of organisations and organisational management. Out of these engagements, scholarly communities arose such as the International Management Studies conference and the Critical Management Studies division within the US-American Academy of Management.

In 2006 and 2012, Peltonen, in the Sage *Handbook of International Human Resource Management*, provided a review of critical theoretical engagements of IHRM and discusses current approaches to the field that consider HRM practices, both domestically and internationally, in terms of 'societal structures, ideologies and power relations that constitute and shape the organisational phenomena and workplace relations' (2012: 532). A particular focus in these critical reviews are on control and governing practices, techniques, and practices within IHRM and its implications on employee and workplace relations. One approach that Peltonen mentions is the critical understanding of the term 'culture' and the use of personnel techniques that are justified in terms of culture. These techniques can be used to exclude or include personnel and legitimise techniques in reference 'to cultural differences and cross-cultural adjustments instead of a more general concern with organisational effectiveness or employee well-being (e.g. Adler, 2002)' (Peltonen, 2012: 535). Peltonen furthers his discussion, under the title '[T]owards a critical research programme within IHRM: current debates and future avenues', and describes critical approaches to IHRM with his focus on multinational enterprises (MNEs), international business (IB), and international management (IM) as well as expatriates. This, in turn, provides a review of the critical approaches to IHRM but limits the approaches to the mainstream IHRM scholars' empirical point of entry.

De Cieri et al. (2007) use the critical perspective of postcolonialism to highlight that IHRM deserves theoretical disputation and that take-for-granted assumptions in the practice should be problematised and questioned. They argue that these assumptions have a direct effect on thoughts and behaviours, which can lead to 'isomorphism' in the description and assessment of IHRM theory and practice. De Cieri et al. (2007) further their argument by using what they term 'imitation', drawing highly from Bhabha's (1994) terms of mimicry and hybridity. Imitation is 'the copying of another's form, practice or claim to legitimacy' (293). This would direct the analysis to how and why existing practices and disciplines are adopted and adapted and, in turn, highlight what is being taken for granted rather than subsuming 'other' past or present differences (ibid).

Postcolonialism, as an epistemology, is interested in relations and structures that reproduce historical colonial legacies and present neoimperialism. This reproduction of situated histories, practices, and discourses socially construct people in ways that exclude and include particular knowledges and voices and enforce powerful barriers to equality in the global economy (Acker, 2004, 2006; McDowell, 2008; Mignolo, 2000). Exclusion barriers are not only ignored but also taken-for-granted among mainstream management (and IHRM) scholars. Postcolonialism, as a theoretical lens, challenges the researcher to deconstruct prescribed practices and theories in IM and IHRM by using methods such as discourse analysis of narratives, histories, visual materials, ethnographies, case studies, and critical readings of canonical texts (e.g. Westwood, 2006 Jack and Westwood, 2009).

In 2008, international management became the subject of critique in management studies as being disengaged with epistemic reflexivity and the field's theoretical development. Within this discussion, a special topic forum in the *Academy of Management* was published with eight contributions that 'attempt to open up metatheoretical conversation with international management' (2009: 870). The call of papers for this forum emphasised 'the articulation of alternative theoretical representations that will allow new conceptualisations in this field [international management], taking into account the unavoidable power relations that sustain the materials realities of international management' (2009: 870).

Within the eight contributions, postcolonialism as an epistemological framework was favoured and methods of analysis were, for instance, linguistic analysis, deconstructionist approaches, metaphor analysis, and discourse analysis. The impression given by the contributors' perspectives and methods is to encourage and facilitate a discussion within international management by 'bringing in other knowledge/other's knowledge' (2009: 880). At the end of the introduction to the special topic forum, the authors comment on 'Reflections on "what we already know"' and mention that they do not want to reinvent the wheel of critical approaches to international management, but rather apply the approaches in analysis. The critical approaches, nonetheless, are for analysis of MNCs and not other sectors in the global economy.

In 2009, Peltonen and Vaara published a chapter on critical approaches to comparative HRM. In this chapter, they argue that comparative HRM is broader than mainstream approaches to IHRM because it takes seriously the 'recent calls for more socially embedded organisational research' (2009: 69). The authors argue that comparative HRM can be linked to critical management studies (CMS) in the sense that the field can make use of the theoretical and methodological approaches that they suggest. These approaches are global labour process theory, postcolonial analysis, and transnational feminism. To structure this argument, the authors give an explanation of each approach but also provide a table divided into the following sections: (1) background influences, (2) focus, (3) research questions, (4) epistemology, (5) ontology, (6) methods, and (7) exemplary studies (2009: 78–79).

The idea of bringing in different critical perspectives to be applied to comparative HRM facilitates the broader discussion on how to include more theories, voices, and methods in the fields. Nonetheless, I feel this chapter is more a suggestion rather than providing 'exemplary studies' in the discipline of management and organisation. For instance, Mohanty is a self-proclaimed 'transnational and postcolonial feminist' and is a professor of women and gender studies. Her work is an anti-capitalist struggle against neoliberal globalisation, and she illustrates her activism by empirically examining the cultural and ideological construction of a woman's representational form through discourse (scientific, literary, judicial, linguistic, cinematic, etc.), and 'women' as real, material subjects of their collective history (Mohanty, 1984: 334). She does not focus on employment relations or management of human capital, per se. She is interested in the inequalities that derive from uneven economic development and cultural imperialism, and her empirical work is not directly linked to management structures, practices, and discourse within the field of IHRM. Suggesting transnational feminism to the discussion of IHRM and comparative HRM is one thing, but, as this book suggests, what is lacking in the field is the application of transnational feminism to the analysis of practices in human resource management as already done for modernism, poststructuralism, and postcolonialism.

One example of transnational feminism being applied to management and organisation studies is by Calás and Smircich (2011) in their chapter entitled '[I]n the back and forth of transmigration: rethinking organisation studies in a transnational key'. In this chapter, the authors use the work of transnational feminists such as Mohanty and apply it to the analysis of transmigrants. They argue that organisation and management studies have considered transnationalism but more as a dichotomous relationship of back and forth, from headquarters to subsidiaries or to the allocation of labour between 'home' and 'not home' such as with expatriate managers or immigrant workers. The chapter begins:

> Along with conditions of globalization, a dominant feature of social life has become the increase of transnational flows of multiple kinds—people, money, ideas, images—(Appadurai, 1990, 1996; Vertovec, 2009). Within the organization studies literature, however, little attention is paid to the fact that transnational flows and interconnections are manifested in a multidirectional back-and-forth of people, practices, and the like. Instead transnationalism in this literature refers mostly to transferring practices from one country to another, such as from headquarters to subsidiaries or to the allocation of labor between 'home' and 'not home' such as with expatriate managers or immigrant workers, and even when offshoring work. In this chapter we suggest the limited understanding of transnationalism in the organizational life whether in big or small organizations, 'local' or 'global'. To this effect, we propose ways for reconsidering organization studies, more generally, in a transnational key.
>
> (2011: 411)

The chapter serves as an introduction to transmigration studies and transnational (feminism) to be applied to the understanding of national borders, various actors in the global political economy, and gendered and racialised processes and practices that are situated and have powerful effects on the workers' lives and physical bodies.

In 2013, Calás and Smircich empirically exemplify gendered, transnational processes by focusing on the intersectionality of women migrants and the implications the 'mobile' intersectionality has on women's subjectivities. The analysis captures the individuals' subjectivities organised transnationally, but the analysis leaves a space for further empirical work on structural, institutional, and organisational practices and processes organising labour across borders.

In the next section, I discuss why and how a transnational feminist lens can broaden the understanding of HRM practices, techniques, and discourses in various contexts in today's global economy. The lens requests going beyond creating models of causal factors influencing HRM policies and practices in MNCs, and the duality between centralisation (or global integration) versus decentralisation (or local responsiveness). The lens facilitates a situated, multi-level analysis of how, why, and by whom (which actors) people are being managed and explicitly acknowledges ruling relations (see Dorothy Smith, 1987, 1990a, 1990b) through discourses and structures that have material implications on employees' lives.

Framing Transnational Feminism as a Lens to Analyse Empirical Data

Transnational Feminisms

Applying the transnational feminist lens to IHRM as a discipline and practice is not only about applying a theory, but also an action associated with values and convictions of social justice. Scholars argue that transnational feminism is a conscious, political shift away from other feminist framings such as third wave/global, black, socialist, postcolonial, and postmodern/poststructural. Although influenced by and in conversation with these feminisms, the emphasis of transnational feminism is to critically examine not only the nation-state and the local in gendering and racialising organisations, but also the transnational capitalistic economy.

Using transnational feminism as a lens means conceptualising the state not as a fixed entity with borders, but rather the state with borders that are permeable and influenced by an historical legacy that may not have occurred physically (the actual) in its geographical area. Through this lens, empirical examination is contextualised in a social and economic history influenced by colonial/imperial legacies and power relations that organise capital and labour in gendered, racialised, and classed ways, impacting the worker's lives in concrete material forms. Examples of scholars working with this lens, for instance, are Acker (2004, 2006), Mohanty (1984, 2013), Calás and Smircich (2006, 2011), Grewal and Kaplan (1994, 2000), Kaplan and Grewal (1999).

Acker does not describe herself as a transnational feminist, and yet her work on gendering globalisation and equality barriers to work organisations is highly influential on management and organisation studies in framing institutional mechanisms that construct the workers and the deeply embedded implications of organising in a global economy. Although her work is concerned with borders of the nation-state and work organisation as she comes from an institutional sociology perspective, her concept of 'gendering globalisation' fairs well with a transnational feminist lens and may be reconceptualised as 'gendering transnationalism'. This reconceptualisation may allow an examination of various forms of movement across time and space rather than focusing solely on socially constructed divisions that maintain boundaries of the nation, gender, and race. For instance, I find the terms 'globalisation' and 'international' problematic and limiting, particularly in my analysis of international human resource management. By focusing on borders as static, justifications of cultural differences and barriers create a conversation of 'us' versus 'them' and legitimise the uneven circuits of labour and capital (e.g. Tsui-Auch, 1999). Globalisation and fixed national/cultural borders, within IHRM, seem to provide space and a dialogue of victimisation of the migrants who are leaving one country for another as a career move. With this mindset, a conversation starts by looking outwards and projecting inequalities on others that exist structurally and discursively amongst those who are assuming a privileged position within the management of human resources.

The use of the concept of 'international' within human resources connotes the existence of nation-states as discrete and sovereign entities, and work organisations can rely on 'dimensions' of cultural differences when managing people from one geographical region to the next (Shenkar, 2001, 2004). This is not to say that relations to the nation-states and work organisations are irrelevant when working with the lens of transnational feminism, but, as argued by Grewal and Kaplan, the lens

> problematize[s] a purely locational politics of global-local or center-periphery in favor of . . . the lines cutting across them. As feminists who note the absence of gender issues in all these worlds system theories, we have no choice but to challenge what we see as inadequate and inaccurate binary divisions.
>
> (1994: 13)

In addition, I acknowledge the influences of postcolonial concepts such as 'hybridity' and 'mimicry' (Bhabha, 1994), and 'orientalism' (Said, 1978). The postcolonial lens' influence on transnational feminism is undeniable, and it provides feminists with conceptual tools to examine various forms and issues of representation. The lens also brings into conversation how imperialism and colonialism 'travels' through time and space and emerges in various forms and practices. Yet, working with a transnational feminist lens creates a discomfort with relations to nations and cultural divisions, which is not always the case when the focus is on colonial/imperial relations and divisions.

In Figure 3.1, I display a framework of some of the epistemologies and ontologies used under the umbrella of transnational feminism(s) within organisational studies and outside of organisational studies.[1] The framework is within two ontological dimensions of 'more structuralist' and 'more poststructuralist', and four epistemologies of examining gender, racialised processes and practices in a transnational, capitalistic economy. The epistemologies are institutionalism and feminist political economy/neoMarxism, within the dimension of 'more structuralist', and feminist postmodernism and postcolonial feminism, within the dimension of 'more poststructuralist'. In terms of 'more structuralist', scholars within this dimension examine structured mechanisms of control and practices within institutions, organisations, and larger governing bodies such as the nation-state. This dimension also concerns itself with borders, barriers, and lines in workplaces, organisations, and political, geographical division of governance (e.g. nation-state divisions). Feminist institutionalism and feminist political

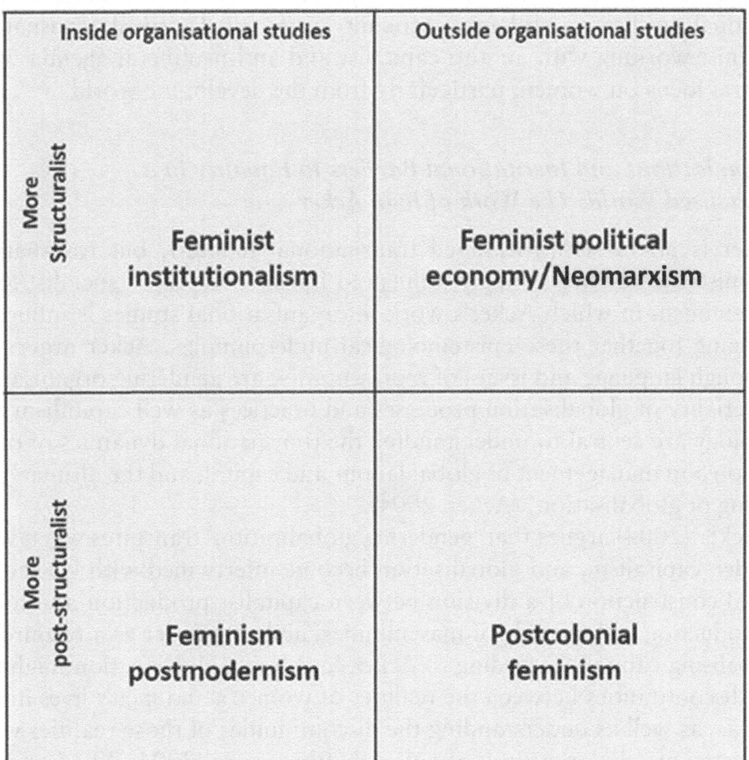

Figure 3.1 Framework of epistemologies under the umbrella of transnational feminism

economy/neoMarxism examine social and organisational phenomena in terms of past and present historical and institutionalised divisions.

In terms of the ontological dimensions of a 'more poststructuralist' view, scholars examine issues of representation and the implications of gendering and racialising the organisations and people's lives rather than institutional mechanisms within the global, capitalistic economy.

In the following sections, I illustrate the epistemological frames under the umbrella of transnational feminism by referencing particular scholars and their ideas. I begin with Joan Acker and describe her work in terms of her concepts 'gendering globalisation' and 'inequality barriers'. I then turn to the work of Calás and Smircich whose theoretical and empirical discussion reconceptualise global processes and practices in terms of a multidimensional rather than a dichotomous relationship of back and forth. The discussion of Calás and Smircich's work is followed with Grewal and Kaplan whose work has been influential from a feminist political economy perspective and analytically deconstructs the concept of 'international'. Their work also falls outside the discipline of organisational studies unlike Acker and Calás and Smircich. Another scholar's work who has been influential for various scholars working within transnational feminism and outside organisational studies is Mohanty. Mohanty is a self-described transnational feminist working with an anti-capitalist and anti-neoliberal agenda with a central focus on women, particularly from the developing world.

Organisations and Institutional Barriers to Equality in a Globalised World: The Work of Joan Acker

Acker is not a self-proclaimed transnational feminist, but transnational feminists' works are strongly influenced by the theories of socialist/Marxist feminism in which Acker's work in organisational studies is influential. Bringing together these epistemological underpinnings, Acker argues that although language and issues of representation are gendering organisations, materiality of globalisation processes and practices as well capitalism as an ideology are central to understanding the transnational dynamics of organisation and management of global labour and capital, and the ultimate 'gendering of globalisation' (Acker, 2004).

Acker (2004) argues that 'gendering globalisation' transpires when/where gender, capitalism, and globalisation become intertwined with (1) the gendered construction of a division between capitalist production and human reproduction, (2) the role of masculinities, and (3) gender as a resource for globalising capital. According to Acker, 'gendering globalisation' highlights the discontinuities between the realities of women's and men's lives in local arenas, as well as understanding the discontinuities of those realities within mainstream scholarly work about global processes (2004: 20). Gendering organisations and global process and capital, to Acker, are not solely about the sexed body, but rather guiding 'gender' analyses with the examination of subjectivities, subject positions, and institutions over time and space as relational products and producers of global processes (2004: 18). The gendering of globalisation, therefore, becomes an analysis of intersections of gender with other subjectivation processes, such as race, ethnicity, class, and sexualities, to better understand specific global processes at specific sites where they appear (2004: 19).

Acker's first argument about a 'gendered division of labour' reflects corporate policies that favor workers without dependents at both the local and global level by claiming no responsibilities for the reproduction of human life through the favouring of workers and labour that create monetary profit.[2] These practices create, at the local level, a gendered system that is supported by unpaid reproductive work as well as the lower paid work in the for-profit economy such as health and social service work. This non-responsibility at the local level that favours capitalist accumulation becomes naturalised[3] as a globalisation process where production is continuously moved from location to location in order to maximise profits by finding cheap labour (e.g. competition between global for-profit organisations and nation-states). This labour is usually produced by a woman. Acker's first argument acknowledges how global processes must be nuanced with local specialties. For instance, the relationships between households, families, and communities as well as the conditions of women in different societies cannot be interpreted only from the perspectives of the gendering effects of Western societies. Thus, while the flows of global capital may move in certain directions, their effects, as well as resistances, must be considered both relationally, and also in their differential local effects and implications (e.g. Acker, 2004; Mohanty, 2007/2011).

Acker's second argument is for the analysis of 'masculinities in globalising capital'. This analysis questions who produces knowledge claims on defining 'globalisation' in both practice and theory. This analysis has both materialistic and symbolic implications. According to Acker, since the beginning of modern globalisation, through colonial conquests by England and other European countries, and later the expansion of 'free markets' and 'economic liberalisation', positions of power within gendered structures, social relations, and practices have been dominated by men. Not just any men, however, but men with particular masculinities or, in many cases, the desired hegemonic masculinities. Referencing both Connell (1987, 2000), Hearn (1993), and Hearn and Parkin (2001), Acker explains the symbolic and materialistic nature of dominating masculinities in the globalised capitalistic processes of colonial conquest and settlement and today's corporate capitalism:

> Masculinities are reproduced through organizational/institutional practices, social interaction, and through images, ideals, myths or representations of behaviors and emotions. Hegemonic masculinity is the most desired and admired form, attributed to leaders and other influential figures at particular historical times. . . . Globalizing masculinities

> around violence and domination seems to have been predominant in these two periods (18th and 19th Century) of conquest and settlement. As corporate capitalism developed, Connell and others for example (Collinson and Hearn, 1996), argue a hegemonic masculinity based on claims to expertise developed along with masculinities still organized around domination. Hegemonic masculinity relying on claims to expertise does not necessarily lead to economic organizations free of domination and violence however (Hearn and Parkin, 2001). Hearn and Parkin argue that controls relying on both explicit and implicit violence exist in a wide variety of organizations.
>
> (1990: 28–29)

Within today's global gendering practices and processes (1990: 31), Acker argues that violence is less explicit as the means of violence is institutional in seemingly neutral, rational business practices. The knowledge claims being dominantly produced comfortably and confidently by leaders as business as usual or of deficit reduction necessity, implicitly affects humans in materialistic forms. For instance downsizing or moving production or representing the 'desirable' (Acker, 1990) worker as flexible, disposable, and a commodity to be bought and sold, creates a workforce of domination.

The third argument by Acker is to 'analyse gender as a resource for globalising capital'. The central resource or 'human resource' of this analysis is women, particularly third-world women, whose transnational mobility contribute to the prosperity of capitalist production. Acker (2004) notes that transnational economies cannot be limited to the understanding of moving labour production to countries that permit lower wages, but rather through transnational labour migration from less affluent countries to more affluent countries. Transnational labour migration patterns can be understood as generating new forms of political economy and a culture of work intensification in receiving countries of the labour in which a flexible, cheaper workforce is needed to maintain modes of capitalist production (such as cheaper labour filling the jobs that have been associated with low pay or non-pay in the past, such as housework or caring).

Postmodernism and Transnational Organising: The Work of Marta B. Calás and Linda Smircich

Calás and Smircich's academic work is critical of the positivist epistemology in management and organisation by both theoretically and empirically using the lens of postmodernism, and, most recently, transnational feminism to examine gendering and racialising processes and practices that reinforce inequalities within social relations, fields, and discourses. According to Calás and Smircich:

> Research in transnational social fields would provide ways to articulate clearly and consistently in organization theory the centrality of gender/

> sexuality/race/ethnicity/class relations invisibly sustaining modalities of neoliberal globalization.
>
> (2011: 424)

In 1996 and 2006, Calás and Smircich theoretically explain transnational feminism through a literature review of feminisms in organisational studies and frame their understanding of the lens as having postmodernist/post-structuralist, socialist feminism, and black feminism roots. They state that

> Transnational/(post) colonial feminisms, while not monolithic, include several critics who challenge Western feminist theorizations of gender and gender relations as furthering the images and social experiences of mostly privileged women (and men) in the 'First World'. These arguments go beyond those raised by black and other race theorists who questioned the white, middle class, heterosexist, representations of gender in feminist theorizing, and interrogate, for instance, the function of 'the nation' in gendering and racializing others through specific patriarchal projects between and within different countries.
>
> (2006: 317)

To explore these transnational social fields, Calás and Smircich use the method of 'intersectionality' with a transnational feminist lens to understand better how the simultaneity of processes take place and disrupts the bounded nation, which creates new transnational social spaces (Calás and Smircich, 2011).

Empirically, through a transnational lens, Calás and Smircich gender their analysis of organisation in transnational social fields by examining subjectivities, subject positions, and institutions over time and space as relational products and producers of transnational processes. They indicate that

> gendering (and the race, ethnic, class, sexualities and other subjectivation processes with which gendering intersects) should produce a better understanding of current global processes at the specific sites where they appear.
>
> (2006: 322)

Outside Organisations and Outside the 'International': The Work of Inderpal Grewal and Caren Kaplan

Grewal and Kaplan began their scholar and teaching careers using the 'colonial discourse analysis' method to empirically examine how inequalities of class, gender, nationality, sexuality, and ethnicity are created through movements over time and space in particular ways (1994; Kaplan et al., 1999). Engaging with this empirical analysis of inequalities, Grewal and Kaplan (2005) want to focus their work not only in terms of civil rights practices and identities but also on forms of discourses with concrete material effects within the history of imperialism. For them, to understand projects of modernisation and development would request a term such as 'transnational' instead of 'international' as transnational destabilises rather than maintains boundaries of nation-state, race, and gender. Transnational, according to Grewal and Kaplan (2000: 1), 'signals attention to uneven and dissimilar circuits of culture and capital'. Whereas, the term 'international' does not allow this recognition as it is based on a configuration of the nation-state as discrete and sovereign entities, even though these boundaries were politically created through a system of inequality and exploitation.

Grewal and Kaplan acknowledge the influence postcolonial studies have had on their feminist trajectories, particularly their engagement with postcolonial theorists on the nation and nationalism. As feminist scholars, they view nationalism 'as a process in which new patriarchal elites gain the power to produce the generic "we" of the nation' (2000: 3). And yet, nationalism and the nation are not limited to patriarchies, but also the spread of Eurocentric discourses and the superiority of one's country and culture through, for instance, victimisation of the colonised/third-world Others (2005). Grewal and Kaplan argue that the relations with the nation-state and nationalism stealthy root themselves deeply in the minds of the citizens, and this blinds people looking outward at the Other to the structural inequalities that exist in their own local surroundings. The scholars give an example of Islamic women obtaining refugee asylum in the United States by pleading that their patriarchal cultures persecute them, and yet, the United States remains a country with extremely high rates of domestic violence (2005).

Outside Organisations and Neocolonial Structural Controls: The Work of Chandra Mohanty

A strong drive behind Mohanty's transnational feminist epistemology is collective feminist solidarity across borders (2003) and her own lived experiences as a scholar and transnational migrant woman of colour from India (Mohanty, 2007/2011). Across borders, to her, does not refer to confining a theoretical and methodological analysis solely within the nation-state, but rather geographically, economically, socially, and historically positioning women's lived experiences both 'particularly'[4] and collectively. As stated in her well-known work, 'Under Western eyes: feminist scholarship and colonial discourses',

> The relationship between 'Woman'—a cultural and ideological composite other constructed through diverse representational discourses (scientific, literary, judicial, linguistic, cinematic, etc.)—and 'women'—real, material subjects of their collective histories—is one of the central questions the practice of feminist scholars seeks to address. This connection between women as historical subjects and the re-presentation of Woman produced by hegemonic discourses is not a relation of direct identity, or a relation of correspondence or simple implication. It is an arbitrary relation set up by particular cultures.
>
> (1984: 197)

An avid reader of feminist theory in the early 1980s, Mohanty began to question what she was reading, and what these theories were teaching her. These questions led her to write 'Under Western eyes' to critique hegemonic feminist theories and 'global feminism' and to create a space for third-world women in Western feminist theory. In an interview, Mohanty reflects that

> 'we' were present in courses on development and political economy, and theoretically, 'we' often emerged as a foil to hegemonic White/Western feminist subjectivities.
>
> (2013)

She also states in another interview that the theories viewed gender as non-racialised, non-classed, and US-American (Mohanty, 2007/2011). There was no space for thinking about marginalised women, who, in her opinion, were often poor, working class, of colour in the North and peasant women of the South. These women communities were assumed to have little understanding as to why they are located in the situation they are in, which is, they have no understanding within the reading of power. She notes that within her reading of socialist feminism, there is something in terms of reading capitalism and how capitalist values become naturalised in the areas we live in. These values allow those with privileges to construct either those without privileges as victims or as people deserving of charity or as people with no critical understanding of power and how to fight it. She reflects:

> That actually is some of the ways I get to thinking about what it means to speak of global capitalism, corporate globalization right now, and of the possibility and potential of transnational anti-capitalist feminist struggle, right? That is how I get to this place where, you know, asking the questions of 'what is it, for instance, about how . . . historical colonialism construct themselves and their relations of rule on the basis of racialized gender? That becomes an important question. And how does that then get picked up in the decades following and how do capitalists relations of rule utilize those gender and racialized legacies of rule in order to, once again, create surplus labour, once again create third world poor women as the preferred workforce, and can we actually talk about anti-capitalist struggle without understanding the importance of race, gender, and colonial legacies in that struggle. . . . One way to think about it in the world we live in, 'how does the colonial traffic in the imperial?'
>
> (2007/2011)

Revisiting the 'Under the Western eyes' article in 2003, 16 years after its publication, Mohanty affirms that her original article

> sought to make the operations of discursive power visible, to draw attention to what was left out of feminist theorizing, namely the materialist complexity, reality and agency of Third World women's bodies and lives.
>
> (2003: 230)

As conversed in this interview and noted in the 2003 article, she analytically strives to

> draw attention to what is unseen, undertheorized and left out in the production of knowledge about globalization. [Because] . . . I believe capital as it functions now depends on and exacerbates racist, patriarchal and heterosexist relations of rule.
>
> (2003: 231)

To illustrate how global capitalism affects women's work in local specifics, Mohanty demonstrates how neutral categories of gender and race hierarchies in labour obscure historical differences around the world. By focusing on women's work, Mohanty argues that a particular form of third-world women's exploitation in the current economy ignores not only historical differences but also commonalities between third- and first-world women within 'the logic and operations of capital in the contemporary global arena' (Mohanty, 1997: 28).

Writing in an academic neoliberal context, Mohanty published an article entitled 'Transnational feminist crossings: on neoliberalism and radical critique' in which she argues that this individualistic mindset endorsed by the neoliberal ideology separates the feminist critique away from questions of gender and racialised systemic inequalities. She states:

> For instance, what happens to the key feminist construct of 'personal is political' when the political (the collective public domain of politics) is reduced to the personal? Questions of oppression and exploitation as collective, systematic processes and institutions of rule that are gendered and raced have difficulty being heard when neoliberal narratives disallow the salience of collective experience or redefine this experience as a commodity to be consumed. If all experience is merely individual, and the social is always collapsed into the personal, feminist critique and radical theory appear irrelevant—unless they confront these discursive shifts.
>
> (2013: 971)

Another concern that she addresses in this article is the limits of "post" (2013: 986) and that the commitment needed for the analysis of systemic and materialistic implications of colonial legacies, issues of representations, and the gendering and racialising of structures. She argues that

> The neoliberal privatization and domestication of social justice commitments can go hand in hand with postmodernist/poststructuralist dissolution of the systemic critiques of structures and institutions evident in intersectional, transnational materialist feminist engagement. This compromising of our politics reminds us that it is always

> important to turn the critique of privilege on ourselves. The dissolving of the systemic analyses of women of colour and transnational feminist projects into purely discursive (representational) analyses of ruptures, fluidity, and discontinuities symptomatic of post-structural critique contributes to a threshold of disappearance of materialist antiracist feminist projects that target the state and other governing institutions. It is the danger of the appropriation of radical women of colour and transnational feminist projects that should be of deep concern to us all.
> (2013: 986–987)

Here, I display Figure 3.2, accompanied by various scholars discussed previously with positions in the ontological dimensions and epistemological frames (Figure 3.1). The transnational feminist scholars work across the epistemological frames, both empirically and theoretically, to capture the transnational nuances of gendered and racialised organising across time, space, institutions, and cultures.

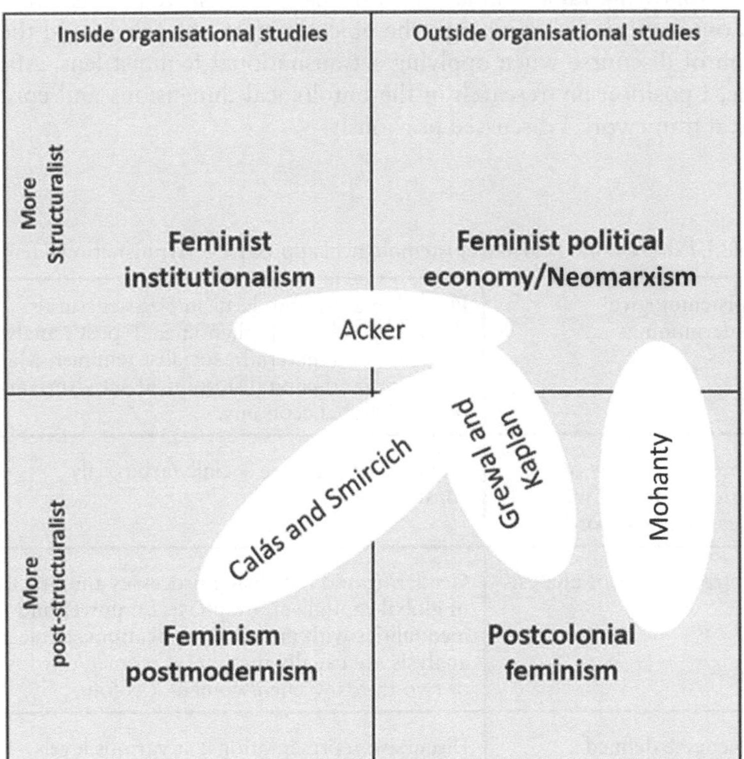

Figure 3.2 Positions of scholars working under the umbrella of transnational feminism

Working With Transnational Feminism(s)

Echoing the comments made by Calás and Smircich, 'transnational feminism(s) is not monolithic' and includes several scholars working with various ontological dimensions such as structuralist (e.g. a concern of borders and the functions of the nation-state) and poststructuralist (e.g. moving beyond or transcending borders considered politically and socially constructed).

My definition of 'transnational feminism' is the following:

> Transnational feminism is critical of capitalist production and processes that transcend borders, national and organisational, and systematically genderise and racialise humans (particularly third-world women) in material forms. This calls for analysis beyond 'post', specifically, examining not only issues of representation but also the concrete structural and material effects of capitalism and neoliberal ideology on women, men, and children's lives.

In the following table (Table 3.1), I display this research's epistemological and ontological underpinnings, the object/subject of analysis and the definition of discourse when applying a transnational feminist lens. After the table, I position my research in the ontological dimensions and epistemological framework I discussed previously.

Table 3.1 My ontological and epistemological approaches to transnational feminisms

Epistemological underpinnings	Postcolonial/postmodernism/poststructural (BUT, beyond the epiphenomenal 'post'; analysis of discourse and material), socialist feminist, Marxist feminism (anti-capitalist political activism), and political global economy.
Ontological view of the nation-state and work organisations (borders)	National borders are socially/arbitrarily constructed.
Object/subject of analysis	Gendering and racialising processes and practices of global capitalism. Emphasis on **power and inequalities with material implications.** Subjects of analysis are usually immigrant women/third-world or two-thirds women/women of colour.
Discourse defined	Discursive representations, at various levels, within text and talk but also tangible material implications of discourse ((re)production, (re) dissemination, and (re)reception).

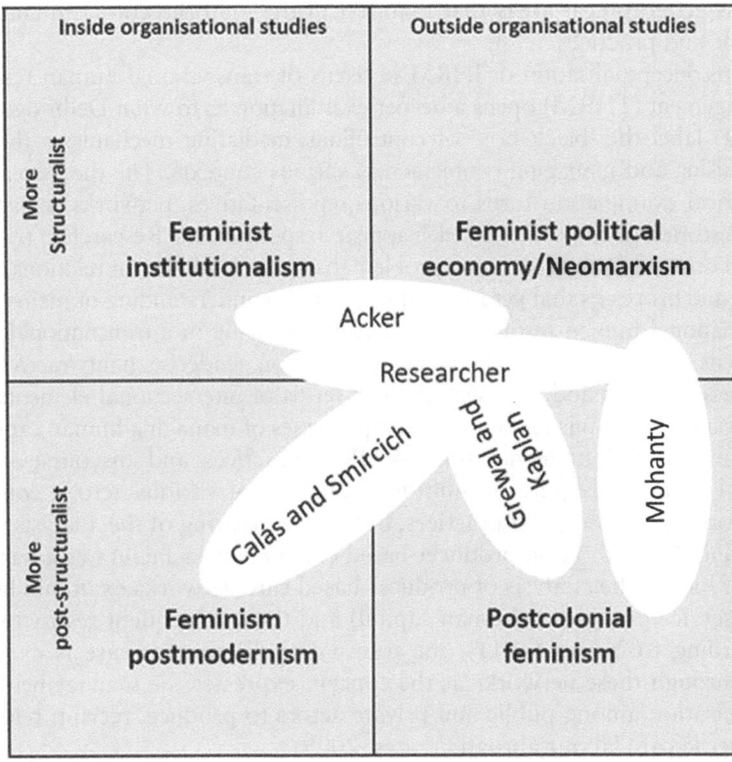

Figure 3.3 My ontological and epistemological approaches to transnational feminisms

Considering this summary, I position myself in the middle of the two dimensions and the four paradigms (Figure 3.3). My transnational feminist lens is critical of the fixed borders of organising and examines discursive representations as Grewal and Kaplan and Calás and Smircich, but I move beyond the limits of 'post' like Mohanty by gauging my focus on the material implications of discourse(s) and structuring effects of discursive practices within institutions and organisations like Acker.

Transnational Human Resource Management: The Case of Producer-Based Care Networks

Transnational human resource management as a concept is applied to examine HR systems' strategic processes, practices, and functional roles in terms of a situated or geographical duality of centralisation (global integration) versus decentralisation (local responsiveness) (Festing, 2011; Ståhl et al., 2012). However, as criticised by Calás and Smircich within the discipline of management and organisation (2011), this 'back and forth' divide limits the understanding of the various flows and interconnections of organising across geographical areas that manifest in the multidirectional nuances of people and practices.

A reconceptualisation of IHRM in terms of transnational human resource management (THRM) opens a deeper examination as to what Delbridge et al. (2011) label the 'black box' of controlling, mediating mechanisms that are organising and managing people across various contexts. The theoretical and empirical examination turns to various representatives, networks, structures, and histories, to name a few, which appear in specific sites. Research of transnational organising and managing problematises the invisibility of relations, practices, and processes that get lost in the prescribed understanding of mainstream international human resource management. Bringing in a transnational feminist lens situates the research and centralises it on gender/sexuality/race/ethnicity/class relations and representations in terms of intersectional elements that materialise in organising practices and processes of managing human capital.

Transnational understanding of HRM practices and discourse in the global economy requires a multi-level analysis of various actors, complex networks, processes, and practices, but also a situating of the analysis. Centralising the method on producer-based care networks facilitates a narrowing of focus. The analysis of producer-based care networks examines health care service provisions (human capital) and their subsequent restructuring. According to Yeates (2011), the transnationalisation of care is exemplified through these networks as the concept expresses the management and organisation among public and private actors to produce, recruit, relocate, and settle care labour abroad (Yeates, 2009).

Yeates (2011) notes that most studies of care transnationlisation are concerned with cross border migration processes, and this is understandable as 'the movement of people as a pre-eminent mode/expression of transnational activity and consciousness' (1117), but she questions the complex networks producing these movements and its various aspects. She states that producers' care networks should be used as conduits for transnational economic flows (remittances of goods and capital) and transnational ideational flows (ideas and ideologies of care); as constituted by and formative of border-spanning social formations (global care networks, transnational families); and as an object of transnational collective action (e.g. advocacy and coalition campaigns, policy formation/responses in and through domestic and/or global fora).

She expands this concept by focusing on skilled workers and their management, but also on the implication of restructuring the health care labour economy. Her analysis draws on her previous work of 'global nurse care chains' as she explains through both nurse labour management transnationally and Catholic Irish religious workers.

In terms of IHRM studies and practices, this term can help situate discourse, practices, actors, and networks at various levels in accordance with both theoretical and empirical entities to the field. The concept and subsequent method of choice made by the research creates an initiative of reflection as the research must question who or what are the producer(s) of knowledge in regards to the IHRM of care workers and what structural implications the production of this knowledge has.

Summary and Concluding Thoughts

As theoretical fields, international human resource management and international management have been subjected to critique by using theoretical approaches such as poststructuralism and postcolonialism and linguistic/discursive methods of analyses. These critiques request bringing more voices into the conversation of IM and IHRM practices, but also question the positivist, functionalist perspective that currently dominates the fields' understandings. This request concerns the analysis with issues of representation within the field and practices, but also highlights dominant knowledge production and its discursive and material consequences for the global economy's workforce. Although suggested, transnational feminism has not been applied to IHRM analysis and can further the examination of the organisation of human labour in today's global economy. A sector dominating in the global economy in terms of labour demands is health care, particularly nursing labour. The health care industry is gendered in terms of employing mostly women into the occupations and involves various levels of governance and management as well as actors and networks from the private, public, and third sectors. Through a transnational feminist lens and reconceptualising the field in terms of transnational human resource management (THRM), the theorisation and analysis of the management of health care workers transnationally can contribute to the discussion of IHRM studies and practice. In addition, using producer-based care networks as an empirical conceptualisation of how transnational processes and practices materialise constructs the transnationalisation of care in terms of broader networks of actors, institutions, organisations, and multiple levels/directions of organising.

Notes

1 This framework is to illustrate various episteomological frames that the scholars either function within, around, or cross over. The frames derive from my understanding of Burrell and Morgan's (1979) two dimension/four paradigm is understanding organisation studies and analysis as well as Kuhn's definition of paradigms of scientific disciplines (1962). The frames illustrated in this thesis are not to serve as boxed ideas but rather the various perspectives that the scholars are interacting with under the multi-faceted theory of transnational feminism(s).
2 Acker's argument references Diane Elson's work (1995) with terms of monetary 'productive' economy and non-monetary 'reproductive' economy.
3 Mohanty also emphasises this naturalisation of transnational capital processes and practices.
4 Mohanty's subjects of analysis are 'particular kinds of women—poor, third and Two-Thirds women, working class/immigrant/migrant women' who are 'the preferred workers in these global, "flexible" temporary job markets' (Mohanty 2003: 245–246).

References

Acker, J. (1990) Hierarchies, jobs, bodies: A theory of gendered organizations. *Gender and Society*, 4(2), pp. 139–158.
Acker, J. (2004) Gender, capitalism, and globalization. *Critical Sociology*, 30(1), pp. 17–41.
Acker, J. (2006) Inequality regimes: Gender, class, and race in organizations. *Gender and Society*, 20(4), pp. 441–464.
Adler, N. (2002) *International dimension of organizational behaviour*. Cincinnati, OH: South-Western College.
Alvesson, M. & Willmott, H. (2012) *Making sense of management: A critical introduction*. London: Sage.
Batt, R. & Banerjee, M. (2009) *How relevant is HRM for the 21st century? A critique of Anglo-American research*. Paper presented at the meeting of the labor and employment relations association, New Orleans.
Bhabha, H. K. (1994) *The location of culture*. New York: Routledge.
Boxall, P., Purcell, J. & Wright, P. (eds.) (2007) *The Oxford handbook of HRM*. Oxford: Oxford University Press.
Brush, B. L., Kingma, M. & Lorenzo, F. M. (2004) Imported care: Recruiting foreign nurses to US health care facilities. *Health Affairs*, 23, pp. 78–87.
Burrell, G. & Morgan, G. (1979) *Sociological paradigms and organizational analysis*. Aldershot: Gower.
Calás, M. B. & Smircich, L. (1999) From 'the woman's' point of view: Feminist approaches to organization studies. *Studying Organization: Theory and Method*, pp. 212–251.
Calás, M. B. & Smircich, L. (2006) From the 'woman's point of view' ten years later: Towards a feminist organization studies. In Stewart R. Clegg, Cynthia Hardy, Tom Lawrence, & Walter R. Nord (eds.) *The Sage handbook of organization studies*. London: Sage.
Calás, M., & Smircich, L. (2011). In the back and forth of transmigration: Rethinking organization studies in a transnational key. *Handbook of gender, work, and organization*. Chichester, West Sussex: Wiley, pp. 411–428.
Clegg, S. R. (1989) Radical revisions: Power, discipline, and organizations. *Organization Studies*, 10(1), pp. 97–115.
Clegg, S. R. & Hardy, C. (2006) 1.13 representation and reflexivity. *The Sage Handbook of Organization Studies*, p. 425.
Connell, R. W. (1987) *Gender and power*. Cambridge: Polity.
Connell, R. W. (2000) *The men and the boys*. Berkeley: University of California Press.
Cooke, F. L., Veen, A., & Wood, G. (2017). What do we know about cross-country comparative studies in HRM? A critical review of literature in the period of 2000–2014. *The International Journal of Human Resource Management*, 28(1), pp. 196–233.
De Cieri, H., Cox, J. & Fenwick, M. (2007) A review of international human resource management: Integration, interrogation, imitation. *International Journal of Management Reviews*, 9(4), pp. 281–302.
Delbridge, R., Hauptmeier, M. & Sengupta, S. (2011) Beyond the enterprise: Broadening the horizons of international HRM. *Human Relations*, 64(4), pp. 483–505.
du Gay, P. (1996) *Consumption and identity at work*. London: Sage.

Elson, D. (1995) Gender awareness in modeling structural adjustment. *World Development*, 23(11), pp. 1851–1868.

Festing, M., & Eidems, J. (2011). A process perspective on transnational HRM systems: A dynamic capability-based analysis. *Human Resource Management Review*, 21(3), pp. 162–173.

Fournier, V. & Grey, C. (2000) At the critical moment: Conditions and prospects for critical management studies. *Human Relations*, 53(1), pp. 7–32.

Grewal, I. & Kaplan, C. (1994) *Scattered hegemonies: Postmodernity and transnational feminist practices*. Minnesota: University of Minnesota Press.

Grewal, I. & Kaplan, C. (2000) Postcolonial studies and transnational feminist practices. *Jouvert*, 5(1).

Grewal, I. & Kaplan, C. (2005) *An introduction to women's studies: Gender in a transnational world*. New York: McGraw-Hill.

Hearn, J. (1993) Emotive subjects: Organizational men, organizational masculinities and the (de)construction of 'emotions'. In S. Fineman (ed.) *Emotions in organizations*. London: Sage, pp. 142–166.

Hearn, J. & Parkin, W. (2001) *Gender, sexuality, and violence in organizations*. London: Sage.

Jack, G., Calás, M. B., Nkomo, S. M. & Peltonen, T. (2008) Critique and international management: An uneasy relationship. *Academy of Management Review*, 33(4), pp. 870–884.

Jack, G. & Westwood, R. I. (2009) *International and cross-cultural management studies: A postcolonial reading*. Basingstoke: Palgrave Macmillan.

Kaplan, C., Alarcón, N. & Moallem, M. (eds.) (1999) *Between woman and nation: Nationalism, transnational feminisms and the state*. Durham: Duke University Press.

Kaplan, C. & Grewal, I. (1999) Transnational feminist cultural studies: Beyond the Marxism/poststructuralism/feminism divides. In C. Kaplan, N. Alarcón & M. Moallem (eds.) *Between woman and nation: Nationalism, transnational feminisms and the state*. Durham: Duke University Press, pp. 349–364.

Kuhn, T. (1962) *The structure of scientific revolutions*. Chicago: University of Chicago.

McDowell, L. (2008) Thinking through work: Complex inequalities, constructions of differences, and trans-national migrants. *Progress in Human Geography*, pp. 491–507.

Mignolo, W. (2000) The many faces of cosmo-polis: Border thinking and critical cosmopolitanism. *Public Culture*, 12(3), pp. 721–748.

Mohanty, C. T. (1984) Under Western eyes: Feminist scholarship and colonial discourses. *Boundary*, 2, pp. 333–358.

Mohanty, C. T. (1997). Preface: Dangerous territories, territorial power, and education. *Dangerous territories: Struggles for difference and equality in education*. New York: Routledge.

Mohanty, C. T. (2003). "Under Western eyes" revisited: feminist solidarity through anticapitalist struggles. *Signs: Journal of Women in Culture and Society*, 28(2), pp. 499–535.

Mohanty, C. T. (2007/2011) Anticapitalist feminist struggle and transnational solidarity: An interview with Chandra Talpale Mohanty (J. Nordahl, Interviewer). Retrieved from http://vimeo.com/28572566

Mohanty, C. T. (2013) Transnational feminist crossings: On neoliberalism and radical critique. *Signs*, 38(4), pp. 967–991.

Nkomo, S. M. (1992) The emperor has no clothes: Rewriting "race in organizations". *Academy of Management Review*, 17(3), pp. 487–513.
Peltonen, T. (2012) Critical approaches to international human resource management. In I. Björkman & G. Ståhl (eds.) *Handbook of international HRM research*. 2nd edition. London: Sage, pp. 532–548.
Peltonen, T. & Vaara, E. (2009) Crticial approaches to comparative HRM. In C. Brewster & W. Meyrhofer (eds.) *Handbook of comparative HR*. Cheltenhuam: Edward Elgar Publishing, pp. 69–89.
Said, E. (1978) *Orientalism*. New York: Vintage.
Shenkar, O. (2001) Cultural distance revisited: Towards a more rigorous conceptualization and measurement of cultural differences. *Journal of International Business Studies*, 32(3), pp. 519–535.
Shenkar, O. (2004) One more time: International business in a global economy. *Journal of International Business Studies*, 35(2), pp. 161–171.
Smith, D. E. (1987) *The everyday world as problematic: A feminist sociology*. Boston: Northwestern University Press.
Smith, D. E. (1990a) *The conceptual politics of power*. Boston: Northwestern University Press.
Smith, D. E. (1990b) *Texts, facts, and femininity: Exploring the relations of ruling*. London: Routledge.
Ståhl, G. K., Björkman, I., & Morris, S. (Eds.). (2012). *Handbook of research in international human resource management*. Cheltenham, UK: Edward Elgar Publishing
Townley, B. (1993) Foucault, power/knowledge and its relevance for human resource management. *Academy of Management Review*, 18, pp. 518–545.
Townley, B. (1994) *Reframing human resource management: Power, ethics and the subject at work*. London: Sage.
Tsui-Auch, L. S. (1999) Regional production relationship and development impacts: A comparative study of three production networks. *International Journal of Urban and Regional Research*, 23(2), pp. 329–344.
Westwood, R. (2006) International business and management studies as an orientalist discourse: A postcolonial critique. *Critical Perspectives on International Business*, 2(2), pp. 91–113.
Yeates, N. (2009) *Globalising care economies and migrant workers: Explorations in global care chains*. Basingstoke: Palgrave Macmillan.
Yeates, N. (2011) Going global: The transnationalization of care. *Development and Change*, 42(4), pp. 1109–1130.

Part 2

Situating

4 Representatives and Social Worlds in the Transnational Human Resource Management of Nurse Labour

How can 'transnational' managerial practices be situated and, therefore, empirically examined? How can transnational feminist theory be analytically practiced by drawing attention to the politics of location and the politics of knowledge production? This chapter grapples with these questions and proposes a methodology to situate empirical elements within the transnational management of nurses: a historically gendered and racialised occupation.

In practice, the transnational management of nurses is not limited to one general situation but multiple diverse situations, and encompasses multiple representatives, organisations, and discourses of authority that are asserting how and by whom nurses are managed. Knowledge production about nurses and nurse labour management is (re)produced both locally and globally, reinforcing discursive representations and unjust hierarchies of the occupation on a systematic and global scale.

The aforementioned statements do not indicate that nurses do not have agency in their mobility (see Smith, 2006) but that transnational management is influenced by reifying uneven geographies in familiar, seemingly natural ways (McKittrick, 2006: xiv). To draw attention to these seemingly natural ways, the examination of the transnational management of nurses demands some analytical and political actions by the researcher. For instance, as a researcher, I situate my work by the following:

1) Moving away from a positivist notion of space, time, social action, and particularly a dichotomous, universal (generalisation) notion of practices and borders of organising workforces. The term 'international' becomes problematised as not objective, Western-centric (Europe and North America), and influenced by values of capitalism. Time and space is anchored in a historical moment (Alexander and Mohanty, 2010).
2) Drawing attention to the gender and racial elements within the situation of a practice (local) through grounded discourses around the practice of transnational management by representatives working in social worlds/arenas that embody collective action at a meso level of organising and institutions.

3) Mapping the elements of transnational management by situating an empirical example of the representatives, their social worlds, and the discourses used to represent transnational management practices of globalised nurses.

In this chapter, I situate and map qualitative data with Adele Clarke's methodology 'Situational Analysis' (2005, Clarke et al., 2017). Clarke's methodology takes grounded theory/social interactionism 'around the postmodern turn', by advocating for constructionist framings of the situation, and addressing problematic positivist recalcitrancies. The methodology problematises the representation of a series of events as progressive and/or linear and strives to create a discursive space in which the focus is on what is said and by whom, and in which context it is said, thus facilitating the analysis of how and why particular accounts were/are received (Paludi et al., 2014). Clarke also insists in 'sensitizing concepts' (2005: 52) to account for the influences of the researcher's lived experiences and the past scholarly research that informs the empirical examination.

Clarke's 'situational analysis' is a theory/method package with 'roots' in Foucaultian analytics of power, nonhuman actants, and a shift from grounded theorists Strauss and Corbin's social worlds (2005: 37–78). In this chapter, I describe these roots, but I also indicate where I differ from her understanding of power and discourse, particularly her emphasis on Foucault. I then highlight how situational analysis and transnational feminism work together to design a research that examines the dense complexity of social processes (practices/actions) in a transnational, gendered, racialised workforce.

Lastly, the chapter discusses both the means of collecting data and the issues of contesting grounds of access to the representatives and organisations involved in the social action of recruiting/placing the nurses in Finland. These negotiations of accessing representatives highlights the research process of the researcher knowing who was involved, but also the representatives acknowledging and becoming aware of themselves through negotiations and interacting. The negotiations also highlight an ordering (see Strauss' negotiated order, 1979, 1982a, 1982b) of who recruits and places the nurses and decides how transnational management is practiced.

A Situated Approach to Mapping the Transnational Human Resource Management of Nurses

Clarke recommends, while approaching qualitative research, 'a theory/method package' (2005: 2–5). Her theory/method underpinnings are grounded theory, symbolic interactionism, and postmodernism. Grounded theory, which is not a theory but a method 'grounded in data', is rooted in the Chicago School in the 1960s (Glaser and Strass) and is interested in an inductive approach to collecting qualitative data. In grounded theory, data is collected at the beginning stages of the research process and analysed soon after through memos, maps, and various ways to try and grasp what the data entails. After this first stage, a 'substantive theory' is considered and 'theoretical sampling' is conducted to create new data sources. Foundational to the method of grounded theory is symbolic interactionism. According to symbolic interactionism, reality is socially constructed, and a 'situation' is that moment where people produce a common meaning of symbols in interaction (Blumer, 1969: 84). Paralleling symbolic interactionism in the 1960s and influenced by Mead's theory on perspectives (1962), Berger and Luckmann published in 1966 their book entitled *The Social Construction of Reality*. In this book, the authors argue that all knowledge, including the most basic, taken-for-granted common sense knowledge of everyday reality, is derived from and maintained by social interactions. When people interact, they do so with the understanding that their respective perceptions of reality are related, and as they act upon this understanding, their common knowledge of reality becomes reinforced. Such approaches emphasise the idea that society is actively and creatively produced by human beings. They portray the world as made or invented—rather than merely given or taken for granted (Burr, 1995; Berger, 1973).

Because of symbolic interactionist and social constructionist underpinning, Clarke argues that grounded theory should be and was (somewhat) positioned in the epistemology of postmodernism. Within what Clarke claims is her postmodernist/poststructuralist understanding of the social, she argues that the analysis of the situation centres on 'the organizational and institutional and the discursive relationalities rather than on organization and institutions'. This does not mean that the elements in the situations are epiphenomenal, and there is no possibility of analysing and discussing data collection of meaning making and relations, but more that partialities, differences, and hybrities exist. Complexities, differences, variations, silences, race, ethnicities, sex/gender, sexualities, and so on all have implications on how meaning is constructed through symbolic interactions and social relations (2005: 297). As in empirical studies working with transnational feminism, discussed in situational analysis facilitates examining who and how individuals interact and create meaning within a material world. As stated by Clarke (2005: 7), '[T]he social is relentlessly material, not "merely" epiphenomenal. As elsewhere, those meanings (Meadean attitudes, points of view, and perspectives) are not to be assumed but to be empirically examined'.

Clarke's empirical examination of the situation builds on Strauss' pragmatist grounded theory tools of social worlds/social arenas and negotiations. As emphasised by her, 'the situation per se becomes the ultimate goal of analysis, and understanding its elements and their relations is the primary goal' (2005: xxii). Moving beyond the micro level of the situation to the meso level, Strauss and Clarke conceptualise social worlds and arenas as 'modes of understanding the deeply situated yet always also fluid organizational elements of negotiations and discourses' (2005: xxix). Clarke agues, after Strauss' death, that he foreshadowed postmodern assumptions in an analysis of the situation and its surrounding social worlds, such as

> the instability of situations; the characteristic changing, porous boundaries of both social worlds and arenas; social worlds seen as mutually constitutive/coproduced in the negotiations taking place in arenas; negotiations as central social processes haling that 'things can always be otherwise', and so on.
>
> (2005: 13)

As a result of these dynamics, negotiations, in social worlds and arenas, can signal the micropolitics of power and the powers of discourses by 'decentring the subject and power in its more fluid and discursive forms (e.g. Foucault, 1979, 1980)—as well as "the usual" meso/macro structural elements' (2005: xxix). To conceptualise visually the postmodern assumptions in the analysis of empirical data in the situation, Clarke creates a matrix where the whole situation and the distinctions between macro/meso/micro dissolve and the focus becomes what is present and not present in the situation (2005: 72).[1]

Using this matrix, Clarke does not dismiss Strauss' social worlds/arenas but rather builds on them. She does this by considering the following assumptions: (1) acknowledge the embodiment and situatedness of all knowledge producers; (2) use the situation as the analytical grounding of the research; (3) shift from normative and homogenous representational strategies to complexities, differences, and heterogeneities; (4) assert the 'sensitivity concepts' rather than pursue formal theory; (5) do situational maps throughout the research process; and (6) turn to discourse (e.g. narrative, visual, and historical) to expand the domain of social life (2005: 19). According to Clarke, maps 'are excellent devices to materialize questions' (2005: 30) around these guiding assumptions to push grounded theory around the postmodern turn. In Figure 4.1, I adapt the definitions of the Clarke's situational maps to clarify the cartographic tools used in this book to examine the transnational management of nurses (the situation).

---

1. **Situational maps** that lay out the major human, nonhuman, discursive, and other elements in the research situation of inquiry and provoke analysis of relations among them;
2. **Social worlds/arenas maps** that lay out the collective actors, key nonhuman elements, and the arena(s) of commitment and discourse within which they are engaged in ongoing negotiations-meso level interpretations of the situation; and
3. **Positional maps** that lay out the major positions taken, and not taken, in the data vis-à-vis particular axes of difference, concern, and controversy around issues of the situation of inquiry.

Figure 4.1 Adapted figure of Clarke's cartographic approaches (Clarke, 2005: xxii)

In Part 3 of this book, 'A Situation', I build on an abductive approach to the transnational management of nurses by sensitising concepts from Part 1 of this book 'Framing' and by situating my data on transnational management with situational analysis and using Clarke's cartographic tools. As I am influenced and constantly working through my theoretical lens of transnational feminism, I am interested in power relations and their subsequent claims and materialist consequences on/through/with/around etc. the practices of recruiting and placing globalised nurses. One of Clarke's challenging questions is 'who is authorized and not authorized to make what kinds of knowledge claims about whom/what and under what conditions?' (2005: xxv). I discuss Clarke's focus for this question later, and then I explain my analysis of knowledge production of the transnational management practices of nurses with the use of Clarke's cartographic tools.

Clarke aims to answer the question of authority through three 'roots' of grounded theory: (1) through Foucault and 'turning' to discourse and gaze/perspective; (2) taking the nonhuman explicitly into account; and (3) shifting from social worlds/arenas to situational maps and analysis. In the first root, Clarke discusses Foucault's work on genealogies of knowledge and how language and discourses are interwoven through structures and institutions that create power relations that have, historically, been negative, repressive, and humiliating (e.g. through disciplining practices, subjectivation techniques or the productions of intelligible bodies). She centres this discussion around his work on the panopticon or the medical gaze. She argues that when Foucault became interested in agency, he became closer to the way that pragmatist social interactionists thought as they 'have a long tradition of attempting to see the world from the perspectives of all those in the situation, including the underdog(s)—those with less (but never no) power' (Clarke, 2005: 58). According to Clarke, both Foucault and Strauss centre their understandings of power around practices and social actions. For Foucault, power was about analysing 'regimes of practices' not institutions, theories, or ideologies in a given historical moment. According to Foucault (1991: 75), practices 'understood here as places where what is said and what is done, rules imposed and reasons given, the planned and the taken-for-granted meet and intersect.' For Strauss, social action was grounded in the actual work people are doing, individually and collectively, and work is usually organised as a set of practices related to the social world(s) in which they are involved and committed to for whatever reason. Serious conflicts may occur between or among segments of social worlds. Power relations for Strauss (1979, 1982a,1993) are constituted in the practices of addressing such conflicts that he termed 'negotiated ordering'. Here, 'the various interactional processes-negotiation, persuasion, manipulation, education, threat, and actual coercion will each have different salience' (Strauss, 1993: 240). According to Castellani,

> Strauss's concepts are significant to a theory of discursive interactionism. . . . [T]hey reveal that practice is a negotiated order, both in terms

> of practice and the interactions of the individuals involved in those practices . . . like power relations, interaction-as-negotiation is fundamental to any and all states of interaction, be they domination or any other form of control. *As such, the overall organization that emerges from practices is a negotiated order.*
>
> (1999: 267; emphasis in the original)

Clarke's work and this book's research differ in terms of understanding discourse. Although she uses social interactionist terminology, she states that she needs and wants to acknowledge Foucault's analytics of power as it emphasises fluid flows of power and 'drags' history into the analysis (Clarke, 2005: 297). I find this confusing as she later indicates that when using a Foucaultian approach to discourses that she is interested in agency and discourse of the situation and that Foucaultian understanding of discourse as a master discourse problematically trumps this (175). In Chapter 5, I discuss my understanding of discourse and its subsequent analysis. I view discourse in terms of a small 'd' rather than the grandiose 'D' as Foucaultian approaches to discourse entail. This does not mean that I am not interested in power, but the analysis of the discourses focuses more on organised control and compliance within the work practices of the transnational management of nurses, which is in the same interest of Strauss' research. I am concerned about the interaction and social actions of those involved in the recruitment of the Filipino nurses. As pointed out in Part 1, nurse work and its management have been empirically examined as institutionally gendered and racialised. There is a deskilling process occurring when nurses migrate and/or are recruited by countries where they are noncitizens that has been empirically documented. This deskilling process and the occupation itself subjects the nurses to lower-paying spheres of their occupation, disuse of their qualifications, and working conditions such as shift work or overtime. The nursing workforce itself has also been constructed as flexible and versatile, where work experience, qualifications, and skill do not discriminate between all the nurses being recruited and placed. As written by Kingma, a nurse is considered generically as a nurse, no matter the background of that individual.

Clarke's second root is nonhuman actors/actants/and elements. According to Clarke, nonhuman elements (e.g. technologies, material infrastructures, specialised information and/or knowledges, material 'things') are significant in analysing the social construction of the situation and the objects within it. Nonhuman elements can be given meaning, agency, and power by human actors through symbolic interactionism. As stated by Blumer:

> The position of symbolic interactionism is that the 'worlds' that exist for human beings and for their groups are composed of 'objects' and that these objects are *the product of symbolic interaction*. An object is anything that can be indicated, anything that is pointed to or referred to—a cloud, a book, a legislature, a banker, a religious doctrine, a ghost,

> and so forth. . . . The nature of an object—of any and every object—consists of the meaning that it has for the person [and/or social world] for whom it is an object.
>
> (1969: 10–11)

This explicit constructionist and materialist view of the nonhuman has also been referred to by Watson (1998, 1995a, 1995b, 1995c) as 'discursive resources', where individuals and readers can socially construct identities and narratives from objects such as human resource magazines. With this in mind, I would argue that texts are nonhuman, be it virtual or non-virtual, and are drawn upon by actors in relations to each other and their collectivities and part of their social action.

Clarke's third root is to enlarge Strauss and Corbin's social worlds/arenas maps into situational analysis. She does this by rethinking the relationship of conditions and the situation. Within Strauss and Corbin's conditional matrices, they frame the structural conditions of actions to levels beyond the micro such as institutional, community, national, and international levels (local to global levels). Clarke, in situational analysis, wants to destabilise the distinction as it is associated largely with modernist thinking. She does not view the world as separable. She argues that 'the conditions of the situation are the situation. There is no such thing as context' (2005: 71). She still sees the analytic importance behind social worlds/arenas maps, but wants to impose the fundamental question, 'how do these conditions appear—make themselves felt as consequential—inside the empirical situation under examination?' (2005: 72). The notion of destabilising the various levels of the social in the situation is also a concern for transnational feminists (Alexander and Mohanty, 2010).

Collecting Data on the Conditions of the Situated Story

In this book, I build on a situated story influenced by interviews, documents, participatory observations, and a research diary. Stories situate a historical moment of time and anchor 'cartographic rules that encapsulate differentiated and hierarchical spatialities, thus foregrounding the links between sites, location, and the production of knowledge about the transnational' (Alexander and Mohanty, 2010: 33). As Alexander and Mohanty argue, 'stories simultaneously "map" in that they mobilize both histories and geographies of power' (2010: 33).

To mobilise the history of the nurse occupation and sites of knowledge production of transnational management, the last part of this book explores the situated story of transnational management of Filipino nurses in Finland. The story spans from the year 2007 to 2011, during which five groups of 75 nurses were recruited from the Philippines by a private company to work in elderly care and hospital surgical wards in Finland. The story is based on interviews with various representatives working in the arena of transnational management of nurses, documents, and websites produced by organisations claiming to recruit nurses transnationally (press releases by the organisations, presentation slides, human resource magazines), and observations of some (but not all) key events from September 2008 to December 2011. I kept a research diary to reflect on how the story opened up and to makes sense of the representatives working with the practice of the transnational management of nurses in Finland. I also wanted to locate myself as a researcher and brainstorm (or 'messy map') the elements of the situation. I used this diverse selection in order to give an overview of and map the various representatives and social worlds, practices, and discourses involved in the arena of transnational management of Filipino nurses in Finland.

Representative Entrepreneurs, Implicated Actors, and Social Worlds

In the process of collecting information on this situated story, actors emerged into the situation, left, or remained. The actors interviewed and text given by the actors or accessible by their associated organisations are considered in this book as 'representative'. In particular, I argue that those interviewed in this situation are representative entrepreneurs who are deeply committed and active individuals in their social worlds and try to mobilise those around them (Hughes, 1971: 54; Watson, 1998). These entrepreneurs also produce meaning within their relations and discursive practices, and socially construct implicated actors in their social worlds and arenas. Implicated actors are socially constructed by others for their own purposes (Clarke and Montini, 1993). There are at least two kinds of implicated actors. First, the implicated actors who are physically present but are generally silenced/ignored/invisible by those in power in the social world or arenas. And, second, the implicated actors not physically present in a given social world but are solely discursively constructed: they are conceived, represented, and perhaps targeted by the work of others; hence, they are discursively present. Neither category of implicated actors is actively involved in the actual negotiations of self-representation in the social world or arena, nor are their thoughts or opinions or identities explored or sought out by other actors through any openly empirical mode of inquiry (such as asking them questions). They are neither invited by those in greater power to participate nor to represent themselves in their own terms. The difference between the two is about physical presence. If physically present, they are largely ignored.

One could argue critically that I actively ignored the implicated actors by not interviewing *all* 75 recruited Filipino nurses, Filipino nurses in the Philippines, elderly care patients, domestic Finnish nurses working in elderly care in Finland as well as hospitals, but I stand strong on how this illustrates which voices were dominating and accessible to the story. Originally, I wanted to conduct an ethnography in the workplaces where the nurses were recruited for and placed. These organisations are private for profit, and over various occasions, I was denied access to interviewing the nurses or entering the organisations to make observations because of threats of 'competition' with other businesses. I then proceeded to interview those whom the organisations involved in the recruitment and placement recommended. In regards to the Filipino nurses I did interview, I consider them representatives as well in this story. Within the interviews, they recant some of their lived experiences, but the interviews, influenced by the interviewer as well as the semi-structured questions, focused on the social actions of interest: transnational management. These nurses could speak for themselves, and serve as representatives of larger social worlds that transcend transnationally over space and time. The Philippines, as framed in Part 1, has a history of labour exportation, imperialism, and colonialization, contributing to hierarchies of place within the transnational (Alexander and Mohanty, 2010: 33). This book does not claim to capture empirically these postcolonial/neoimperial/transnational practices and processes nor how the nursing profession is gendered and racialised. The book hopes to explore the transnational management of nurses beyond human resources through a situated story of how a group of nurses are recruited in the Philippines and subsequently transnationally managed to work in Finnish health care. In other words, transnational management as a praxis through a situated story.

Interviews: Gaining Access to Social Worlds

In-depth interviews were conducted with 17 representatives in the management of nurses from the Philippines (from 16 organisations, two organisations had two representatives in the interview), and 10 Filipino nurses (6 recruited by a private agency for practical nursing and 4 not recruited but educated and working as practical nurses in Finland).[2] The process of contacting these representatives over two years (March 2009–December 2011) consisted of internet web research of the organisations' websites which were suggested by representatives, social networking (both virtually on Facebook and non-virtually), and asking each individual interviewed if there were other individuals I should interview or key events that I should attend. Many recommendations were made in regards to whom I should interview, and it also led me to key events such as both formal and informal group meetings of Filipino nurses both recruited and not recruited and conferences in Helsinki on the international recruitment of a foreign diverse workforce. This form of interviewing could be considered 'theoretical' and 'snowballing' sampling as patterns were examined in successive interviews and the directions to explore were influenced by the predecessor interview (Miles and Huberman, 1994).

In addition, I asked, in the interviews, for text or any policies/laws that I should consider. Through these questions, I received pamphlets on working in Finland and recruitment, multiculturalism in the workforce, and governmental projects, some of which received European Union funding (European Social Fund [ESF]). The search for documents did not end at the interviews, nonetheless. While writing the methodology and data analysis sections, websearches for laws and project details concerning labour migration in Finland were extensively performed in order to clarify who the actors are in the transnational management of the Filipino nurses and what institutional practices and structures existed as well as the political, economic, and social context of the time. This 'writing up' and clarification of the details were directed by the previous social interactions, and to illuminate the social worlds and arenas that I had entered, am working in, and/or that the representatives are potentially working and interacting in.

As the interviews were of representatives, the analysis proceeded on a meso level. I considered that those interviewed were working in various social worlds that intertwined the transnational nature of the recruitment and placement practices but also the European Union context as well as the national local context of Finland. And, as the interviews were post-hoc accounts, where the respondents are able to take into consideration the end result of the process, the documents collected before, during, and after the interviews were complimentary as well as informative as to how the claim making/social understanding of the transnational practices and processes of the interviewee unfolded (Wrede, 2010).

At the beginning of this research, it was not clear as to who were the representatives. The access part of the interviews proceeded with social contacts and then asking each participant interviewed if they could recommend someone who is also a stakeholder in the management of the Filipino nurses. It also included reading various newspaper clippings on Filipino nurse recruitment in Helsinki that various participants mentioned (at the time there were over 300 Finnish media articles written on the recruitment), and then asking if the contact information was as such then why can I not contact them and request information. Now writing this up, I realise that I was entering various social worlds myself and acting as a representative for social worlds and organisations (e.g. Academics, English speakers in Finland, non-Finns professionals). For instance, I was told by a representative working in the Ministry of Interior building that I was the first foreigner the representative had met that entered the building. At the time, I was startled by this statement as the Finnish Ministry of Interior (circa 2011) was responsible for immigrant labour organisation and management.

Interviews included open-ended, semi-structured questions. Questions were created before the interviews and varied between groups of participants. For instance, the questions for the nurses were more oriented to their experiences and how they perceived the recruitment and placement processes in the Finnish health care system. Questions were asked about how they were recruited, did they receive training and by whom, what are their qualifications, where are they working in Helsinki, how they perceive their management, what were they doing before arriving in Finland, do they have families, and are they in the Philippines or in Finland. Questions towards the recruiters focused more on the initiation of the recruitment and training such as how the recruitment began, why the Philippines, what the future of the recruitment is, how the recruiters perceive the advantages and disadvantages of hiring foreign nurses, Finnish language proficiency, and what work they do for the recruitment organisations. For the other representatives, the questions focused on what their responsibilities in their workplace consisted of; how they or their organisation are involved in the recruitment, placement, and retention of foreign workers, and, in particular, of foreign nurses; if they are collaborating with other organisations in the recruitment and placement of foreign nurses; and if they had views of the management of foreign nurses (e.g. advantages or disadvantages of recruiting foreign workers).

At the time, there was an air of sensitivity and tension when asked to be interviewed about the Filipino nurses and their management. Emails and phone calls to reassure about the research process were sometimes not followed up or ignored. For instance, here is an email received from a private business representative involved in the recruitment of the Filipino nurses in regards to accessing the organisations for interviews (email and research diary entry 18.12.10):

> I am still against this, but lets (sic) see. [representative] will explain my opinion why I don't see our proposal too Optimistic.

All the interviews were conducted and accessed through English. Although the recruitment and the majority of the training that the Filipino nurses received were in English, some actors who were asked to be interviewed declined because they did not want to speak in English (I write 'did not want', but I was also told that they 'could not speak fluently in English'). In the beginning, while accessing data through interviews, I had the impression that I was not succeeding with access in some organisations because I did not speak fluent Finnish. However, after many discussions with scholars and practitioners who are also interested in the recruitment and spoke fluent Finnish, I was informed that they were also denied access or had a confusing time trying to locate certain actors. There was an ambiguity as to who was involved in the recruitment and who was willing to share their expertise on the topic.[3]

In each interview, the representatives signed a consent form of complete confidentiality. To honour the representatives' anonymity, the data analysis revolves around social worlds constructed by the researcher through the interview questions and the text suggested by the representatives. This construction of social worlds for the purpose of mapping will be discussed more in Chapter 5.

Documentary Method: Material Presence of Social Relations and Actions

Documentary methods (DM) involve the use of already existing materials. Documents are bound to a specific point in time, and they can be used to examine, for instance, how a specific actor argued in a specific stage of a policy process. Nonetheless, the nature of the documents should not be considered as stable, static, and predefined artefacts (Prior, 2003: 2). Documents also have agency so it is important to analyse not only their contents, but also how they were used, how they travel, etc. (Kendall and Wickham, 2004; Prior, 2003: 21–26; Clarke, 2005). As indicated by Dorothy Smith, documents also reflect their social relations:

> Texts are situated in and structure social relations (extended social courses of action) in which people are actively at work. Texts enter into and order course of action and relations among individuals. The texts themselves have material presence and are produced in an economic and social process which is part of a political economy.
>
> (1990: 162)

It is common for a researcher to combine document research with interviewing. DM involves the active role of the researcher who chooses the documents to include in the study, often from a great number of possible materials. These particular conditions do not, however, exclude multiple uses of documents if such conditions are taken into consideration (Prior, 2003).

One key aim of DM is to allow the identification of the central actors or stakeholders and map their ties with each other as well as the arenas where they act and the strategies they use (Shaffer et al., 2005). The mapping of key actors and other important empirical data served the planning of interviews but also the organisation and analysis of the data, which is explained in more detail in Chapter 5 where 'situational analysis' is introduced and the data is illustrated in 'situational maps' (ordered), social worlds and arenas, and positionalities.

Documents for this situated story were collected over three years (September 2008–December 2011), five months after the first group of Filipino nurses were recruited to Finland. Documents were found virtually and non-virtually. All representatives that were interviewed were asked if they have any documents that could be of use to the research or if they knew or wanted to highlight policies and laws in Finland in regards to immigrant-based labour or a diverse workforce and actors in Finland interested in recruiting from abroad. Table 4.1 describes the documents given by the representatives in interviews and the events that I attended in which the documents were publically obtained. The table also indicates which discursive genre the documents fall under. Genre is defined as 'a socially ratified

Table 4.1 Genres of documents

Documents given or publically disseminated by representatives	Genre of discursive resource
Conferences power point presentation slides	Public event
European Migration Network's annual reports	European Union
HR magazines and book on business and culture, power point slides of public events, websites, media clippings	Private business and corporate
Nurse union reports, power point presentations, advocacy pamphlets, websites	Public and advocacy
Ministries, municipality, and national supervisory authority's websites, pamphlets, reports	Public and governmental

way of using language associated with a particular type of social activity' (Fairclough, 1995: 14). The genre of the discursive resource also can denote which social world the interviewee is conducting his or her activity.

By using various data sources, the interview questions were influenced by internet sources of the different organisations in the story as well as by attending events in which the representatives attended or gave a formal presentation with power point slides. In addition, after the interviews were conducted, a final question was posed as to whether or not the interviewee had documents related to the research topic. What was revealing about this triangulation or direction and redirection was the similarities in what was expected from the nurses and the processes of recruiting and placing the nurses within the various data sources. Although Chapter 7 covers in detail what discourses were used in the talk and text of managing the Filipino nurses, throughout the data collected, comparing the documents and interviews almost reinforced and contradicted themselves, revealing how stories about the social practice of recruitment can change. For instance, after speaking to one of two representatives separately from the same private business organisation, the representative indicated that the representative recently wrote a chapter on the case with another colleague of the organisation. In both the interview and the chapter, the representative refers to the Filipino nurses as 'warm and friendly and not that Asian' when asked why recruit from the Philippines and not another country. Table 4.2 shows a few examples of this parallel between talk in the interview and naturally

Table 4.2 Reinforcing or contradicting empirical examples between talk and text

Representative's social world	*Quote from Interview*	*Naturally Occurring text*
Private business and corporate 'Reinforcing'	'They bring a warmth, a very outgoing sort of natural that, i am not saying that we don't have it here, we do, we are warm people, but it is just a different way. It comes across in a different way. They—I have to wonder at the start when they came, some people are going to fall over backwards here because of their outgoing, bubbly, warm, very tactile sort of nature that, from what l gather, and it is mostly through conversations with the likes of [Opteam HR consultant], maybe, is that, you know that certainly from a patient welfare point of view and things like that, they actually like it. They bring a dimension that, to us, and that is where the cultural advantage bill fits in. We all learn a little bit from each other'.	Book chapter: Managing mindsets Under the subtitle of the chapter entitled 'Friendly and Warm': 'They [the Filipino nurses] are seen as remarkably friendly and warm. Obviously, this can also be said of many Finns, if only one know what kindness and warm-heartedness look like in Finland. Finns themselves appreciate the friendly attitude of Filipines. The Filipino nurses are talkative, caring and warm towards patients and colleagues, and it comes "naturally"'
Private business and corporate 'Reinforcing'	'So, we checked China, India, Thailand, and, I believe it was afterwards that we chose the Philippines. We checked out Vietnam, and, yeah, there are many things that speak for the Philippines. They value education and the quality of nursing education is good. It was basically planned by the Americans, so it is no wonder that there are so many Filipino nurses in the United States. So the quality of the degree and of course the culturally bound politeness and, when we think of the elderly people here, they [Filipinos] have a natural respect for the elderly which we could learn from actually. And, also, that they speak English and they have studied in English. Even though not everybody speaks as well as earlier because the schooling language can also be the local language in the	Text from the private business organisation's Website: 'Filipinos have a long tradition of working abroad. Over 8 million Filipinos work abroad presently. A fairly large number of the Filipinos in Europe are nurses. 10% of the gross national product in the Philippines consists of money overseas Filipinos send back; it is the biggest source of foreign currency. Filipinos also have very good English language skills which often is the strongest language for many Finns too'.

	primary schools and the secondary, I believe. But, the nursing schooling is in English. So, that makes it easier. We have, in a way, a common language then in Finland so we don't need interpreters which is, actually, you couldn't have as a doctor or a nurse within health care or even within elderly care as a practical nurse, you can't have an interpreter with you all the time. And, most Finns speak English somehow. At least. So, it is easier to communicate and make sure that the recruited one and the employer understand one another'. 'The Philippines has placed a lot of value in the training and development of nurses. I mean there are a lot of nurses in the Philippines. So, they had more nurses that they can ever hope for to look after their own, if you like, national and domestic requirements. And, the Philippines is a country that relies heavily on exporting their skills and talents, so they're big earners, probably the major earner for the Philippines. But, why do we do that from a nursing point of view? They get good training, they speak English, which is-which irrespective of coming here—I think the Philippines in general has a good international record . . . the Philippines for us is, I suppose, in some ways, like it is a natural, I don't want to use the word resource—it sounds terrible—but, for us, we would go to the Philippines because one, the training is good there.'	**Business HR magazine** 'Filipinos are the most western people in Asia, which makes it easy for them to adapt'.
National security and police 'Contradictive'	When referring to travelling to other countries to gain information on possible recruitment of nurses to Finland: '[the EU-funded project] make some sort of continuation here that not everybody has to start from zero every time'. [Representative] later indicates that countries such as Bulgaria have been visited for the project.	<u>Power point presentation at Spanish Embassy (three years after interview)</u> Indicated that Spain was chosen because of 'a lucky guess' and 'professional tactics'.

occurring text ('naturally' means that it was not influenced by the researcher or the research topic, see Phillips and Hardy, 2002).

Participatory Observations: Maps, Memos, and Reflection of the Situation and Its Social Worlds/Arenas

Using participatory observations allowed me to consider various avenues into accessing information on the how, why, who, and when foreign nurses were being managed in the Finnish health care system. These observations took many forms: informal interviews, direct observations, participation in groups of the Filipino nurses and conversations with other actors and scholars interested in the research topic, analyses of personal notes taken during and after group meetings, self-analysis, and results taken after participating or reading online activities such as Facebook events and recruitment information, which sometimes had an online forum of discussion in Finland or the Philippines. I would argue that I tried to maintain a 'moderate participation' (DeWalt & DeWalt, 2011), but I was also passionate about how the Filipino nurses were being managed as I considered myself a professional immigrant being managed by Finnish actors. As such, I would argue that there are limitations with this method and that is why it was important to include other methods. DeWalt and DeWalt (2011) argue that limits to consider are that (1) recorded observations about a group of people or event are never going to be the full description, (2) there is a selective nature of any type of data process: it is inevitable that the data will be influenced by the researcher's personal beliefs of what is relevant, and (3) the analysis of the collected data is influenced by how the researcher decides to interpret and evaluate the data. This last limit reflects the worldviews or social understandings of the researcher.

Another aspect that arose from the participatory observations was my own individual background. I do not speak Finnish fluently nor do I speak or understand Tagalog. My mother tongue is English, and all the data was collected in English.

At times, I would participate in events when the other participants would switch to another language, and, as such, I was 'technically' excluded from the conversation. Also, my immigrant background created a different relationship with the key informants. There were times when it felt that I could relate to the participants in the sense that I understood the migration and integration process of Finland. Nevertheless, there were also times that, as a Canadian, the key informants were interested in my perspective or experience, not as an immigrant, but as a Canadian. For instance, with the businesses and governmental officials, there were many comparisons made between Canada and Finland. With the nurses, I was asked questions as to how to migrate to Canada or the United States, and what have my experiences been so far with the Finnish language and finding employment in Finland.

During the data collection in 2010 and 2011, I was also pregnant with my first child. My child was born in May 2011. Physically, it was apparent that I was pregnant, and I could not help but wonder if my pregnancy may have influenced what the participants wanted to talk about in the interviews, particularly around the practice of care.

Research Diary Entries and Personal Reflection/Self-Analysis

The research diary facilitated writing down reflections, ideas, observations, and maps of representatives and processes. At the beginning of the research process in 2008, it was still unclear who were involved in the management of Filipino nurses in Finland. Over the short span of two years, responsibilities of the human resource shortage shifted from one Finnish ministry to the next, and new actors became involved.

In addition, as the data analysis is interested in discourses, both content (e.g. claims) and the social interaction of text, the diary entries refocus the data as to how claims about recruitment and placement of Filipino nurses were made, and how the perspectives of the representatives unfolded. The diary entries also paint a picture as to how I was interpreting the data and the context.

Discursive analysis and research acknowledges how the data is situated and the research process of collecting the data as well as the role of the researcher. Data is a reflection of a certain time and space, and the researcher participates in this construction of social reality (Taylor, 2013). One criterion for discursive analysis is that the researcher is not disassociated with the research process, from its initial to final stages. The researcher is always present, for instance, in the selection of the research topic, the collection of the data, the interpretation of data and analysis, and the writing of the dissertation (Wetherell et al., 2001). Another criterion is that the researcher acknowledges his or her own presence in the data and its interpretation, but maintains a systematic, rigorous approach to his or her analysis grounded in other scholarly theoretical and empirical work (Taylor, 2013).

Throughout this book, I continuously acknowledge my presence in the research process. Nonetheless, as described in Chapter 7 on discourse analysis and situational analysis, I attempt to ground the interpretation of the data in tools that will allow the reader to understand the details of the story I am trying to tell. The tools can illustrate how the narratives and claims were made by the representatives in their interviews and became visible to the researcher. These tools also simultaneously apply to the documents to see their relations to the interviews. By using these tools for analysis as well as the data collection methods, I believe I facilitated the process of abductive reasoning by making tangible organisational tools in order to 'systematically combine' (Dubois and Gadde, 2002) the data with the theoretical framework of transnational feminism and previous literature on the management and organisation of transnational nurse labour. Here is an example of a messy map in my journal entry (Figure 4.2).

Figure 4.2 Situational analysis's messy map before ordered map (circa year 2013)

Research Interest Situated in Lived Experience

The idea of this book began with an experience. Between the years 2006 and 2008, I started and finished a master's degree in health care management at the University of Helsinki. This degree is in collaboration with the World Health Organization (WHO) and, because of this, many of the visiting professors are practitioners and researchers at WHO. The programme is international and unlike most masters in Finland, the degree requested, at the time, a tuition fee.

During these years in the degree, there were no Finnish students and no Europeans. All of the students came from countries considered 'non-EU/EEA'. I was the only North American and the only one from the Americas. The rest of the students were predominantly from South and Western Africa (e.g. Nigeria, Cameroon, Ghana), Asia (e.g. India, Pakistan, Japan, Bangladesh), and the Middle East (e.g. Iraq).

Many of my colleagues in the degree had various working experiences in their respective fields of study and most practiced medicine, dentistry, pharmacy, and nursing in their home countries. Some lectured at universities, others are teachers of children.

As non-Finns with student visas, my colleagues and I could work for a maximum of 25 hours/week, and many of us wanted to work to not only afford daily life in Helsinki but also the tuition fees. When my close friend and colleague and I began to express the need to find work, a Bangladeshi colleague said that he could get us a job at Viking Line, a Finnish cruise liner, cleaning rooms during the docking period. I went to the interview at Viking Line and the manager who interviewed me expressed concern that I may not be satisfied with the work as a Canadian. In the end, my friend and I took the job. The job consisted of working from Monday to Fridays for 45-minute shifts. We were paid 7 euros a shift or 35 euros/week. My friend and I were assigned to clean toilets.

I worked at Viking Line for only three months until I found another job waiting tables through a Finnish recruitment agency. At the time, I considered this a career advancement. Nonetheless, during my time at Viking Line, I learned that a lot of us cleaners were non-EU citizens and many of us held a bachelor and master's degree, and, in quite a few cases, medical degrees. The professionals holding medical degrees, I was told, had to find flexible, paid work as they worked as unpaid apprentices to get experience in order to work in Finland.

The questions that kept coming into my head during this time was 'why do some nationalities and not others work in low-paid, flexible, unskilled jobs like cleaning when living abroad although highly qualified? And, why are highly skilled professionals such as medical doctors working as cleaners and not in their profession?' While these questions came from experiences, in the classroom, my colleagues and I researched, quantitatively, patterns of migrating medical professionals. The explanations associated with these patterns consisted of a discourse of 'push' and 'pull' factors of economics, demographics, and institutional health care restructuring. These macro explanations, although important, seemed limited and I wanted to know more about what is happening to health care workers during the process of transnationally moving human resources from one country to the next, and how the workers are subsequently managed in the destination country.

Summary and Concluding Thoughts

This book began with a research interest situated in my own lived experiences. While studying for my masters' degree, I studied and worked in social worlds where my colleagues, who are mostly medical professionals, were deskilled through transnational processes and practices of qualification/education recognition by institutions in Finland as well as employment practices that favoured particular nationalities with student visas for cleaning and service jobs. These jobs are flexible, low paid, and do not require Finnish language. My initial research questions were 'why are important health care human resources (such as doctors, nurses, and dentists) not being used in institutions that have largely documented labour shortages?' and 'do the human resource practices in Finland of non-Finns labour entail labour segmentation in terms of nationality, ethnicity, and language use?'

With these questions in mind, the situated story of the recruitment of Filipino nurses by Finnish private companies emerged into analytical focus, and I saw a way of conceptualising the transnationalisation of care and human resource management through the analysis of representatives, organisations, and institutions recruiting and placing Filipino nurses into Finnish nursing institutions. Initially, I viewed the representatives in terms of their respective organisations, but after further investigation and with the help of discourse and situational analysis, various social worlds in which the representatives live and interact materialised through maps. The maps of the social worlds and situational analysis are discussed in more detail in the next chapter. This cartographic analysis materialises who are the representatives, organisations, and institutions interacting and transnationally producing nurse labour for Finnish institutions as well as positioning the representatives in social worlds of discourse(s).

Notes

1 There are close alternatives to the aforementioned chosen approach on 'structuring the social world'; for instance, neoinstitutional organisation theory and actor-network theory. These theoretical approaches are frequently used in organisation studies to make sense of the structuring networks of network in and across formal organisations.
2 Interviews can be found in the Appendix.
3 As will be discussed in Chapter 7, this limitation of understanding the various organisations and roles involved in the recruitment and placement of the Filipino nurses as well as other immigrant labourers was described in the Finnish European Migration Network (EMN) report on migration-based labour to Finland (Asa and Muurinen, 2010).

References

Alexander, M. J. & Mohanty, C. T. (2010) Cartographies of knowledge and power. In A. L. Swarr & R. Nagar (eds.) *Critical transnational feminist praxis*. Albany: Suny Press, pp. 23–45.
Asa, R. & Muurinen, H. (2010) *Temporary and circular migration: Empirical evidence, current policy practice, and future options in Finland*. Helsinki: European Migration Network.
Berger, P. L. (1973) *The social reality of religion*. London: Penguin Books.
Berger, P. L. & Luckmann, T. (1966) *The social construction of reality*. New York: Anchor Books.
Blumer, H. (1969) *Symbolic interactionism: Perspectives and method*. Englewood Cliff: Prentice Hall.
Burr, V. (1995) *Introduction to social constructionism*. New York: Routledge.
Castellani, B. (1999) Michel Foucault and symbolic interactionism: The making of a new theory of interaction. *Studies in Symbolic Interaction*, 22, pp. 247–272.
Clarke, A. (2005) *Situational analysis: Grounded theory after the postmodern turn*. Thousand Oaks, CA: Sage.

Clarke, A. E., Friese, C., & Washburn, R. S. (2017) *Situational analysis: grounded theory after the interpretive turn*. Thousand Oaks, CA: Sage.

Clarke, A., & Montini, T. (1993). The many faces of RU486: Tales of situated knowledges and technological contestations. *Science, Technology, & Human Values*, 18(1), pp. 42–78.

DeWalt, K. M., & DeWalt, B. R. (2011). *Participant observation: A guide for fieldworkers*. Lanham, MD: Rowman Altamira.

Dubois, A., & Gadde, L. E. (2002). Systematic combining: An abductive approach to case research. *Journal of Business Research*, 55(7), pp. 553–560.

Fairclough, N. (1995). *Critical discourse analysis: The critical study of language*. Essex: Longman.

Foucault, M. (1979) *Discipline and punishment: The birth of the prison*. New York: Vintage.

Foucault, M. (1980) *Power/knowledge: Selected interviews and other writings*. C. Gordon (ed.). Brighton: Harvester.

Foucault, M. (1991) *The Foucault effect: Studies in governmentality*. Chicago: University of Chicago Press.

Hughes, E. C. (1971) *The sociological eye*. Chicago: Aldine Atherton.

Kendall, G. & Wickham, G. (2004) The Foucaultian framework. In C. Seale, G. Gobo, J. F. Gubrium & D. Silverman (eds.) *Qualitative research practice*. London: Sage, pp. 141–150.

McKittrick, K. (2006) *Demonic grounds: Black women and the cartographies of struggle*. Minneapolis: University of Minnesota.

Mead, G. H. (1962) *Mind, self and society*.

Miles, M. B. & Huberman, A. M. (1994) *Qualitative data analysis: An expanded sourcebook*. London: Sage.

Miles, M. B. & Huberman, A. M. (1994) *Qualitative data analysis: An expanded sourcebook*. London: Sage.

Paludi, M., Mills, A. & Helms Mills, J. (2014) Disturbing thoughts and gendered practices: A discursive review of feminist organizational analysis. In S. Kumra, R. Simpson & R. Burke (eds.) *The Oxford handbook of gender and organizations*. Oxford: Oxford University Press, pp. 53–75.

Phillips, N. & Hardy, C. (2002) *Understanding discourse analysis*. Thousand Oaks, CA: Sage.

Prior, L. (2003). *Using documents in social research*. London: Sage.

Shaffer, E. R., Waitzkin, H., Brenner, J. & Jasso-Aguilar, R. (2005). Global trade and public health. *American Journal of Public Health*, 95(1), pp. 23–34.

Smith, C. (2006). The double indeterminacy of labour power: Labour effort and labour mobility. *Work, Employment and Society*, 20(2), pp. 389–402.

Smith, D. E. (1990) *Texts, facts, and femininity: Exploring the relations of ruling*. London: Routledge.

Strauss, A. L. (1979) *Negotiations: Varieties, contexts, processes and social order*. San Francisco: Jossey-Bass.

Strauss, A. L. (1982a) Interorganizational negotiation. *Urban Life*, 11(3), pp. 350–367.

Strauss, A. L. (1982b) Social worlds and legitimation processes. In N. Denzin (ed.) *Studies in symbolic interactions*, 4. Greenwich: JAI Press, pp. 171–190.

Strauss, A. L. (1993) *Continual permutations of action*. New York: Aldine de Gruyter.

Taylor, S. (2013) *What is discourse analysis?* New York: Bloomsbury Academic.
Watson, T. J. (1995a) In search of HRM: Beyond the rhetoric and reality distinction or the dog that didn't bark. *Personnel Review*, 24(4), pp. 6–16.
Watson, T. J. (1995b) Rhetoric, discourse and argument in organisational sensemaking: A reflexive tale. *Organization Studies*, 16(5), pp. 805–821.
Watson, T. J. (1995c) Shaping the story: Rhetoric, persuasion and creative writing in organisational ethnography. *Studies in Cultures, Organizations and Societies*, 1(2), pp. 301–311.
Watson, T. J. & Bargiela-Chiappini, F. (1998) Managerial sensemaking and occupational identities in Britain and Italy. *Journal of Management Studies*, 35(3), pp. 285–301.
Wetherell, M., Taylor, S., & Yates, S. J. (2001) *Discourse theory and practice: A reader*. London: Sage.
Wrede, S. (2010) How country matters: Studying health policy in a comparative perspective. In I. D. Bourgeault (ed.) *The Sage handbook of qualitative methods in health research*. London: Sage, pp. 88–105.

5 Mapping Social Worlds Through Discourse, Text, and Materiality

Introduction

Sites of knowledge and politics of geographies play central roles in the transnational management of nurses. This chapter explains how discourse and its analysis locates the production, dissemination, and reception of representational knowledge on nurses and their management. Discourses materialise in tangible ways that affect the transnational management practices of nurses as well as their daily working lives.

The chapter ends by situating the discourses of the recruitment and placement of Filipino nurses by Finnish organisations between the years 2007–2010. The health care context in Finland is also historically described to situate the knowledge producers and their associated social worlds.

What Is Discourse and Why Analyse It?

Discourse and its analysis are largely associated with the 'linguistic turn'. This turn to language signifies a departure from Enlightenment/positivist thinking that language is functional, detached from the social context, and referential rather than bearing strongly on how meaning is constructed. Scholars such as de Saussure (structural linguistics; 1974), Wittgenstein (1967), and Winch (1958; both linguistic philosophers) recognised that language is constitutive and constructive of meaning rather than reflective and representative.

This epiphenomenal understanding of language and its constructivist role in viewing social reality calls into question what passes as truth and knowledge and scrutinises what things mean rather than how things work (Winch, 1958). The inner and outer dialogue of the researcher examining the social subsequently is fraught with questions such as 'what is the social constructive meaning behind this object of analysis? Who is constructing meaning and why? Who is not constructing meaning and why? How is the meaning produced, disseminated, and received by others?' The idea of language and its use to construct meaning, in this line of thinking, becomes malleable, ambiguous, and excessive. A single term or construct signifies multiple meanings, voices, and significances. The researcher as objective, neutral, and independent is problematised.

The constructionist view of a social phenomenon is largely accepted in many disciplines (Gergen, 1999) and various scholars contemplate issues of representation and legitimisation within their work (Denzin and Lincoln, 2000). In this vein, discourse analysis is not only a method but also a methodology. Qualitative researchers use various methods of analysing discourse but are mostly concerned with not only understanding and interpreting the object of analysis but how the object is produced and by whom.

Discourse is defined as 'an interrelated set of texts, and the practices of their production, dissemination, and reception, that bring an object into being' (Phillips and Hardy, 2002: 3). Interrelated texts transpire from systems of thoughts composed of ideas, attitudes, courses of action, beliefs, and practices (Lessa, 2005), situating the knowledge producer in their surrounding context. These practices could be, for instance, talking with the use of a group of statements that provide a language about a particular topic at a particular historical moment.

Social reality is produced and materialised through discourses (Carabine, 2001: 268), and social interactions cannot be fully understood without reference to the discourses that give them meaning. Discourses are embodied and enacted in a variety of texts, although they exist beyond the individual texts that compose them (Hardy, 2001). Texts can thus be considered 'discursive units' (Chalaby, 1996) or 'discursive resources' (Watson and Bargiela-Chiappini, 1998) and a material manifestation of discourse. Text may take a variety of material forms that become accessible to others (Taylor et al., 1996: 7), including written texts, spoken words (such as interviews), pictures, symbols, artefacts, and so forth (Grant et al., 1998).

Discourse analysis can be understood through three dimensions: text, discourse, and context (Phillips and Hardy, 2002). This consideration signifies that text and discourse are interrelated but also that they are constructed, produced, disseminated, and received by an audience living and working in realms within and beyond their physical bodies and minds. As stated by Fairclough and Wodak:

> [D]iscourse is not produced without context and cannot be understood without taking into consideration . . . discourse are always connected to other discourses which were produced earlier, as well as those which are produced synchronically and subsequently.
>
> (1997: 277)

Criticism towards discourse and its analysis has been expressed by scholars arguing that the emphasis has become too focused on language use and language as a mirror. Subsequently, important elements of the situation get lost:

> [M]ost of these studies look at texts and talking rather than looking through discourse to see the specific ways the world is produced. The

> problem of language as the 'mirror of nature' that preoccupied the positivists was replaced by simply focusing on the 'mirror' as an object. The central 'turn' issues of how different worlds emerge, the power relations in this emergence, and the mechanisms of protection, get lost.
>
> (Deetz, 2003: 423)

In addition, as addressed later, by solely focusing on language use and issues of representations (as in the case of most 'post' epistemologies), the material elements of discourse and the construction/meaning of the social becomes lost in the empirical analysis.

Varieties of Discourse Analysis

This section discusses the varieties of discourse analysis of empirical data. It begins with Alvesson and Kärreman's (2000) article that focuses on what they call 'core dimensions' of discourse analysis. The sections then turn to framing discourse analysis in terms of theoretical approaches taken up by Phillips and Hardy (2002). Lastly, I discuss the importance of the material relationship to discourse and its subsequent analysis with empirical data by referencing Phillips and Oswick (2012) and Hearn (2014).

Core Dimensions of Discourse Analysis

Alvesson and Kärreman (2000) argue that discourse analysis of empirical data needs to recognise two key dimensions: (1) the relationship between discourse and meaning and (2) the attentiveness to detail and specific context versus an interest in more standardised forms of language use. What this means is that, although language use is central, the researcher still needs to clarify and reflect on how much 'determination' or 'autonomy' discourse is given to meaning, particularly how much the effects of discourse, or discursive practices (e.g. how language is used), shapes and defines subjectivity. It also indicates that the researcher needs to make the distinction between if the discourse is representative of a local micro context or a more general macro context. This highlights what the authors call 'climbing the ladder of discourse' in the sense that the researcher moves between Discourse (big D) and discourse (small d).

Climbing the ladder from Discourse to discourse refers to moving from general or mega discourse (long-range interest) that allows the researcher to make connections with categories that have been historically, socially, and institutionally embedded in the larger society to specific discourse production, for instance, in a local context that is definitive for that locale (close range interest). The former also allows the researcher to make distinctions with the discourse and 'non-discursive' elements such as power/knowledge relations. The large 'D' discourse tries to comprehend how social reality is discursively constructed and maintained within particular, historically situated discursive moves, whereas the small 'd' discourse works with text and talk within everyday interactions in organisations.

Moving horizontally on the scale from discourse and meaning (inseparable) to discourse and meaning (unrelated) refers to the position the researcher takes when making sense of language and language use within context and temporal space. Specifically, as posed by Alvesson and Kärreman, does the researcher give discourse 'muscle' or is discourse more 'transient'? If discourse and its associated meanings are given a lot of muscle or determination, discourse and its practices can drive subjectivity (our sense of ourselves, including thoughts, feelings, and orientations). Meaning and discourse, therefore, are overlapping.

On the other side of the horizontal spectrum, discourse and meaning are considered not related. This means that the subjects and their subjectivities are not determined by discourse and that language may not have such a determining factor on the social construction of reality. For instance, the subject may be conscious of the use of language and tell particular stories or use particular emotions depending on which audience the user is in front of.

The authors conclude that when conducting discourse analysis, it is problematic when the researcher moves between the different spectrums when making sense of the empirical data. For instance, the researcher making fixed categories that are generalised to grand or macro discourses with empirical data from a local context such as interviews and other 'social text' of everyday interactions.

The authors end by suggesting that when examining empirical data, particularly data from a local context like interviews, the researcher should consider not only language use but also the social context in which the data was extracted. Hence, the researchers should provide various ways in which the interviews and other accounts in social text can be interpreted as the accounts can vary in different settings that the interviews were conducted, the variety of discourses available to the subjects, and the verbal skills and creativity of the interviewee in producing their accounts.

The authors further this warning by suggesting how discourse analysis could be conducted beyond language by systematically examining all empirical data before considering what it can be used for. This critical evaluation would be for the researcher to decide whether the empirical material is associated with situated meaning or that the material and its meaning are consistent enough to be transported beyond the local context (e.g. interviews). With this in mind, the authors offer three interpretations of how statements made in the empirical data could be considered:

> (1) statements say something about social reality (e.g. leadership behaviour, events); (2) statements say something about individual or socially shared 'subjective reality' (experience, beliefs, stereotypes, cognition, values, feelings or ideas); (3) statements say something about norms of expression, ways of producing effects (impressions, identity work, legitimacy) or something where accounts must be interpreted in terms of what they accomplish rather than what they mirror-as action rather than in terms of true or false.
>
> (2000: 1146)

The fourth interpretation, which overlaps the three aforementioned statements (particularly, two and three), relates to the question of Discourse (capital D). The authors reflect on this by posing the question as to when can a researcher with empirical data move down the discursive ladder from small 'd' to big 'D'? One concern that arises is by moving too quickly from discourse to Discourse, the nuances and social significances of the empirical data at a local level are lost by quickly moving to grandiosise or muscularise the discourse. This may be a reflection of the researcher excited to explain extradiscursive elements beyond the text. Nonetheless, this jumping from one level to the next may not reveal elements of the data that the researcher set out to explore in the first place.

Discourse analysis of this situated study is conducted within what Alvesson and Kärreman call 'close/determination' perspective. The empirical data was extracted from a local context through interviews and documents, reflecting social text of past, present, and, perhaps, future intended social action of recruitment. Social text, at this local level, includes both talk and written text. Talk is considered less tangible than written text when examining the use of language in the sense that written text is more self-documenting of particular settings. Nonetheless, by focusing on both text and talk (by representatives), both a construction of social worlds (e.g. collectivities creating meaning around the representatives) can be displayed through the data as well as material implications of the interrelated texts (e.g. talk/text working in tandem).

When referring to 'close', discourse analysis is not at the micro level but at a meso level (Wetherell and Potter, 1992): being sensitive to language use in context but interested in finding broader patterns and going beyond the details of the text and generalising to similar local contexts. For this study, discourse is understood in regards to the use of language and its structuring effects. The social constructions of those involved in the social context are constituted through a 'myriad of what post structuralists term "discursive practices": practices of talk, text, writing, cognition, argumentation, and representation generally' (Clegg, 1989: 151). Social construction, therefore, is a driving principle of discourse. As stated by Weedon (1987: 41), discourse is 'a structuring principle of society, in social institutions, modes of thought and individual subjectivity'.

The tension, as discussed by Alvesson and Kärreman, at this level of discourse is how much meaning can be related to the discourse, and what conclusions can be drawn about this relationship (e.g. can categories or generalisation be made and if so, are there nuances or other significant elements of the case that are lost?). In interviews, the dynamics of the interviewee and the interviewer may have an effect on what is said or not said in the statements due to both the participants in the discussion and also the social context and the topic that is spoken about. This does not mean that the statements cannot reflect local construction (including feelings and norms) on the research topic or subjects, but that the statements are not taken solely as a true representation of the social world. To implement a close range/determination analysis of discourse, the account in the data should have some structuring effects, either on the social construction of the interviewee (and other people in the site of question) and/or in terms of framing action. This implies that the researcher would examine whether normative ideals are translated into practices in the study under review. It would also entail understanding what effects these normative ideals have on the social construction of the interviewee and/or other people in the context/situation that the interview accounts or documents are located in. From this perspective, the researcher can draw on non-discursive elements such as power and knowledge production, but only for the particular, local domain of social reality under study such as conceptualising or mapping social worlds and arenas.

Phillips and Hardy (2002) also offer a framework that categorises approaches to discourse analysis according to two key dimensions: the degree to which the emphasis is on individual texts or on the surrounding context and the degree to which research focuses on power and ideology (critical studies) as opposed to the process of social construction (more constructionist studies). They use this to provide a tool for understanding the diversity of theoretical approaches and for sensitising researchers to the important epistemological and methodological characteristics of different styles of discourse analysis.

The vertical axis is similar to Alvesson and Kärreman's as they advocate for explicitly stating the range in which the researcher is studying the discourse. For instance, although the continuum flows from text to context, this does not mean the text does not have a context. What the authors are trying to explore is a distinction between what Wetherell (2001) entitles 'distal' and 'proximal' contexts. Distal context

> includes things like social class, the ethnic composition of the participants, the institutions or sites where discourse occurs, and the ecological, regional, and cultural settings. The proximate context, on the other hand, refers to immediate features of the interaction including the sort of occasion or genre of interaction the participants take an episode to be (e.g. a consultation, an interrogation, a family meal-time), the sequences of talk in which particular events occur and the capacities in which people speak (as initiator or instructor or respondent).
>
> (Wetherell, 2001: 338)

Whereas the proximate context is always incorporated in one way or another, the distal context can be more or less included in the analysis depending on practicality and theoretical orientation.

On the horizontal axis, the choice for the researcher is between constructivist or critical. For the authors, this continuum becomes a question as to how much focus the other has on a particular reality construction (constructivist) or, more explicitly, on the dynamics of power, knowledge, and ideology. As stated by Phillips and Hardy (2002: 20), the question becomes 'to what degree do studies focus directly on the dynamics of power—"the relation of language to power and privilege" (Riggings, 1997: 2)—as opposed to focusing more directly on the processes of social construction that constitute social reality'.

The Material-Discursive and Multi-Domains Approach to Discourse

In organisational and management studies, scholars such as Phillips and Oswick (2012) and Hearn (2014) question the importance of materiality in discourse analysis and the relationship between material and discourse. As argued by Hearn:

> [M]aterialism can now be understood as more complex, as the economic/technological, the 'reproductive', and the bodily/corporeal (including sexuality and violence), as well as materiality of discourse.
>
> (2014: 7)

Phillips and Oswick (2012) conduct a review on organisational discourse: the domains, debates, and directions. In this review, the authors define organisational discourse analysis as involving 'analysis of collections of texts, the ways in which they draw on different discourses, how and to whom they are disseminated, the methods of their production, and the manner in which they are received and consumed' (Phillips et al., 2004: 636). The authors continue their discussion by highlighting existing classification approaches to organisation discourse(s) and create two categories for these approaches: (1) classification by level of analysis and (2) classification by type of method (Phillips and Oswick, 2012: 445). They argue that these approaches are inherently problematic and present alternative ways to rethink discursive inquiry by approaching discourse(s) in terms of within domains and across domain characterisations, and by taking up the material aspects of organisational life. As stated by the authors:

> [I]n addition to the problem of parochialism, a significant impediment to the further development of the field of organizational discourse analysis is an enduring tendency toward isolationism (i.e. an unwillingness to engage with phenomena beyond discourse). In particular, organizational discourse analysts have been criticized for not paying attention to the material aspects of organizational life (Fairclough, 2005; Iedema, 2007; Reed, 1998, 2000). Indeed, Reed (2004) has noted: 'Much of the intellectual inspiration and drive for the development of discursive forms of analysis in social science and organization studies has come from an avowedly anti-realist ontology and epistemology' (413). Drawing upon an earlier polemic on a 'descent into discourse' (Palmer, 1990), Conrad (2004) enlists the term 'discoursism' to represent the tendency to focus on discourse in organization studies to the exclusion of any consideration of material reality.
>
> (2012: 464)

The authors also provide a table to illustrate the perspectives on materiality in discourse-based organisation research and divide the positions of discourse in relation to materiality. The categories are (2012: 466): discourse/constructionism not materiality/realism (competing); discourse/constructionism or materiality/realism (complimentary); discourse/constructionism and materiality/realism (connected); and discourse/constructionism as materiality/realism (co-constituted).

The authors conclude, with empirical examples of organisational scholars, that:

> The problem is not just the need to work across levels that has been so often discussed, but also working across epistemological positions to move to a position that embraces the 'discourse and materiality' and the 'discourse as materiality' positions.
>
> (2012: 470)

Discourse Analysis of this Research: Some Comments About Linguistic Language Use and Situated Knowledge

In this book, discourse from various accounts is analysed in terms of content (claim making in the talk and text). The aim behind this is to understand the particularities of the situation and the discourses' structuring effects on the recruitment and placement of the nurses, but also to recognise that the interviews cannot be taken as 'essential' truths. The interviews were conducted in a particular social setting as well as time (after the recruitment and placement of all the Filipino nurses). As an interviewer, I, who am a woman, solely English speaking, an immigrant, and, at the time of the interviews, visibly pregnant may have evoked different accounts by the interviewees. In the interviews, I was also asked my opinion on the research topic, and the dialogue, at times, of the interviews was quite informal. Particularly, as a Canadian, I was asked what my experiences were, even though, when living in Canada, I was not working in health care management nor was I an immigrant nurse. One important aspect of analysing discourse, in this social setting, is the use of English language.[1] As written previously, discourse is about the use of language to socially construct the objects and the social context in question. What should be noted about this language use is that the interviews are conducted solely in English in Finland, a country in which the primary language is Finnish. Although the use of English in the interviews and as an observer was first seen as a limitation by the researcher, through observation and practice, the use of English became very pronounced in the practice of recruiting the Filipino nurses. All the recruitment as well as the Finnish-language training in the Philippines is primarily conducted in English. The marketing of recruitment of nurses from abroad, particularly the Philippines, is also primarily in English.

Considering the varieties of discourse analysis and their parallel approaches to empirical data, Table 5.1 displays my approach to discourse and the methods of analysis.

Table 5.1 Discourse analysis of this research

Object of analysis (social action)	*Primary discursive focus*	*Sources of data*	*Methods of analysis*	*Sensitised concepts*
Recruitment and placement practices of Filipino nurses in Helsinki	Close range, but discourse is ***situated*** and interrelated with other 'situated elements or conditions' (see Clarke's matrix in Chapter 4)	Interviews Documents Participant observations Research diary	Situational analysis: ordered situational maps and social world maps	***Power*** (constructionist and relational) '***d***'iscourse (close range local context and meso level), but transnationalisation of levels of organising: ***materiality*** of discourse (***interrelated***)

Situational Analysis as an Approach to Discourse, Power, and Materiality

In Chapter 4, I introduce Clarke's situational analysis as a method to analysing a situation through qualitative data collection. Clarke advocates examining the situation through various elements/conditions that make up the situation, with a focus on discourses, power relations, and material 'things' (or nonhuman actants). The method approach is cartographic and includes situational maps, social worlds and arenas maps, and positional maps. To organise my data before its analysis, I use Clarke's cartographic approaches. I begin with the ordered map and proceed to the social world/arenas, and then the positions taken by the actors (based on interview questions). In addition, I provide two text boxes with contextual background information: (1) immigration to Finland and (2) Finland as a Nordic welfare state. After organising the data, the following two chapters analyse and discuss categories that I perceived as informing my research questions in the talk and text of the data. Therefore, in Chapter 6, I focus on the individual human elements and representatives (entrepreneurial and implicated) as well as their collective social worlds. The subsequent chapter discusses the discursive construction of individual actors (representational and implicated) and the implications of these discourses within the practices of transnational management and the material implications on the Finnish labour market of nurses and the transnationalisation of care labour.

Ordered Situational Maps

The use of ordered situational maps is to 'open up the data' and reach what grounded theorists call 'saturation' (Strauss and Corbin, 1998: 143–162). And, I would argue, the maps pedagogically frame/illustrate for the reader which elements of the situation emerge and what elements become important for the researcher to tell the story they want to tell. The ordered situational maps also allowed me to focus in on relations between the different actors and frame discursive constructions of the social practice of recruitment and placement, the representative and implicated actors and their social worlds, and, lastly, actors and the nonhuman actants (material) discursive constructions. These maps facilitate a larger discussion of different levels in transnational organisation and management. The maps create a visual understanding of complex relations that involve negotiations of power, human agency, material welfare, and social infrastructure such as care provisions that stretch among countries (see Table 5.2).

I interpret Clarke's categories as follows and apply the subsequent ordered map to my data:

Individual human elements and actors: these elements are conceptualised as human actors who are considered representatives in the talk and text of

Table 5.2 Clarke's ordered situational map

Individual Human elements/actors e.g. key individuals and significant (unorganised) people in the situation	**Nonhuman elements/actants** e.g. technologies; material infrastructures; specialised information and or knowledges; material 'things'
Collective human elements/actors e.g., particular groups; specific organisations	**Implicated/silent actors/actants** As found in the situation
Discursive constructions of individual and/or collective human actors As found in the situation	**Discursive constructions of nonhuman actants** As found in the situation
Political/ economic elements e.g. the state; particular industry/ies; local/regional/ global orders; political parties; NGOs; politicised issues	**Sociocultural/symbolic elements** e.g. religion; race; sexuality; gender; ethnicity; nationality; logos; other visual and/or aural symbols
Temporal elements e.g. historical, seasonal, crisis, and/or trajectory aspects	**Spatial elements** e.g. spaces in the situation, geographical aspects, local, regional, national, global spatial issues
Major issues/ debates (usually contested) As found in the situation; and positional map	**Related discourses (Historical, narrative, and/or visual)** e.g. normative expectations of actors, actants, and/or other specified elements; moral/ ethical elements; mass media and other popular cultural discourses; situation- specific discourses
Other kinds of elements As found in the situation	

(adapted from Clarke, 2005: 90)

the interviews and documents. For instance, the actors may have been interviewed or are predominately visible in the documents collected (e.g. power point presentations done by the representative's organisation by themselves or on their behalf and the human resource recruitment magazines).

Collective human elements/actors: this refers to the dominant organisations, groups, and projects that emerge in the data and are associated with the recruitment and placement of the Filipino nurses in Helsinki.

Discursive construction of individual and/or collective human actors: these constructions are detailed in Chapters 6 and 7, but I aim to understand who the actors are and what type of discourse is being constructed (produced) and disseminated to further understand who is claiming authority to recruiting and placing the nurses and how.

Political/economic elements: these elements are contextual as municipal and national governance in Finland: regional (governance in the EU) and transnational (importing and exporting human capital). These elements also centralise around labour markets, the Finnish economy, and financing recruitment and placement of foreign labour (e.g. researching actively where to recruit and investing personal capital in the recruitment of nurses from abroad). In addition, the analysis considers ideologies of the Finnish nation-state (social and health welfare and care) (also view context boxes).[2]

Temporal elements: these elements in the case are the contractual training periods of the nurses and the period of recruitment (e.g. how long the pilot studies last).

Major issues/debates (usually contested): data used for this category are both documents and interviews. The major issue/debates reflect discursive positions in the data that are not limited to the representatives or their social worlds.

Nonhuman elements/actants: important elements here are the material economic infrastructure in the nursing profession as well as the Finnish nation-state, the financing over everyday lives, and the specialised tacit knowledge in the nursing occupation, as well as Finnish-language use. The last element, Finnish-language use, is in terms of qualification or level of the Finnish language by a non-native Finnish speaker.

Implicated/silent actors/actants: this is a category that I add to Clarke's recommended ordered map. In the interviews and the documents, I want to capture actors that are implied or physically present in the situation but silent. The silence arises as another representative is referring to the actor on his or her behalf.

Discursive constructions of nonhuman elements: these elements are discussed in Chapters 6 and 7; the aim of illustrating these elements is to emphasise the materiality of the discursive constructions of the Filipino nurses and other actors in the situation as well as the practices of the recruitment and placement by Finnish actors.

Discursive constructions of implicated actors by representatives: this category, as with the aforementioned one on implicated actors, was added by myself for analysis. I want to illustrate, in the data, how implicated or silent actors discursively emerge in the talk and text.

Sociocultural/symbolic elements: this category is based on the literature as I do not use mega discourse ('D') in my analysis. I aim to examine a discourse at a meso level that cannot claim to capture a 'grand narrative'. Therefore, the literature review that encompasses more mega discursive claims is used for these potential elements in the situation: for instance, the discourse of gender and race in the nursing profession.

Spatial elements: these elements in the data comply to the need of multi-domain research as argued by Phillips and Oswick (2012). The idea here is the workforce in question is transnational and actors are working in various social worlds and domains.

Related discourses (historical, narrative, and/or visual): these elements are also constructed based on the book's literature review (also view Context Boxes 5.1 and 5.2).

Social Worlds/Arena Maps

Social worlds and arena maps provide a meso-level analytical framework as they are actor defined and permit identification and analysis of collectivities construed as meaningful by the actors themselves (Clarke, 1991; Strauss, 1993: 209–260). The actors are representative of social worlds and arenas, and the maps facilitate an understanding of collective action by the actors committed to their respective social world through negotiations, maintaining boundaries and gaining social legitimation for the world itself (Strauss, 1982). Discourses within social worlds and arenas are not explicitly present per se as social worlds are universes of discourse (Strauss, 1978) in arenas that are constituted and maintained through discourses. As such, the map analysis focuses on collective social action (Clarke, 2005: 114). To describe and capture the various social worlds and arenas, Clarke (2005: 115) recommends making detailed memos of the following questions for social worlds and arenas maps (see Table 5.3).

As the data consists of interviews and documents collected parallel to the interviews and within the interviews, the maps and the subsequent memos underline the fact that representatives (individuals interviewed) are not organisations/institutions and social worlds, but rather working in a social collectivity with various discourses and 'conditions of possibilities' (see Foucault, 1975; it has also been said that Foucault's concept to explain this is 'episteme') and/or negotiations (see Strauss, 1978). This argument is also made in Chapter 4 and refers to Clarke's situational matrices, which illustrates various elements possible in a situation.

The maps in Figures 5.1–5.3 are my final social worlds and arenas maps. Each social world is based on collective social action; specifically, the intense focus is on actions taken by a particular world on particular issues. In this study, the central issue is the recruitment and placement of the Filipino

Table 5.3 Questions for social world and arena maps

Questions for social world maps	*Questions for arenas in which social worlds are involved or implicated*
• What is the work of each world? • What are the commitments of a given world? • How do participants believe they should go about fulfilling them? • How does the world describe itself-present itself-in its discourse(s)? • How does it describe other worlds in the arena? • What actions have been taken in the past and are anticipated in the future? • How is the work of furthering that social world's agenda organised? • What technologies are used and implicated? • Are there particular sites where the action is organised? What are they like? • What else seems important about this social world?	• What is the focus of the arena? • What social worlds are present and active? • What social worlds are present and implicated or not present and implicated? • Are there any worlds absent that you might have expected? • What are the hot issues/contested topics/current controversies in the arena's discourses? • Are there any surprising silences in the discourse? • What else seems important about this arena?

(Table adapted from Clarke, 2005: 115)

nurses in the capital of Helsinki, but the issue also blurred or transformed into the management and organisation of immigrant nurse labour and/or immigrant labour, in general. In the interviews, I began by asking the participant the following questions:

1) What do your responsibilities and position entail at [your organisation]? Can you describe your daily activities?
2) How is [your organisation] involved in the recruitment and placement of foreign nurses?

The interviews always ended with the follow question:

10) Is there anything else you would like to add to this interview? Are there any documents that are relevant to this research both in English and in Finnish? Are there other people that I should be in contact with in regards to this research?

These questions, as well as the method of data collection, endeavour to examine not only the talk and text of the representatives but also the text of the collective whole (organisation/institution).

Table 5.4 My rendition of Clarke's situational ordered map with my empirical data

<u>Individual Human elements (representatives)</u> – Representatives from private for profit businesses – Filipino nurses (non-recruited/recruited and working in Finland) – Representatives of Finnish nurse unions – Representatives of European Union–funded projects and networks in Finland – Representatives of the City of Helsinki – Representatives of Adult Education in Finland – Representatives of Finnish state ministries (Ministry of Interior, Ministry of Labour and Economy)	**<u>Nonhuman elements/actants (material 'things')</u>** – Financial investments by recruiters – Nurse wages in Finland and the Philippines – Qualifications and certificates of nurses (nursing education – Employment contracts and residential permits – Standardisations in Finnish language use – Health care infrastructure in the Philippines
<u>Collective human elements/actors (Organisations, institutions, projects)</u> – Private for profit companies – Finnish national ministries of Interior and labour and economy – Vocational adult education centre – Nurse Unions – Municipality (of Helsinki) – National supervisory board for welfare and health – Nurse occupation – European Union	**<u>Implicated/silent actors/actants</u>** – Filipino nurses – Finnish nurses – Elderly patients – 'Clients' – Immigrant skilled labourer – 'Family in the Philippines' of the recruited nurses
<u>Discursive constructions of individual and/or collective human actors</u> – Representatives legitimising control of the recruitment and placement of Filipino nurses in Finland – Social constructions of the Filipino nurses in talk and text	**<u>Discursive constructions of nonhuman actants</u>** – Personal and private equity as an investment in recruitment; individuals and organisations that invest privately should receive financial gain in return (production capital) – Nursing is a 'calling' and should not be about wages – Contracts are temporary and flexible – American education in nursing is of high value – Nursing as a registered nurse is more professional and skilled (more educated) than nursing as a practical nurse – Finnish language as difficult to learn and practice (tacit, specialised knowledge) – English language as working language (tacit, specialised knowledge) – Health care in the Philippines: a problem for the Philippines not Finland; Finnish actors are 'ethically' recruiting

(*Continued*)

Table 5.4 (Continued)

Individual Human elements (representatives) Political/economic elements(structural) – The Philippines as an exporter of nurses – Finland's history of immigration and non-Finnish labour – European Union financing and having an impact on the Finnish domestic labour market through projects – Finland as a Nordic welfare state Temporal elements – Training Filipino nurses in Finnish language and requalifying the nurses to practice in Finnish health care organisations – Employment contracts – Nurses migration from Philippines to Finland – Requalification and training of Filipino nurses – Proficiency of Finnish language skills by non-native Finnish citizens – Commercialisation of health care services (for profit): making a business in the recruitment of nurses from abroad	Nonhuman elements/actants (material 'things') Discursive constructions of Implicated actors by representatives – Filipino nurses as available human resources for importation – Packaging desirable products for the clients Sociocultural/symbolic elements – Catholic workers as charitable – Nurses sexed bodies as female – Migrant workers as victims Spatial elements – Trasnationalisation of care – Local provision of care services to the elderly in the municipality of Helsinki and Espoo – Care in a hospital versus care in an elderly care facility Related discourses (Historical, narrative, and/or visual) – American imperialism in the Philippines – Philippines as an exporter of workers – Nursing as women's work – Caring in the private realm and later institutionalised – Nordic countries as welfare states and gender equal – Finland immigration based on refugees and family ties policies – Finnish workers immigrating abroad – Coping management in the nursing occupation – Nursing as a gendered and racialised profession

In the centre of each map below (see Figures 5.1, 5.2, 5.3), there is an arena entitled 'producer-based care network'. The producer-based care network serves as an arena or a domain in which representatives and their associate social worlds—based on their work, social action, and/or collective commitments in the THRM practices—enter to assert authority in the talk and texts of the situation. Each social world, which is constructed through the data collection and analysis, reflects the commitment of the representatives and their organisational work, mandates, and social actions. Implicated representatives and social worlds are outside of the domain. Although these social worlds may be physically present or mentioned in talk and text, the worlds do not dominate in the arena of producer-based care networks (see Figures 5.1, 5.2, 5.3).

The maps are solely an introduction and are described in detail in the next chapter. In particular, the next chapter analyses who the actors (representatives) and collective actors are in the situation. The chapter then proceeds to describe the various social worlds emerging from the discourses in the data and thematic issues that emerge. To facilitate explaining the worlds, I also provide a table (Table 5.5) that reflects my memos on the questions posed by Clarke (Table 5.4).

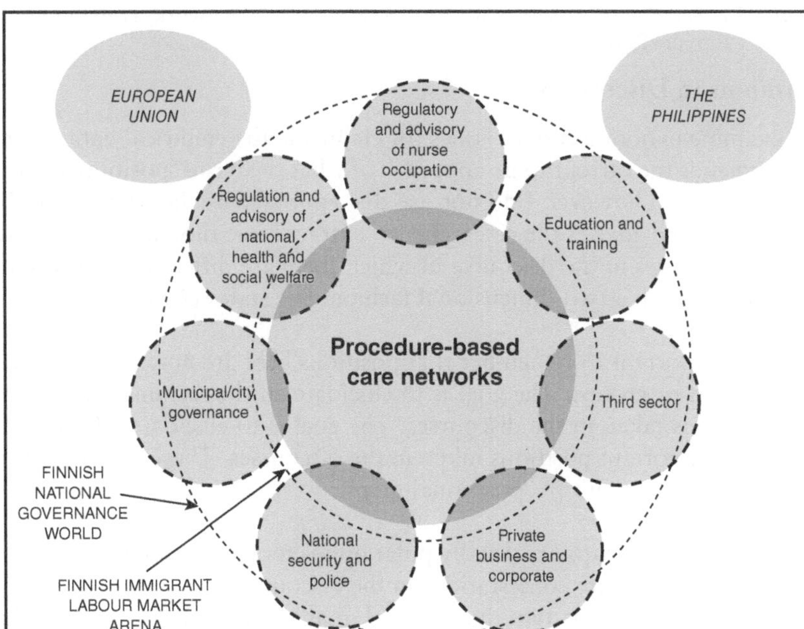

Figure 5.1 Social world maps with producer-based care network as the arena for year 2007

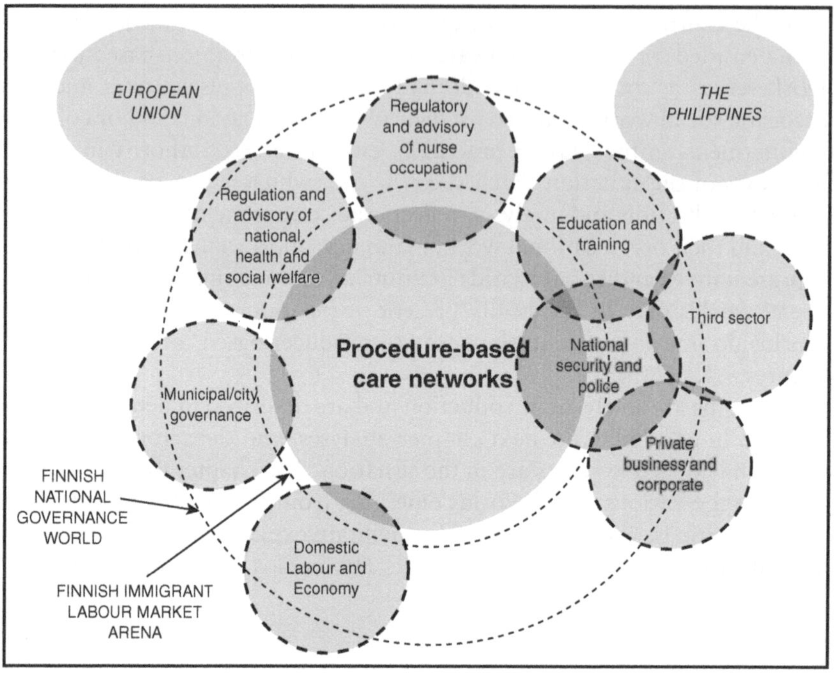

Figure 5.2 Social world maps with producer-based care network as the arena for years 2008–2009

Positions in Discourses

To examine major discursive issues (or claims) in the empirical data, Clarke recommends the cartographic approach of what she terms 'positional maps'. In my analysis, however, I do not use this approach as she suggests. In her suggestion, she advises the researcher to extract basic (not always but often contested) issues in the discourse in which there are different positions and organise them in a two-dimensional fashion. She states (2005: 197):

> It is important to remember that positions here are not correlated with persons or groups. The goal is to elucidate all the seemingly important positions taken in the discourses. The goal is to elucidate all the seemingly important positions taken in the discourses. There may therefore, of course, be multiple positional maps.

The axes in these maps are usually polar opposites (e.g. positive or negative) that serve to illustrate contestations in the discourse.

For me, I found this two-dimensional analysis difficult to use and illustrate, even if she does suggest various positional maps in the data. Instead, I refer to both the ordered situational map and the social world maps to create thematic categories that emerge in the talk and text. An underlying assumption in this analysis is that the discursive claims or positions are

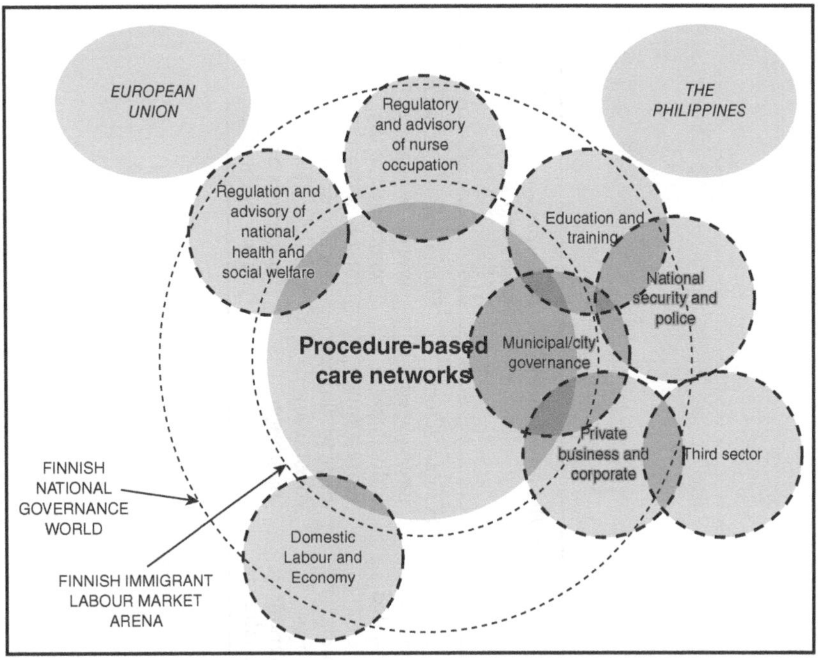

Figure 5.3 Social world maps with producer-based care network as the arena for years 2009–2010

not limited to one representative or social world but rather transpire across the arena of producer-based care networks. This analysis aims to capture the close range, situated discourse of the situation that is the recruitment and placement of the 75 Filipino nurses during period 2007–2010. In my analysis, a particular focus is placed on the discursive construction of representatives and implicated actors, and the interrelationship between power, discourse, and materiality.

Summary and Concluding Thoughts

Discourse and its analysis vary in terms of epistemological and ontological assumptions. The research questions in this book are framed in terms of discourse (small d) as the analysis is close range and situated. Discourse and its implications on the social construction of THRM practices, as well as issues of representation, are also considered as material, having direct physical and nonhuman effects on human bodies and lives.

Social worlds and cartographic approaches as noted previously are used to go beyond the 'knowing subjects', and create material products in a story told by the researcher. The story is a retelling of a journey of collecting and analysing data, and the investigation of a social phenomenon framed in terms of research questions set out by the researcher.

Table 5.5 Social world categories and thematic issues in the data

Social worlds	*Organisations and institutions*	*Commitments and work of the social world*	*Projects*	*Representatives*	*Implicated and/or silent actors and social worlds*
My categories from memos based on Clarke's questions (Table 5.4)	The official name of the organisation or institution or workplace	e.g. commitments of the given world, mandates of the organisation/ institution, the work the given world does, etc.	Temporary projects that are funded for the topic of immigrant labour or immigrant nurse labour	Human actors interviewed; individuals representing their workplace /organisation/ institution	Human actors or social worlds who were mentioned in the interviews or the documents given during the interviews (e.g. the Philippines and Filipino nurses in the Philippines)

The interviews and documents collected 'open up' information on the research question:

1) Who are the representatives, organisations, and institutions involved in the recruitment and placement of Filipino nurses in Finland?
2) What social worlds are they representing?
3) How do the representatives, organisations, and institutions socially interact and relate?

To highlight how the representatives talked and produced texts, the representatives are associated with social worlds in maps created through categories and themes based on the collected data. The situated knowledge of the researcher, the representatives, Finnish organisations, and the transnational management practices are influenced by intersectional identities of whiteness, language, and nationality. This emphasis draws attention to various situational elements in the case, which give significance to practices of inclusion and exclusion in the nursing occupation within Finland and transnationally. These research questions are addressed in Chapter 6.

Furthermore, another question is viewed in terms of positions. The question is this:

> How, through discursive positions in the claims of the produced talk and text, are the representatives and organisations socially constructing the practices of recruitment and placement of Filipino nurses in Finland?

The positions that emerge are associated with the representatives but also encompass positions taken in the data as a whole. In other words, positions also go beyond the knowing subjects and transpire in the various social worlds and arenas in which the representatives interact. This question is address in Chapter 7.

In the following chapter, I present the data collected to tell the story of how various representatives, organisations, and institutions and their associated social worlds emerged and either dominated or did not dominant the arena of the producer-based care networks in Finland.

Contextual box 5.1 Immigration to Finland

The discourses surrounding immigration practices and policies within the Finnish government and municipalities, before 2006, revolved around issues of security and refugees, and the subsequent integration of these individuals (Integration Act, 1999). The propensity was reflected in the small amount of immigrants moving to Finland (Bartram, 2007), and their reasons for resident permit applications (mostly family ties), but also the organisation of different governmental ministries, municipality policies, practices, and projects

(Korkisassari and Söderöling, 2003). Before 2006, the Ministry of Interior (Intermin) was the main institution involved in the design and enforcement of immigration policy and law, but the municipalities provided social provisions and programmes to facilitate integration. As such, one of the stated mandates of the Ministry of Interior is national security and border control: the municipalities that are structured to provide social services that include elements of integration, policies, and practices around immigration were strongly correlated with regulation of security and, subsequently, a need for security that derived from the integration of non-Finns.

In the 1990s, the sharp rise of immigration was reflected in changes in refugee quotas as well as a progamme implemented by the then government that promoted the return of Ingrains of Finnish descent (Aliens Act (301/2004)); Korkiasaari and Söderling, 1998). The rise also coincided with a deep recession in Finland that led to record levels of unemployment. Subsequently, this meant that immigrants, returnees, and refugees found it extremely difficult to find work, and many refugees that had arrived in the previous decade lost their jobs (Tanner, 2011). At this time, the municipalities were providing social services such as housing to these individuals, plus the changing demographics led the government to reformulate how to manage and 'integrate' foreign nationals. Particular issues considered were in the sphere of employment and training.

In 1995, the government at the time appointed an immigration programme and refugee policy commission who later created a report in 1997. This report resulted in the first immigration and refugee programme. The programme focused on the immigrants that were in Finland at the time, which were largely refugees and not labour-based immigrants, and had the stated objective to facilitate the flexible and efficient social labour market integration of all immigrants (Seppelin, 2010).

The commission's report and immigration programme also resulted in the act entitled 'integration of immigrants and reception of asylum seekers' (493/1999) which took effect on 1 May 1999. This act contains provisions on measures

> to promote integration, equality, and freedom of choice of immigrants through measures which help them to acquire the essential knowledge and skills they need to function in society, and to ensure support and care for asylum seekers and beneficiaries of temporary protection in the context of a mass influx for their reception. The further purpose of this Act is to assist victims of trafficking in human beings.
>
> (1269/2006)

Integration in this law is defined as (1) 'the personal development of immigrants, aimed at participation in working life and society while preserving their own language and culture' (362/2005), and (2) 'the measures taken and resources and services provided by authorities to promote and support such integration, and consideration for the needs of immigrant in planning and providing other public services and measures' (1215/2005).

The law sets out who is responsible for this integration, and its design and implementation. It requires the close collaboration of various authorities. Before 2008, the Ministry of Interior was responsible for the general development, planning, steering, monitoring, and coordinating of the integration of immigrants. After December 2011 (1251/2011), the Ministry of Employment and Economy (TEM) became the main institution responsible.

The regional centres for Economic Development, Transport, and Environment (ELY), which also fall under the Ministry of Labour and Economy (TEM) since its establishment in 2008, are responsible for the coordination of the integration of immigrants under the law. ELY distributes funding and decides on which projects and provisions will be implemented by the various Employment and Development Offices (TE). TE offices are responsible for the provision of labour markets services and promoting and supporting the integration of immigrants, as well as providing instruction in reading and writing and of basic education for immigrants registered as job seekers. Coinciding with the TE and ELY offices, municipalities are responsible for drawing up, implementing, and developing an integration programme and for monitoring its implementation and impact. An integration programme contains a plan concerning both measures, services, cooperation, and responsibilities involved in promoting and supporting integration and consideration for the needs of immigrants in planning and organising other public services and measures. It also covers the promotion of ethnic equality and good ethnic relations, and the prevention of discrimination (Seppelin, 2010).

Contextual box 5.2 An emerging destination for migrant nurses: Finland, a Nordic welfare state

New destination countries for migrant nurses have been created through a demand influenced by structural changes within national welfare structures, policies, and practices. As in the case of Finland, which was predominately an emigrating nation before the 1990s, changes in policy permitting more labour emigration in the 1990s, as well as structural and policy changes in the health care and social governance in the 1990s and early 2000s, created a new market for receiving external labourers as well as shifts in management ideologies.

In Finland, there has been an evolution of socially defined care that went from the private realm (the home) to the public realm (the institutions). Care work, before the 1960s, was predominately done by Nordic women in the home, but as women began entering the paid labour market, a care gap was created that the Nordic welfare state had to respond to (Wrede et al., 2008). This response was illustrated through welfare policies, provisions, and programmes. Through this institutionalisation of care, daycare and care for dependents such as the disabled and elderly was socially defined in contrast to the medically defined needs that were already historically professionalised.

Even as this care entered the public sphere, it was still defined as women's work. As the care definition changed, Waerness argues that care work associated with traditional feminitity was commonly devalued and portrayed as irrational in the welfare state rhetoric (1984). Furthermore, as care work becomes more professionalised through paid care, private patriarchy was shifted to a public one (Hernes, 1988) as masculine assumptions about rationality structured the way care was framed in the welfare states (Dahl & Eriksen, 2005). As Wrede et al. argue:

> The professionalisation of social care in the welfare state resulted in a series of separations and exclusions, where the 'irrational' and 'dirty' aspects of care became framed as non-professional and therefore inferior work.
>
> (2008: 24)

Since the early 1990s, the Finnish welfare state has shifted ideologies from a social definition of care work to a more managerial understanding of welfare services. The managerialist understanding of welfare provisions, particularly in regards to cost efficiency, hit the care occupations more severely than other welfare programmes (Julkuenen & Nätti, 1999). Many care workers in the early 1990s lost their jobs due to government and municipalities cutting their spending on public health services and welfare programmes.

Many Finnish experts argue that this shift from welfare to neoliberal ideology has resulted in a 'competition state' (Heinonen, 1999; Sipilä, 2005). Others argue that expenditures in the social sector has not decreased and the 'Finnish model' continues to be successful in balancing growth, education, employment, and social policy (Saari, 2006).

Within this context, the Finnish government is currently dealing with shortages in the health care workforce that has been a result of spending cuts in the 1990s, but also health care as an occupation has lost its attractiveness as a career option over the last 15 years (Kankaanranta & Rissanen, 2008).

The Finnish governmental programme has been trying to combat this shortage by promoting international mobility to Finland by foreign-educated professionals. The government has developed recruitment programmes such as the Government Migration Policy Programme (2006), which promotes labour migration to Finland, and The National Development Programme (KATSE), which aims to recruit unemployed migrants to work in the health care sector through long-term strategic objectives for the social health care system.

With these programmes and institutions in place, international recruitment of health care professionals has still relied heavily on private companies. The private recruitment for the care occupation has allowed for the business sector to work closely with the government in defining the occupation and care.

Notes

1 There are various uses of the English language, particularly as a non-native language by the speaker. English use varied in the interviews as the language is used and understood differently in accordance to the background of the speaker. Use and command of English language varied between the interviewer, a Canadian speaker, and the interviewees, Filipino, Finnish, and British. Although each interviewee had a strong command of the language, the accents and use of vocabulary were different as the interviewees learned and used the language in different cultural contexts.

2 The phenomenon of nation branding has been analysed and discussed by sociology and marketing scholars such as Kleppe et al. (2002); O'Shaughenssy, J. and O'Shaughenssy, N. J. (2000).

References

Alvesson, M. & Kärreman, D. (2000) Varieties of discourse: On the study of organizations through discourse analysis. *Human Relations*, 53, pp. 1125–1149.Carabine, J. (2001) Unmarried motherhood 1830–1990: A genealogical analysis. In M. Wetherell, S. Taylor & S. J. Yates (eds.) *Discourse theory and practice: A reader*. Thousand Oaks: Sage, pp. 380–399.

Bartram, D. (2007) Conspicious by their absence: why are there so few foreign workers in Finland? *Journal of ethnic and migration studies*, pp. 767–782.

Chalaby, J. K. (1996) Beyond the prisons-house of language: Discourse as a sociological concept. *British Journal of Sociology*, 47, pp. 684–698.

Clarke, A. (1991) *As organizational theory. Social organization and social process: Essays in honor of Anselm Strauss*. New York: Aldine de Gruyter, pp. 119–157.

Clarke, A. (2005) *Situational analysis: Grounded theory after the postmodern turn*. Thousand Oaks, CA: Sage.

Clegg, S. R. (1989). *Frameworks of power*. London: Sage.

Dahl, H. M. & Eriksen, T. R. (2005) *Dilemmas of care in the Nordic welfare state: community and change*. Aldershot, UK: Ashgate.

De Saussure, F. (1974) *Course in linguistics general*. London: Fontana/Colins.

Deetz, S. (2003) Reclaiming the legacy of the linguistic turn. *Organization*, 10(3), pp. 421–429.

Denzin, N. K. & Lincoln, Y. S. (2000) Paradigms and perspectives in transition. *Handbook of Qualitative Research*, 2, pp. 157–162.

Fairclough, N. & Wodak, R. (1997) Critical discourse analysis. In T. A. van Dijk (ed.) *Discourse as social interaction*. London: Sage.

Foucault, M. (1975). *The birth of the clinic: An archeology of the medical perceptions*. New York: Vintage.

Gergen, K. (1999) *An invitation to social construction*. London: Sage.

Grant, D., Keenoy, T. & Oswick, C. (1998) Organizational discourse: Of diversity, dichotomy, and multi disciplinarity. In D. Grant, T. Keenoy & C. Oswick (eds.) *Discourse and organization*. London: Sage, pp. 1–14.

Hardy, C. (2001) Researching organizational discourse. *International Studies of Management & Organization*, 31(3), pp. 25–47.

Hearn, J. (2014) Men, masculinities and the material(-)discursive. *Norma: The International Journal for Masculinity Studies*, 9(7), pp. 5–17.

Heinonen, J. (1999). Kohti yksilöllistä pirstoutumista vai demokraattista yhteisöllisyyttä? *Yhteiskuntapolitiikk*, 65(3), pp. 270–278.

Hernes, H. M. (1988) Scandinavian citizenship. *Acta Sociologia*, 31(3), pp. 199–215.

Julkuenen, R. & Nätti, J. (1999) *The modernization for working times. Flexibility and work sharing in Finland*. Jyväskylä: University of Jyväskylä.

Lessa, I. (2005) Discursive struggles within social welfare: Restaging teen motherhood. *British Journal of Social Work*, 36(2), pp. 283–298.

Kankaanranta, T. & Rissanen, P. (2008). Nurses' intentions to leave nursing in Finland. *The European Journal of Health Economics*, 9(4), pp. 333–342.

Kleppe, I. A., Iversen, N. M. & Stensaker, I. G. (2002). Country images in marketing strategies: Conceptual issues and an empirical Asian illustration. *Journal of Brand Management*, 10(1), pp. 61–74.

Korkisassari, J. & Söderöling, I. (1998) Finland: from a country of emigration into a country of immigration. Teoksessa I. Söderöling (ed.) *À changing pattern of migration in Finland and its surroundings*. Helsinki: Väestöliitto, pp. 7–28.

Korkisassari, J. & Söderöling, I. (2003) *Finnish emigration and immigration after World Ware II*. Turku: Migration Institute.

O'Shaughnessy, J. & O'Shaughnessy, N. J. (2000). Treating the nation as a brand: Some neglected issues. *Journal of Macromarketing*, 20(1), pp. 56–64.

Phillips, N. & Hardy, C. (2002) *Discourse analysis: Investigating processes of social construction*. Newbury Park: Sage.

Phillips, N., Lawrence, T. B. & Hardy, C. (2004). Discourse and institutions. *Academy of Management Review*, 29(4), pp. 635–652.

Phillips, N. & Oswick, C. (2012) Organizational discourse: Domains, debates, and directions. *The Academy of Management Annuals*, 6(1), pp. 435–481.

Saari, J. (2006). *Suomen malli–Murroksesta menestykseen*. Helsinki: Yliopistopaino.

Seppelin, M. (2010). *Finnish integration policy. Act on the integration of immigrants and reception of asylum seekers*. Helsinki: Ministry of Social Affairs and Health.

Sipilä, J. (2005). Minkä instituutioiden varaan uskallamme turvamme rakentaa. *Sosiaaliturva*, 93, pp. 13–16.

Strauss, A. (1978). A social world perspective. *Studies in Symbolic Interaction*, 1(1), pp. 119–128.

Strauss, A. (1982). Interorganizational negotiation. *Urban Life*, 11(3), pp. 350–367.

Strauss, A. (1993). *Continual permutations of action*. New York: Aldine de Gruyter.

Strauss, A. L. & Corbin, J. (1998) *The basics of qualitative analysis: Grounded theory procedures and techniques* (3rd ed.). Thousand Oaks, CA: Sage.

Tanner, A. (2011) Finland's Balancing Act: The Labor Market, Humanitarian Relief, and Immigrant Integration. Migration Information Source, 31 January, available (in English) on http://www.migrationinformation.org/feature/display.cfm?ID=825

Taylor, J. R., Cooren, F., Giroux, N. & Robichaud, D. (1996) The communicational basis of organization: Between the conversation and the text. *Communication Theory*, 6(1), pp. 1–39.

Waerness, K. (1984). The rationality of caring. *Economic and Industrial Democracy*, 5(2), pp. 185–211.

Watson, T. & Bargiela-Chiappini, F. (1998) Managerial sensemaking and occupational identities in Britain and Italy. *Journal of Management Studies*, 35(3), pp. 285–301.

Weedon, C. (1987). *Feminist practice and poststructuralist practice*. Oxford: Basil Blackwell.

Wetherell, M. (2001) Debates in discourse research. In M. Wetherell, S. Taylor & S. J. Yates (eds.) *Discourse theory and practice: A reader*. Thousand Oaks: Sage, pp. 380–399.

Wetherell, M. & Potter, J. (1992) *Mapping the language of racism: Discourse and the legitimation of exploitation*. New York: Harvester.

Winch, P. (1958) *The idea of a social science*. London: Routledge & Kegan Paul.

Wittgenstein, L. (1967) *Philosophical investigations*. Oxford: Blackwell.

Wrede, S., Henriksson, L., Høst, H., Johansson, S., & Dybbroe, B. (2008) *Care work in crisis: Reclaiming the Nordic ethos of care*. Lund: Studentlitteratur.

Part 3

A Situation

6 Transnational Management of Nurses in Producer-Based Care Networks in Finland

Managerial work is usually organised as a set of practices related to the social world(s) in which managers are involved (see Strauss, 1978). In other words, managers are committed to particular work objectives, mandates, and practices, depending on which social world they are navigating through their daily work activities.

Social worlds are collectives or 'universes' of discourses in which common symbols, organisations, and activities emerge. These worlds provide insight into deeply situated and yet fluid organisational elements of negotiations and discourses. Social worlds also engage with other social worlds in an arena, which is a space where the social worlds interact around a central social action.

In this chapter, I argue that an examination into the transnational management of nurses necessitates an examination into sites of knowledge production and the politics of geographies. To facilitate this examination, I use Adele Clarke's (2005) cartographic tools of situational analysis to construct social worlds, which are interacting and negotiating, in an arena where the central action is the transnational management of nurses.

To illustrate negotiations and interactions between Finnish representatives and work organisations involved in the transnational management of nurses, the social worlds maps focus on 'producer-based care networks' as an arena. As defined by Yeates (2011: 1120), producer-based care networks link public and private actors that produce, recruit, relocate, and settle labour abroad into the care chain of global nurses. With this definition in mind, I argue that producer-based care networks are powerful sites of knowledge production in which representational discourses of global nurses emerge and practices of transnational management are materialised. To visualise and explain this site of knowledge production, I employ 'the producer-based care networks' as a metaphorical platform to display the representatives and their work organisations practicing transnational management as a central action in the locality of Finland. This platform captures how the representatives and their social worlds interact and negotiate through discourses of talk and texts around the action or praxis of transnational management.

More specifically, in this chapter, I endeavour to capture an arena where representatives and their associated social worlds interact to dominate, pacify, or remain silent within the social action of recruitment and placement of nurses from the Philippines. What this reveals is the 'who' of the situation or 'who cares' when it comes to the recruitment and placement of these global nurses.

Within the arena of producer-based care networks, private and public representatives work in their associated social worlds to produce, recruit, relocate, and settle labour transnationally; in this situation, the networks produce knowledge and practices of recruitment and placement of Filipino nurses for Finnish clients. How the representatives practice the transnational management of care is constructed in terms of the organisation's work, commitments (e.g. selling and packaging recruitment of nurses from the Philippines), how the representatives of the organisations practice the work and commitments, and how the organisation and its work is described through discourse.

The following sections map discourses and practices of the transnational management of nurses through a situation, or what I like to call a situated story, of the recruitment and placement of Filipino nurses by Finnish organisations. The first recruitment of nurses outside the European Union for the Finnish welfare state happened in the year 2007. The situated story here details, through discourse analysis of talk and text, how and by whom transnational management was practiced in Finland at this time, and illustrates through maps of 'producer-based care networks' which representatives and practices emerged with their associated social worlds.

Establishing the Arena of Producer-Based Care Networks

In Finland, prior to the year 2007, immigration was mostly related to family ties and refugee seekers as well as immigrants with Finnish ancestry reclaiming citizenship.[1] The discourses and material practices that surrounded this immigration were viewed in terms of 'integration' into the social infrastructure (social and health benefits; learning Finnish language; 'personal development')[2] rather than the work-related or economic 'integration' of skilled and/or professional immigrants. In an interview I conducted in 2011 related to the question 'why was there a shift in immigration responsibilities from the Ministry of Social Affairs and Health (STM) to the Ministry of Interior (Intermin)?', the representative of Intermin reflects (interview #12),

> The Ministry of health and social services was long passed, like fifteen years ago in the eighties. And, why for the background, the whole idea was before that only those who [seeked] asylum were refugees or immigrants. We didn't have . . . we had very few . . . or hardly any . . . still it is only three percent of the whole population is immigrant background. And, in the past, the majority of those people who came were asylum

seachers [sic]. And, the whole idea was immigrant/foreign people would come first that there was social security questions. So, we would need social security aid. And, that is why the integration, it was only key users of security [those who, by law, are entitled to social security in Finland (KELA)].

Shifting responsibilities of immigration between ministries illustrates the social action of organising and managing immigration as moving between different social worlds and different representatives of those worlds. It also reveals shifts in the discursive construction of immigrants as refugees and/or families (prior to 2007) to immigrants as labourers and/or individuals (post 2007). The immigrants for 'integration' before 2007 were managed in accordance to the social infrastructure of Finland, whereas after 2007, the discursive construction of the immigrant becomes the 'much needed labourers' and is subsequently managed in accordance to the economic and labour market infrastructure of Finland.

The representative (interview #12) continues:

And then you have this time that, of course, you need labour . . . labour market is important and we try to recruit these people [immigrants] and help them integrate into our labour market. That is, of course, nowadays, the whole idea [as] ninety percent of immigrant people come to work here, or family members, or come to study. Only ten percent of immigration are for other reasons.

Parallel to the discursive shifts as well as movements of responsibilities between National ministries on immigration, the City of Helsinki began initiatives of active recruitment from abroad for labour shortages in the Helsinki public sector with the Inkeri project in 2007.[3] The project recruited from regions where the recruitees were of Ingrian descendants such as Russia, Karelia, and Estonia.[4] Those recruited for the project were property managers, housekeepers, practical nurses, teacher aides, and school secretaries. The project recruited the employees through two years of advertisement and provided all the settlement necessary for integration, such as Finnish-language courses, mentors, housing, schooling for their children, and counselling. Nonetheless, even with the basic knowledge of Finnish, the project concluded that the City would not do any more direct recruitment. According to a representative of the City of Helsinki (interview #9b):

It showed us just how difficult straight recruitment from abroad is. Even though it was really small scaled, people spoke some degree of Finnish, and they were professionals who just went through advertisement in order to get this Finnish credentials. There were a lot of issues which ate a lot of time of the person coordinating the project. And, basically, we made some conclusions as to not to do straight recruitment ourselves

> anymore, but to use professional companies who are making a business case out of it in the future.

The representative notes that, because of the experience with the Inkeri project, Helsinki would contract recruitment services from an external source. The representative (as well as another representative interviewed at the same time) also notes that Helsinki has had many discussions with key players involved in the recruitment of foreign labour. They both believe that the city of Helsinki as well as Finland are in the beginning stages of learning about the processes and practices of recruiting from abroad. Key concerns arising from the discussions are language and the involvement of non-Finns in top decision-making processes. In regards to the language, the representative indicates that the discussions revolve around 'what is enough?' (interview #9b):

> The official line is that we try to promote it very much that there should not be any difference as long as the person has Finnish plausible credentials and enough of language skills. So, the basic discussion goes around the issues 'what is enough? 'What credentials are plausible enough? What is the 'enough' of Finnish language? And, that is where the most discussion is growing.

Both representatives expressed apprehensions in regards to the lack of immigrant involvement in the decision on integration policies within Finnish social welfare infrastructure and the Helsinki labour market (interview #9a):

> We [city of Helsinki] hope to get more and more of immigrant voices in the positions of, at least good professional position, a better position of power. But, let's see how long it takes before we have at least the first member of parliament with immigrant background.

The representative at the city of Helsinki reflects on work-related immigration by stating that the discussions need to go deeper and communicate domestically rather than researching other cities and countries abroad. One suggestion of the representative is to collect experiences and knowledge from Helsinki's own staff to inform and develop Helsinki's HR system. The representative states (interview #9a):

> I think, in general, we are in the beginning of the whole recruitment [process] because we don't have any senior position of immigrant background. And, this is where the issue goes deeper because we don't debate with the HR people to really develop the system and what are their experiences, for example, their countries and benchmark through that way. For example, we are circulating surveys to our colleagues of

> various cities and Europe to give us [information] rather than our own staff people giving experience and knowledge.

Obstacles to developing a locally informed and more inclusive public HR system based on the experiences of city's staff are further enforced, the representative argues, through the shift in ministries on managing immigration (interview #9a):

> I think the thing is that when the whole immigration business started, they were the lead Ministry [Ministry of Interior] in immigration but then it has been swapped from the Ministry to the Ministry of Labour in 2009, it was swapped again to the Ministry of Interior. And, you may ask the Ministry [Ministry of Interior] itself. I mean what are the reasons behind, we have our guesstimations, but I am quite curious the concrete. But, this is one of the, maybe, the challenges we are now facing. The more we get into receive immigrants; we would need more direct positions coming from the ministry of health and social issues.

Prior to and during the year 2007, there was an ambiguity as to who was responsible for the social and educational infrastructure of immigrant workers within the labour market. This ambiguity transcended to various public social and health sectors in need of human resources. The national ministries' shift in responsibilities of the organisation of immigrant labour gives the impression to public servants that immigration to Finland was in its beginning stages and, therefore, neither the national ministries nor the City of Helsinki had a clear direction on how to proceed with governance. A space in the arena of producer-based care networks became available to other representatives interested in asserting themselves as the authority in the management of immigrant labour, in general, and immigrant health care labour, in particular.

At this time, other representatives concerned with the organisation and management of care labour in Helsinki and Finland derive from the institution, Valvira, the Finnish regulatory body of patient care and safety. The representative of Valvira clarify that their institutional purpose is not to recruit and place health care professionals in workplaces but rather supervise and advise on procedures and regulations to safeguard patients' safety and quality in health care (interview #8a):

> Well, to attract that is not really Valvira's main aim to attract professionals. Valvira's main aim, as I have just told you, is to be a safe guard for patients' safety and quality in health care. But, of course, we want to work together with those officials and many, many institutions that work with this aim to have enough workforce in Finland. Well, we have been to many meetings and conferences where this has been the topic and even our point of view and our part to this work, for example,

> explaining all these procedures and in taking into account that it is important to start this process early enough so that, so that really the persons that come here to work know that what kind of authorisation they can get and so on that they do not just be transported to Finland and then first start the process and after, perhaps half a year, see that it is not possible to get an authorization with this education. So, what we see as important for this recruitment for foreigners is that they very proactively take contact with us and look through that really the procedures is fair enough for those that are coming to Finland. So, that there are no misinterpretations and no false beliefs.

The representative of Valvira asserts that the institution, because of its purpose, does not directly contribute to the discussion of how and whom should recruit and place internationally educated nurses, and yet, the organisation is still concerned about the future labour shortages in the health care sector and the nurses from outside of Finland being informed of Valvira's qualification process. This means that Valvira is participating more in meetings about recruitment of non-European nurses, but also re-examining procedures of licensing and registering nurses in order to allow the nurses to integrate as paid professionals. These discussions transpire among different ministries, recruitment agencies, employers, and polytechnics/vocational training schools who are responsible to retrain and requalify the nurses and provide them with language courses. As such, Valvira can be considered a 'gatekeeper' for both domestic and foreign nurses applying for jobs in Finland, but also for the recruiters wanting to recruit and integrate labour into the nursing occupation in Finland. For instance, although in practice in the Philippines the diplomas nurses receive are for registered nurses (a four-year bachelor's degree of nursing science), Valvira considers the degree in Finland to not be equivalent for working as a registered nurse but as a licensed practical nurse (LPN, licensed vocational nurse, state-enrolled nurse in English, *lähihoitaja* in Finnish). According to Valvira, a person without LPN training can perform duties of an LPN if the person has related education, experience and professional skill. Practical nurses are qualified to work within elderly care, for instance. Also, Valvira's criteria for practicing as a health care professional differs among non-Finnish applicants as Valvira cannot request Finnish or Swedish qualifications from EU members but can from non-EU citizens. In Table 6.1 are the qualifications requested from EU members and non-EU members[5] (my bold font highlights the different criteria).

Valvira's criteria has material implications on where the nurses can work, their salaries, their career trajectories, if they need to attend professional training, if they are requested to complete tests on Finnish or Swedish language and their nursing qualifications, if they will be required to do apprenticeships as well as their day-to-day time schedules. In other words, although

Table 6.1 Valvira's licensing guidelines for EU nurses and non-EU nurses

European Union Nurses Required Work Permission Application Documents	*Non-European Union Nurses Required Work Permission Application Documents*
1. a copy of a valid passport or other registration document for verifying your nationality;	1. a copy of a valid passport or other registration document for verifying your nationality;
2. copies of your diploma and study records;	2. copies of your diploma and study records;
3. **a copy of a certificate issued by a competent authority that your qualification complies with EU regulations;**	3. **a copy of a certificate issued by a competent authority for a valid license to work as a nurse, if you have been granted such a license in another state. The certificate must be no older than three months;**
4. a copy of a certificate issued by a competent authority for a valid license to work as a nurse, if you have been granted such a license in another state. The certificate must be no older than three months;	4. copies of certificates of employment for the period following graduation, if necessary;
5. copies of certificates of employment for the period following graduation, if necessary; and	5. **a copy of the National Certificate of Language Proficiency in Finnish (minimum requirement: level 3–4) or a certificate for passing the Civil Service Language Proficiency Test minimum requirement: satisfactory level). Separate certificates for completing Finnish Language studies are not accepted;** and
6. a copy of a document certifying a change of name, if the name appearing on the enclosed documents is different from the one you are currently using.	6. a copy of a document certifying a change of name, if the name appearing on the enclosed documents is different to the one you are currently using.

Valvira claims no responsibility for the recruitment and placement of the nurses, the organisation's practices of setting the criteria to requalify trained professional nurses as well as attending to the Finnish language use is formative in the transnational management of nurses. Furthermore, through criteria and the reinforcement of laws to protect patient safety, Valvira claims authority in how the Filipino nurses' skills and education are constructed and in which position they can occupy in the local labour market.

Valvira, as an organisation, enters the arena of producer-based care networks in Helsinki within what I label the social world of regulation and advisory on national health and social welfare. The organisations' participation in producing human capital in the nursing occupation is not direct recruitment or placement for profit. And yet, the organisation and representatives negotiate with other representatives in the transnational management of internationally trained nurses as well as the systemic regulation of the nursing skills and language in Finland.

In another interview, the representative of the European Migration Network (EMN) also took the stance that the EMN, although under the umbrella of the Finnish ministry of Interior (Intermin) and physically located in Finnish Immigration Services (MIGRI), is representative and in accordance to EU directives and not involved in the recruitment and placement of migrants labour (interview #14):

> Actually, I am physically at the immigration services but I am doing an EU job. This European migration network (EMN) which is an EU wide organisation. Each EU member state has to have this type of contact point where we gather information regarding migration issues and citizenship issues. And, it is eighty percent EU funded, twenty percent government funded. And, in Finland, the contact point happens to be at MIGRI. So, that is why I am here.

The representative clarifies that the purpose of EMN is to produce two annual reports as well as hold seminars and events on this topic to disseminate information. The representative states (interview #14) that

> This is, at the moment, the top research organisation. So, we have two annual reports that we repeat every year. We call it the policy report which means migration and asylum policy, and the other, annual report is migration and protection statistics report. And, then we have two to three thematic reports every year. And, depending from the topic of the thematic reports, where we acquired information from varies, but as far as the two, the annual reports that we repeat-annual reports—of course the people that make the report, the ministries, and how the policies are implemented. And, then we get the information about how the policies are implemented, i.e. from this immigration department, border control, police. So that is always the first part of that report, the legislation and how it is implemented on a policy level, a national policy level. Because, this actually, this is like the main bulk and then you have local actors, the third sector, media, and then we look at the research section, which research has been done in regards to immigration policy used here in Finland. Because these research reports are to give as wide as possible view, societal view, as to how migration policy is in each member's state.

In 2007, the thematic report produced by EMN was entitled 'Conditions of entry and residence of third country highly skilled workers in the EU', and although Finland's national contact point at MIGRI was not yet officially established, the networking to disseminate EU 'thematic' issues on immigration was being implemented. According to the representative (interview #14),

> When the EMN was established as an EU wide entity with a council decision in May 2008, it was already in our so called constitution. It states that when we have this national contact points, you need to have a minimum of 3 persons full time work effort per year for the contact point. And, each national state has to establish a contact point to support its work. Going back to your question, where do you get your information from, and that is the purpose of EMN to get as wide as possible view of the whole society on any issue that it is looking at. So, we establish this national network so people, and it is for individual member and institutional members, who, through their work or their study interests have a special interest in finding out about immigration issues and sharing information, and also disseminating their own work.

EMN's purpose in the production and practice of disseminating information on and about EU derivatives, particularly on immigration, interweaves discourses within the EU on the management of immigrants in the EU members' nation-states. In 2007, the network was yet to be established in Finland, but the EMN's themes and focus of the network, before and during the time of the Filipino nurses being recruited and placed, parallels the context of Finland as a nation conducting its policy and practices in the context of being part of a regional entity: the European Union. The contact point may explicitly say that the EMN does not have direct involvement with the recruitment and placement of the nurses, but by the EMN disseminating and collecting information on particular themes contributes to the discourses of transnational management of immigrants and immigrant labour. This discursive entry point gives EMN space in the arena of producer-based care networks.

In terms of national governance in 2007, the Finnish national government (a representative democracy) was led by the Centre Party. Tarja Halonen was the then President, and Matti Vanhanen was the then Prime Minister. The governmental structure accords to the principles of parliamentarism, meaning that legislative power is vested in the Parliament of Finland, and executive power is exercised by the Cabinet, officially termed Council of State, which is led by the Prime Minister, the head of Government.

In 2006, the then government of Prime Minister Matti Vanhanen introduced, for the first time in Finland, an immigration programme that included the intention to promote employment-based immigration, but also define 'migration policy values, with the aim of respecting human and fundamental rights, to reinforce a culture of good governance and to combat migration-related threats' (Government Migration Policy Programme, 2006: 22). The programme also strives

> to form a comprehensive framework for migration policy planning and implementation, especially with regards to immigration into Finland

> from outside the EU and the EEA. Moreover, the programme aims to promote the development of a multi-value, multicultural and non-discriminating society and thus foster Finland's internationalisation process, improve international competitiveness and serve as means of responding to the challenges posed by an ageing workforce and population as a whole.
>
> (Government Migration Policy Programme, 2006: 22)

In 2007, an Action Plan for the 2006 government's migration policy programme was drafted by the Ministry of Interior (Intermin) to be implemented during period three (March 2008 to 1 December 2008). The action plan is a document providing more detail on the policy guidelines stated in the migration programme. It is also the first action plan for labour migration in Finland and is essential to the programme's implementation. The action plan states that Finland should engage in short-term and long-term policies to improve the 'attractiveness of Finland' (Government Migration Policy Programme, 2007) and promote recruitment from abroad that is led by employers and based on actual needs. The action plan further required the assessment of opportunities for arranging orientation training in the departure country, actions related to the recognition of skills gained outside of Finland; the promoting of opportunities for traineeship and employment for foreign students; the remigration of Ingrian Finns, and some research on needs of the local labour markets as well as the potential for legislative reforms (Ministry of Interior, 2009c; Asa and Muurinen, 2010).

The Finnish government's migration policy programme and the action plan to make Finland 'attractive' are foundational for the producer-based care networks to function in this situation. If political discourse is not conducive with the action of the corporate actors, the representatives' authority in claiming practices on the recruitment of foreign labour, in general, and foreign nurses, in particular, may lose legitimacy or be stalled or not be able to start. An arena established the space for actors to claim responsibility and authority in the recruitment and placement of foreign labour. Public, EU, and state organisations, discursively in talk and text, are present in the discussion of enforcing laws and policies in regards to the provision of care in Finland. And yet, the representatives and their associated organisations do not claim that their work involves the transnational management of nurses. Through the lack of authority being asserted by public representatives, the arena of producer-based care networks becomes available to non-public actors such as private businesses 'to make a case' (interview #9b) out of recruiting Filipino nurses for Finnish health care organisations. In other words, the production of knowledge on the transnational management of nurses is asserted from a social world claiming to know how to practice the management in Finnish health care.

The Finnish government does not have a particular place in the producer-based care network arena but interweaves through all the social worlds in terms of political discourse and structural mechanisms of policies and laws.

The discourse, at this time, is making Finland 'attractive' to immigrant workers from outside the EU and based on the employers' actual needs.

Preparing for Import: Making a Case Out of the Recruitment of Nurses From the Philippines

On 30 August 2007, the Finnish president, Tarja Halonen, met the Filipino ambassador to Sweden, Maria Zeneida Angara Collinson, in Helsinki, Finland. There was yet to be an embassy of the Philippines in Finland. This meeting was a year after the Philippines President Gloria Macapagal-Arroyo met the Finnish head of state. President Arroyo was the first Philippine top official to visit Finland, and President Halonen agreed to reciprocate the visit by going to the Philippines in 2009.[6]

After meeting with other governmental officials and representatives of the private sectors in Finland, the Ambassador secured an agreement from the Helsinki Region Chamber of Commerce to conduct promotional and business matching activities concerning the Philippine health industry. Following the visit from the ambassador, a Finnish company that produces elderly care and other care services announced its plans to recruit about 100 nurses from the Philippines in 2008 and 2009 in partnership with a private Finnish recruitment company, and a private Finnish adult education centre.[7,8]

After the collaboration, the private recruitment company partnered with a private company in Manila[9,10] as, according to the Philippines Overseas Employment Association (POEA) (2002), international recruitment companies cannot directly recruit unless in cooperation with a local representative. The Finnish recruitment company actively involved itself in the recruitment process in the Philippines as representatives were present for the first and second interview processes (selection stage) as well as being directly involved in providing services in language training and relocation of the selected employees (e.g. work contracts [two years], working visas, housing; interview #1a). At the time, the Finnish recruitment company had offices in Manila and Davao (interview #1a).

Through the collaboration on the transnational management of nurses from the Philippines, the three Finnish businesses interacted to establish authority in Finland as representatives in the recruitment and placement of Filipino nurses. Discursively, this authoritative assertion is discussed as a new business and leadership initiative in Finland. The organisations negotiate positions of authority publically in the media as well as meeting with state officials and through their own private financial investments. Each organisation's commitment to the recruitment of Filipino nurses requires them to invest money in the hope of financial gain. A representative of private Finnish adult education centre explains (interview #10a):

> it was brand new when we started with group. Anybody haven't did it before. And it was something all days that we teach them we had to

> learn something new. This is a company, we have to always sell and get profit but when we target this process we understood that we don't get nothing. We can only get some new learnings, and we can understand the whole system after this process. And we agreed that.

The recruitment became not about short-term financial gain, but a business case or pilot to legitimise the organisations' authority in the future recruitment of health care workers from abroad. The recruitment established authoritative practices in the arena of producer-based care networks in Finland through the assertion of professional expertise and financial investment.

As the three organisations emerged in the arena, the representatives of the organisations began to work more closely with public officials and national policy decision makers in order to assert expertise in the preparation of internationally skilled labour. These discussions were not only about the recruitment of one group but how to create a future infrastructure to manage a non-Finnish workforce for health care provisions. As one representative from the private Finnish recruitment company reflects on this period of time (interview #1b):

> But, we do work close with the ministries and Valvira, for that matter. Because Finland is not really prepared for this type of immigration. We need educational system, for example, because the ones [immigrant nurses] that have come to Finland, they are like one now and another then. So, it hasn't been in groups and it hasn't been organised, and the lead hasn't been there in the same way. So, that is something that will change. Laurea [polytechnique] is working on this, together with the rest of the polytechnique or university of applied sciences, I think they call themselves nowadays. So, that is something now that needs to be created. So, when a nurse comes to Finland, through us, for example, they can't really wait, you know, when a certain content is only given within a year or two, because from an employer's point of view, they have to get their license as soon as possible. So, it is impossible for them to wait. And, we do know what is needed, basically now. What sort of contents for example need to be trained. And, these people need training, they can't just, you know, present what they can do—there will be clinical tests, but they can't just appear there because the language also needs, you know, the professional language, in order to develop needs, one-to-one training or training in groups. Like we done now. But, in a bit different way, since this is a pilot.

By declaring that Finland is not ready for this 'type of immigration' and that it is important for the private, for-profit organisations such as the Finnish recruitment company to work with other representatives on the recruitment of labour from abroad illustrates the arena of who is responsible in the transnational management of care. The foundation of the recruitment is such that it is talked about as being in the beginning stages and the Finnish recruitment company has the expertise and knowledge on how it should be practiced. The Finnish recruitment company claims authority as the recruiters of the Filipino nurses for Finnish health care organisations by emphasising the need for recruitment and language-training models like their organisation has already created and implemented.

The initial networking of representatives in Helsinki and the meeting of the Philippines Ambassador to Sweden and the then Finnish President illustrates a catalyst of recruiting Filipino nurses through the trio of the for-profit Finnish organisations. Nonetheless, the Finnish recruitment company was researching other possible countries for the recruitment of nurses. These countries included China, India, and Thailand, but the recruitment company decided to choose the Philippines, and the representative highlights 'many things that speak for the Philippines' (interview #1b):

> So, we checked China, India, Thailand, and, I believe it was afterwards that we close the Philippines. We checked out Vietnam, and, yeah, there are many things that speak for the Philippines. They value education and the quality of nursing education is good. It was basically planned by the Americans, so it is no wonder that there are so many Filipino nurses in the United States. So the quality of the degree and of course the culturally bound politeness and, when we think of the elderly people here [in Finland], they [Filipinos] have a natural respect for the elderly which we could learn from actually. And, also, that they speak English and they have studied in English. Even though not everybody speaks as well as earlier because the schooling language can also be the local language in the primary schools and the secondary, I believe. But, the nursing schooling is in English. So, that makes it easier. We have, in a way, a common language then in Finland so we don't need interpreters which is, actually, you couldn't have as a doctor or a nurse within health care or even within elderly care as a practical nurse, you can't have an interpreter with you all the time. And, most Finns speak English somehow. At least. So, it is easier to communicate and make sure that the recruited one and the employer understand one another.

The response from another representative from the recruitment company coincides with the previous quote as to why the Philippines became the country to recruit from (interview #3):

> There are plenty of evidence to support that. The Philippines has placed a lot of value in the training and development of nurses. I mean there are a lot of nurses in the Philippines. So, they have more nurses than they can ever hope for to look after their own, if you like, national and domestic requirements. And, the Philippines is a country that relies

heavily on exporting their skills and talents, so they're big earners, probably the major earner for the Philippines. But, why do we do that from a nursing point of view? They get good training, they speak English, which is-which irrespective of coming here—I think the Philippines in general has a good international record. All of the nurses that come here have had previous international experience, so we know that they are not coming raw, they haven't been anywhere else.

These claims to their selection of the Philippines create implicit actors in their conversations. The Philippines and the other countries such as India and China are present in the conversation but are constructed in terms of country-specific, cultural representations such as cultural-bound politeness, respect for the elderly, positive international reputation of overseas workers, 'big earners', and US-Americanised. The Finnish recruitment company's claims to research ideal countries for recruitment also represent the Philippines to other Finnish representatives. The claims consist of the Philippines being ideal as the 'evidence supports' that the country has a good education in an American university system model, the nurses speak English, there is a surplus of trained nurses, and the national system of the Philippines is experienced and reliant on the exportation of human capital such as nurses. These claims naturalise the institutionalised control mechanisms in the Philippines to produce nurses for import by other countries.

In regards to implicated representations and issues of inclusions to the arena of transnational management of nurses, two interviewees, a Filipino nurse working and living in Finland (interview #2) and a representative from the union of registered nurses (TeHy) (interview #5), recollect the process of the first group of Filipino nurses being recruited in 2008 and their involvement in the talks prior to the recruitment. Both interviewees felt that they were left outside of the process, particularly with the first recruitment. This is telling of the authority in the recruitment of non-Finnish nurses as the actors were physically present in the discussions within the arena (e.g. the Filipino nurses) but were made silent.

In the interview with a Filipino nurse working in Finland, the nurse vocalises frustration at the Finnish recruitment company and the private elderly care company (interview #2):

INTERVIEWEE #2: But, in a way, I was also angry because we were approached by [the private elderly care company] if we could go to there, if we could come to their office, and they informed us that there were these eight Filipino nurses coming. Can we go have a meeting with them?

INTERVIEWER: With the nurses or [the private eldery care company]?

INTERVIEWEE #2: With [the private elderly care company]! So, we did! We did go, we did go. They asked me personally what they can do to make them [recruited nurses] a bit more . . . uummm . . . so they can settle down. What they could do more to keep these people here because they don't know anything about Filipinos. And I put down, I gave to them, actually, it was only this project manager who was there, let me see, [name]? I don't know what name now . . . I hope this is anonymous. I hope you don't name.

INTERVIEWER: Absolutely, I actually have a consent form for you to let you know that it is anonymized. Everything is going to be confidential.

INTERVIEWEE #2: Good. Yeah, because we didn't like what [the private elderly care company] did, to be honest.

INTERVIEWEE #2: What I did tell them that is Filipinos are this, this, and this. Filipinos would like to have this, this, and this. But, all of those were trashed.

INTERVIEWER: They didn't even consider it.

INTERVIEWEE #2: They didn't. Not at all! And, the last statement that was really insulting, but I didn't dare say it to the Filipino nurses who are now presently working. I did tell to [an employee at the private elderly care company] that sooner or later after the contract is finished and you still don't support these Filipino nurses, they will leave. They will go somewhere else. And, you know what [an employee at the private elderly care company] said? We don't care. It is alright.

INTERVIEWER: It is really interesting because they are making so much investment. . . .

INTERVIEWEE #2: Exactly!

INTERVIEWER: In language training, especially this recruitment agency, who is recruiting actively for these organisations in Helsinki.

INTERVIEWEE #2: Exactly. We were 3 people there [names the two others]. So, umm, it was really sad that [the private eldery care company] asked us to help them, and then we told them, especially when it came out of my mouth. I was thinking 'fine' if this is what they are thinking, we can't affect the situation. They are private entrepreneurs and when I heard that HUS [The hospital district of Helsinki and Uusimaa] started copying the pilot, I was hoping that it would be totally different in a way that these Filipino nurses would be treated equal. Well, yes, salary wise they are being paid, according, minimum wage or ummm according to collective bargain agreement. But, what we were wanting is that, we were wishing that these Filipino nurses could also take their families here, build their own lives here, have a mortgage . . . umm . . . ummm . . . get an education, develop their profession, and not just, you know, stay where they are. . . . Because what I noticed is every time we have a meeting [referring to a support network of Filipino nurses in Finland], they tell everything: their frustrations, their anger, their . . . umm . . . what they don't know . . . why things happen this way . . . and, so, what I did is I set a goal that we would have a peer support and each one would think and write down their problem, and then we pick one problem and then we discuss. And, if possible, we could ask a lawyer, for example.

Although the nurse from the Philippines is physically present in the arena, the discourses of the nurses in the arena are disregarded. The nurse vocalises various issues in terms of how the recruitment and placement should be practiced but the Finnish elderly care company dominates the authoritative space by disregarding her claims on the treatment of the recruited nurses. The nurse is frustrated and enraged at the lack of care in retaining the recruited nurses in terms of changing recruitment practices and structural mediating mechanisms of family reunification, career development, and equal treatment.

The nurse also notes that the Helsinki public hospital (HUS) is copying the pilot of the private elderly care company in the transnational management of nurses from the Philippines. The power of this site of knowledge production of the recruitment practices influences other Finnish organisations, reflecting the identification of these organisations with each other and the values the members uphold.[11]

The power of these discourses influences the construction of practices, which have material implications in how the nurses are subsequently managed in the Finnish health care system.

In terms of unions and as representatives in transnational management of nurses, the representative of TeHy (The Union of Health and Social Care Professionals in Finland) states that the unions are involved in the monitoring of recruitment of nurses from abroad, but also that the Finnish recruitment company, before recruitment, contacted TeHy about unionising the nurses (interview #5):

> [The private recruitment company] has worked also then with us, like the centre organisation in so that they inform us of what is going on, and we have a continuous discussion, we just met in December, so we have a discussion all the time how is the processes going and what are the problems and so on because they want to keep us informed.

The interviewee also states that the private recruitment company has invested a lot of capital in the recruitment from abroad rather than focusing on local structural reforms within the nursing occupation. The representative later states that by recruiting registered nurses to be deskilled in the recruitment process to become practical nurses, the Filipino nurses will leave Finland to look for better career opportunities. The representative adds that the recruitment in English as well as training the Filipino nurses in Finnish or Swedish to work in Finland creates barriers to equal opportunities for the nurses to move up the career later. It also takes away from viewing the nursing occupation locally as gendered and constructs a hierarchy of place within the transnational in terms of occupation and social status (interview #5):

INTERVIEWEE #5: Yes, that is what we have asked also because we see it as a threat that, you know, [the private recruitment company] has spent so much money, it has been so expensive because they have been pioneers and, of course, then they need to put more effort and more money. Are the Filipino nurses, are they really going to stay here? That is a threat because then, but what can you do because, you know, you can't tell them to stay here. It is a free world, you can go if you want to. And, so that, that is a little bit worrying that of course if they want to spend the money, and have a worker for two years, that is fine. But, for example, our thinking is that all that money that [the private recruitment company] has spent on this process and HUS [hospital district of Helsinki and Ussimaa] has spent on this process, they could have used the money to give a little raise for the nurses to pay a little bit better and they won't have the problem. And, you know, it is not only the money issue like the wage but, we have bad leadership here in Finland. We have very like unflexible working hour system or that people can't really affect themselves when they . . . it is very unflexible these systems, we have . . . it is very hierarchy. How do you say that?

INTERVIEWER: Hierarchical?

INTERVIEWEE #5: Yeah, that is very strong, in Finnish health care. Doctors are here and nurses are there and you are there. So it is. . . . There are a lot of difficulties that we have and we tell them that if something has changed in the hospitals and in there at the workplaces because it is the foreign nurses, they are going to face the same problems that the Finnish nurses are facing which is the reasons that they do not want to work in the health care system. They want to go somewhere else. So, how can we guarantee that these foreign nurses they, they don't do the same thing, they go and work somewhere else in some other field, not in the health care system. So, something should change in the health care system, and at workplaces, and we always say that, we now talk a lot about this lack of workforce in the health care business. But, we shouldn't talk about that, we should talk about how to have good workplaces. So that people enjoy working, they get enough pay and there is good leadership and all that. And, if all that is in order then we would have enough workers. Because our statistics show that there are 35,000 nurses and practical nurses who work outside of health care. So, they work wherever at shops or there at home because they get better pay and they are tired of this shift work and everything so there are 35,000 people. Of course, many are those that don't like working in the health care, and they would never, ever come back. But, you know, there are many people who would like that things would change at the workplace. So, we think that that is a waste of resources, you know, we train people and they become nurses, practical nurses, then they work one, two, three years, then they find out that, you know, I just can't work here. I will go and work somewhere else. And, that is a waste of resources because then it doesn't help that we, we increase the input in the schools, and we train more nurses and practical nurses if they then stay at the health care that is a waste of resources. So, something should change at the workplace that is a problem. We discuss too much about this lack of workforce that we need to have more, more people instead we should deal with the people, and deal with the workplaces. What are the problems there, why don't people stay there?

INTERVIEWER: I was finding that in my research too, it is like you replace the workforce that you already have without dealing with the internal problems, and you replace it with a workforce that is lower on the hierarchal scale, in the sense, that they are coming from poorer countries that they are willing to do any job that you request them to do and that they are willing to integrate the way that they see the employer wants them to. So, these jobs, instead of changing the nature of them, it is reinforcing them and actually making them worse.

INTERVIEWEE #5: Yeah, and what we are worried about is that, you know, this plan that because like in the Philippines they don't have practical nurses, they don't train practical nurses so we are very worried that we have as system now that we recruit nurses, they train here to become practical nurses, and they stay and work as practical nurses and that is not ethical because they wanted to do that job that they are trained to do. And, they are trained to be nurses, so in Finland, we lack kind of that path so that that way you are now a practical nurse, you learn Finnish, and then what. How you, what is the path for you, this personal career path that how you can become a nurse in Finland. And, that is what we are worried about that we should have this a lot of these migrant nurses who work here as a practical nurse and then they stay there. And, that is not what we would want to happen.

This passage reveals three central aspects of the nursing occupation in Finland. First, there exists a hierarchy in the medical profession where nurses are subordinate to doctors. Second, there is a lack of leadership in the management of the nursing professionals. Third, nursing is devalued in terms of pay, shift work, and other tangible working conditions resulting in Finnish nurses leaving their positions.[12]

In many countries, including the Nordic welfare states, a common trend in the health care sector is to adopt a business agenda by commodifying services and human resources through measurements and calculations of costs. Subsequently, the managerial strategy of the health care profession becomes about saving costs rather than investing in the workforce.

These discourses and practices of managing nurses in Finland does not disappear when businesses offer a solution for the nurse shortage by recruiting a workforce to comply with the demands of cost savings and flexibility. It does the opposite. The managerial practices continue to reinforce gender and racialised representations of the nurses as malleable and disposable (Davies, 1995) while creating a carousal of nurses leaving the occupation or migrating to another country for better career prospects (Kingma, 2006).

The nurses coming from abroad face the threat of being deskilled because of Finnish regulations of education, skills, and language use. While interviewing a representative of SuPer (Finnish union for practical nurses), the representative echoes this same point that the union is advocating against the deskilling of nurses from abroad (interview #6):

> We think it would be ethical if a nurse would be employed as a nurse and a doctor would be employed as a doctor. Not a cleaner. That is our aim. That is also our common aim with the PSI [Public Service International] which is—we have, it is not a union, but a collaboration with 9 public sector trade unions [global federation]. We have made our own ethical rules that we want to encourage. So, this is one of the main points that we have been discussing with the recruitment agencies that if they bring someone/somebody, we want it to be ethical. And, it means that a nurse should be working here as a nurse. And, what has happened is that they don't always do it like that but they do something else. . . . Some recruitment agencies but I know that the union for the recruitment agencies, they have very strict and very good ethical guidelines that every recruitment agency, if they are members. They don't have members who don't—I don't know, it is difficult to explain in English—but some recruitment agencies, they don't care. If a Filipino says that it is ok for me to work as a cleaner that is ok. So, they say that the person that is immigrating, they choose but—they can choose whatever but we don't think it is similar. We want it if you move people from another part of the—you should take care that can do the things that they have studied or learned.

Turning back to the social world maps and sites of knowledge production on transnational management of nurses, the unions represent the social world of advocacy and advisory in a country where unions have a strong influence on the regulation of the labour market. This gives the unions such as TeHy and SuPer the authority to claim space in the arena of producer-based care networks. For both legal and pragmatic reasons, the recruitment company works closely with the unions but also disseminates information to the nurses who are being recruited about how to become a union member. Although in practice the private recruitment company complies with union and labour regulations on ethical recruitment, the workplaces for nurses in Finland are structurally hierarchical in terms of gender, race, and occupation. The recruitment company's assertion in replacing a workforce already experiencing high turnover due to unfavourable working conditions such as wages and working hours does not change the workforce but rather reinforces it by deskilling the nurses through transnational recruitment practices that do not recognise the nurses' education and skills. The recruitment company produces nurses for the current Finnish health care labour market in which the clients request educated, malleable, and less paid professionals.

In 2007, actors in the producer-based care networks began to emerge, remain, or stay silent in the talk of the interviews with representatives in Helsinki. The uncertainty expressed by the public actors in the recruitment of the Filipino nurses, and foreign-skilled health care professionals in general, leaves a space in which private businesses such as the recruiting companies can stake claims in the dialogue as to which nationality of nurses should be recruited and how they should be managed. Although the Finnish recruitment company's representatives note in the previous excerpts that the Philippines was chosen because of what the representative term as 'evidence', Finnish institutionalised practices illustrate how certain policies favour particular immigrants (e.g. EU) and enforce standardisations of language and skills that place the recruited Filipino nurses in a position of deskilling and segmentation. Also, by placing representatives outside the producer-based care networks, such as the Filipino nurses working in Finland and the Philippines as a nation-state, creates a discursive sphere that materialises into restructuring the local care labour market to favour the corporate practices of the recruiters and private clients.

Figure 6.1 is the social world map for the year 2007. In the centre is the producer-based care network, which is considered the arena in which

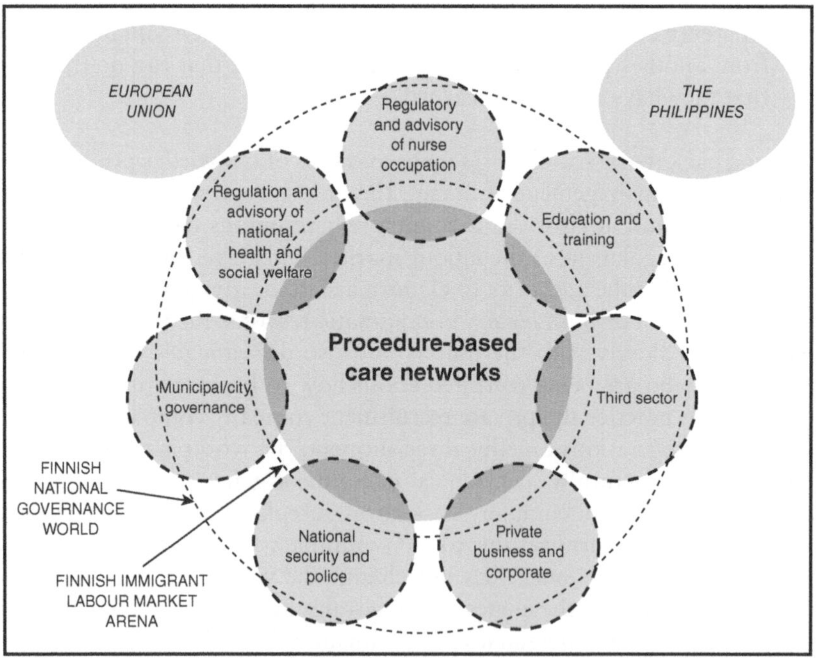

Figure 6.1 Social world map of year 2007

authority is asserted through discourses of representatives within their social worlds on the transnational management practices of nurses.

Outside the producer-based care networks are the social worlds of the Philippines as well as the European Union. As illustrated previously, the entities or social worlds are referred to on various occasions by the representatives in both the talk (interviews) and the text (documents). The presence of these social worlds is acknowledged and is socially constructed by the representatives.

Each social world, in which I socially construct for the purpose of analysing the data, are described later. Again, the social worlds are constructed based on Clarke's suggested questions (Chapter 5, Tables 5.1 and 5.2) and derive particularly from the represented commitments and work of the social worlds. In each category, you will note that I associate interviews with the representatives of each social world. The aims of these methodology practices are two-fold: (1) to situate the voices of the representatives in the discourses of their social worlds based on their own professional work, and (2) to describe sites of knowledge production of practices through the interactions and relations of Finnish organisations. The cartographic illustration, shown later, reveals representatives and their social worlds interacting within the arena of producer-based care networks.

The social worlds and representatives are described in no special order here.

Advocacy and advisory of nurse occupation: this social world has organisations and representatives with the mandate to advocate for the labour rights of nurses, either practical or registered and both domestic and transnational. The purpose of this world is also to influence labour and education policies. This social world emerges from the data through the representatives of nurse unions (interview #5; interview #6).

Education and training: this social world has the purpose to provide services in education and training in Finland. This social world consists of representatives from the private adult education centre (interviews #10a and #10b), who are involved in the requalification of internationally educated nurses in the Finnish language.

Third Sector: this social world received its title as it encompasses the Red Cross; it can also be termed 'voluntary sector' as the Red Cross works in collaboration with local authorities but is nonprofit. In 2007, the Finnish elderly care company in this situation was mostly owned by Red Cross. The representatives in this world are from the private elderly care company (interview #17). Nonetheless, as noted in the social world maps, this company became privately owned after 2008.

Private business and corporate: this social world encompasses organisations and representatives whose purpose or mandate is to produce profit and is privately owned. The work in this social world receives no funding from the nation-state or European Union. The representatives in this world are the private recruitment company (interviews #1a and #1b; interview #3).

National security and police: this social world has the mandate to control and regulate national borders, security, and immigration in Finland. The organisations and their representatives are Finnish Ministry of Interior (Intermin), immigration services (MIGRI), and European Migration Network (EMN) (interview #12; interview #14; interview #7)

Municipal/city governance: in this social world, the mandate is to provide, govern, and regulate social and health services in the city of Helsinki. The organisation and representatives in this social world are the City of Helsinki (interviews #9a and #9b)

Regulation and advisory of national health and social welfare: the mandate of this social world is to supervise and provide guidance to health care and social services providers with the nation-state of Finland. Valvira's representatives and the organisation are in this social world (interviews #8a and 8b).

European Union and the Philippines: both the European Union and the Philippines (as well as the nurses in the Philippines) are mentioned at various times in the interviews with the representatives and in the documents collected. Displayed in the map, these social worlds are placed outside the producer-based care networks. The worlds are considered implicated as they are discursively present.

In 2007, the social worlds and representatives are emerging into the arena of producer-based care networks in Helsinki. Simultaneously, as illustrated in the first of the social world maps (Figure 6.1), the elected government and its associated policies, laws, and practices permeate the rest of the social worlds functioning in Finland. For instance, former PM Matti Vanhanen's 2006 and 2007 Government Migration Policy Programme, as well as the subsequent action plans, influences the commitment and mandates of the social worlds interacting in Finland. The action plan set forth to make Finland 'more attractive' to immigrant workers from outside the EU and encourage policy and practices that suit the labour needs of Finnish employers.

To situate social worlds in the producer-based care network means to situate knowledge production of transnational management practices of the nurses. The social worlds identify the public and private actors that produce, recruit, relocate, and settle labour abroad for the Finnish health care organisations. In other words, the actors that link managerial practices within the Global Nurse Care Chain (Yeates, 2009). The maps also situate representatives in 'universes' of discourses that construct the nursing occupation in Finland according to their work commitments but also reflect a transnational representational history of the nurses as gendered, racialized, and unequal. These discourses serve to reinforce taken-for-granted notions of how nurses are managed, both locally and globally, as commodified resources to be managed and not nurses as people to be developed and engaged in the work they are trained and experienced to do.

Pioneering the Supply Practice of Transnational Nursing Labour

In January 2008, the Finnish Ministry of Employment and the Economy (TEM) was established. This new ministry brought together the Finnish Ministry of Trade and Industry, the Finnish Ministry of labour, and the Department for Development of Regions and Public Administration, formerly under the Ministry of Interior (Intermin). According to the then Government Programme of Prime Minister (19 April 2007), Matti Vahanen, the new Ministry would

> assume responsibility for the duties of the existing Ministry of Trade and Industry, the tasks of the Ministry of Labour, excluding migration and integration matters, and the functions of the Department for Development of Regions and Public Administration of the Ministry of the Interior, excluding the Regional and Local Administration Unit.[13]

In 2008, TEM was responsible for the operating environment of Finnish entrepreneurship and innovation, the effectiveness of the labour markets, the employability of employees, and the regional development in the global economy.

To execute these responsibilities, TEM compiles employment services' statistics from the regional Employment and Economic Development Offices (TE) such as job seekers using the services, those unemployed, registered open positions by employers, and labour policy actions to promote the employment of job seekers. TE offices fall under ELY (the Centre for Economic Development, Transport, and Environment) who provides funding and approves different projects according to the municipality or region that the centre is responsible for.[14] Under this legislation, nonetheless, means that TEM, in 2008, is responsible solely for the domestic labour and economy and not the integration of immigrants into the labour market unless the immigrant worker has an 'A' status. An immigrant can only obtain an 'A' status if the immigrant, first, has a working or permanent residence permit, second, is living in Finland, and, third, is registered as a job seeker either as a requirement for social benefits or actively seeking a job. In other words, because of TEM's mandate and practices, the social world of Finnish domestic labour and economy falls outside of the arena of producer-based care networks. This separation creates a divide between labour of Finnish citizens and working residence with migrant background and non-Finnish residences or those recruited and working (therefore, not an active job seeker).

In April 2008, the first recruited group of Filipino nurses arrived in Helsinki. The Finnish recruitment company selected eight practical nurses, four men and four women, from the Philippines to work for their collaborative partners' elderly care services. This recruitment began in the Philippines in 2007 with the trio of the Finnish private companies (interviews #1a and #1b). According to the representative from the private recruitment company, the Philippines is an exporting country of human capital and because of the structured production of supply, demanding care for another country does not affect the health care system in Philippines (interview #1a).

> They [the Philippines] always had the excess production for purpose to send abroad . . . we [the recruitment company] do not worsen the health care system in the Philippines.

Before the initial group arrived, the recruitment company had offices in Manila and Davao. Through these offices, recruitment and language training took place. The recruitment process involved the receiving of applications, interviews, and selection by the Finnish recruitment company. The nurses recruited were highly skilled registered nurses (a bachelor's degree of four years) with various years of work experience. Most of the nurses were older and also had lived and worked abroad (interview #1b). In an interview, the representative of the recruitment company reflects back that it was not a good idea to recruit overly qualified and experienced registered nurses for practical nurse jobs in Finland (interview #1b). The representative believes, however, if initially the recruited nurse complains about being overly qualified, the nurse will later comply with the new position and its limitation because of the Finnish language use.

INTERVIEWEE #1b: so, we didn't want to have long working experience. We didn't expect them to have worked, for example, in OR [surgical hospital ward] like we did with HUS. So, the criteria are really different.

INTERVIEWER: So, for the first eight that were hired for [private elderly care company], they were quite qualified—-

INTERVIEWEE #1b: they were older, men/women and basically, the best we had then [in 2008]. And, we were also as we are still looking for, you know, the ideal person who will make it here. What qualifications do they need for.

INTERVIEWER: Making the transition? And, why was that problematic that they ranged in different skills, that they were overqualified in some aspects?

INTERVIEWEE #1b: Like in Finland, you are overqualified for a job, you probably don't settle for less, in a way.

INTERVIEWER: Ok, and you found that out because the nurses complained or because they left or?

INTERVIEWEE #1b: They experienced or some of them experienced that well . . . ummm . . . this is something I know I can't, I work as a registered nurse. But, then of course, as soon as they, in practice, they realize—I remember an occasion where a nurse went to a doctor with a client and found it extremely difficult. And, after that, he said 'well, now I see why I can't work as a registered nurse yet'.

At the beginning of the recruitment, the eight Filipino nurses selected by the Finnish recruitment company were deemed as overqualified and not the ideal candidates (persons) to work in Finnish health care. Although the recruitment representative legitimises the deskilling of the nurses through an anecdote of a recruited nurse finding it difficult to practice nursing within the professional dynamics in Finnish health care, the previous excerpt reveals the organisational hierarchy of professional status and working relations between Finnish doctors and nurses.

The initial recruitment entailed training the nurses in the Philippines before arriving for work in Finland. This training consisted of working conditions, basic rules of employment, the workplace, culture, and the basic Finnish language and were completed in collaboration between the Finnish recruitment company and the Finnish adult education centre in the Philippines. The Finnish adult education centre continued their training efforts when the Filipino nurses arrived in Finland. Their main objective was to further train the nurses in the Finnish language but also provide vocational training for six months in which the nurses would have their knowledge and skills assessed and tested to become equivalent to Finnish standards for practical nursing (interview #1b). When asked about this training period, the Finnish recruitment representative indicates that the training was done in a mixture of Finnish and English language:

> Oh yes [the training was in English], and also during the schooling period here. Which, for practical nurses, is approximately six months. And, this takes place in Finnish. They use some English, especially at the beginning but the idea behind all this is that they are trained to work in Finnish because all, let me see what do they say, patient charting, everything is done in Finnish in Finland. And, it is, there is a law that dictates—

When the first group of eight recruited nurses arrived in Finland, they were placed immediately in the employment of the Finnish elderly care company as trainees. The training period lasted six months and was in joint effort with language and vocational training with Finnish adult education centre. With the joint effort of all three organisations, a steering and project group was created to coordinate the actions of the recruitment and placement (interview #1b). The organisation wanted to be innovative and pioneers in managing the labour shortage in health care in Finland. At the time, the CEO of the Finnish elderly care company noted on the company's website that the company 'wants to become the Nokia of the caring field' (translation from Finnish).[15] In addition, it also appears that the companies did not want to restructure the practices and system within the Finnish health care. As discussed by the representative of the Finnish elderly care company, the ideal candidate would be a nurse willing to work as a practical nurse and continue to be satisfied with the hired position.

After the initial recruitment and placement among the three organisations, a forum was organised for those interested in multiculturalism and health care in the Helsinki region (this was not for the three joint organisations in particular but for all those interested in the topic). The conference was entitled 'the First Nordic leadership forum: multicultural management in health care'. It was considered the first leadership forum on a subscribed theme, which, at this forum, was health care and multiculturalism. Future forums would be on other chosen themes by the organisers, the Nordic Institute for Advance Training in Occupational Health (NIVA). According to the forum's objectives, the conference was to

> Provide insight into multicultural leadership through illustrations on specific strategies from multicultural workplaces. The idea is to not only discuss challenges related to work organization and management of multicultural working environments, but also to highlight the potential that multicultural workforce provides. The health care sector was chosen because it is one of the sectors that are at first instance most affected of these changes in all Nordic countries.[16]

The target audience was

> senior executives and government officials as well as managers and professionals working in the field of health care or alternatively, in any other field where obtaining, integrating and keeping multicultural workforce is an issue. Managers and professionals from other than health care fields dealing with similar problematic areas are therefore also encouraged to participate in the Forum. The language of the leadership forum will be English.[17]

Although this forum was not solely meant for the trio of Finnish companies recruiting nurses from the Philippines, the forum acted as a debut for these organisations as leaders in multicultural workplaces and human resource management of health care workers in Helsinki. The trio of companies had representatives at the forum as speakers. Within each of their presentations, it appears that the representatives of the organisations structured their power point slides in accordance to the forum's objective: to share insight and illustrations of 'multiculturalism in health care' and leadership. Each power point presentation begins with what the organisation is and does (e.g.

services, work, purpose, mission) and illustrations or cases in which the representatives construct their organisation as engaging with a more non-Finnish, more 'foreign' labour force. In particular, the representatives' examples for engaging in the dialogue on multicultural workplaces and leadership centralise on the organisation's involvement in the recruitment and placement of Filipino nurses. They argue that there is a domestic labour shortage in Finland for the elderly health care sector, and the organisations they represent have strategies to resolve this problem. According to the representatives, they have addressed this problem successfully with their transnational management practices and models in their pilot study of nurse recruitment from the Philippines.

Making Finland Attractive to Recruit Immigrant Professional Workers: Public Representatives Asserting More Dominance

At the end of 2008, the City of Helsinki began the Polku ('path' in English) project that was led by SEURE Henkilöstopalvelut Oy, a recruitment and placement agency owned and operated by and for the city.[18] The Polku project offered counselling to employers regarding the recruitment processes for foreigners in the cities of Helsinki, Espoo, and Vantaa and assisted in the practical resettlement of foreign workers who are recruited by those cities. According to a representative from the city of Helsinki, the Polku project began with the objective to facilitate recruitment and placement from abroad when it started in 2007 (interview #9b). Nonetheless, when the economic recession hit in 2008, the project refocused its aims to advise in the hiring of immigrants already in the country. A representative from the City of Helsinki states (interview #9b) that

> the situation changed dramatically and what was supposed to be the project where we would get a lot of international staff coming in, and the 'Polku people' would basically provide a first advisory point for those people. Basically, resettlement services. It turned out that there was only a trickle of people coming to work from abroad, and much more need from current employers to advise them on employing immigrants already in the country. So the projects profile changed, and it was advising immigrants within the country on their varying needs working for the city of Helsinki as well as Vantaa. And, it was also advising the employing supervisors in the bureaucracy issues connected to employment of immigrants . . . Polku has also started in the capital area in discussion about recruitment and retainment practices so that there will be more similar to each other in different cities. They have organised a series of forums where these issues were discussed. And, if by now the project is finished, it was finished in 2010, there

> is still something called Polku network. It is basically meeting of HR personal who are interested in discussing these issues that are connected to that.

From 2008 to 2010, the National Institute of Health and Welfare (THL) conducted a research project entitled 'Attractive Finland'.[19] The purpose behind the project was to provide informed direction on the ways for recruiting foreign nurses in the European labour market. The project was in collaboration with the City of Helsinki (human resource centre) and the Helsinki Uusimaa Hospital District (HUS). The project was funded by the European Social Fund (ESF).

There were five aims to Attractive Finland. First, to forecast the health care workforce needs; second, to map nursing resources by understanding further nurse training and qualification as well as their international mobility, particularly in respects to the EU directive on the Recognition of Professional Qualifications (2005/36/EC); third, to establish networks and relations for successful cooperation in the acquisitions of employees; fourth, to consider ethical recruitment and draft alternative operating models based on bilateral cooperation; and, lastly, to compose a model of international recruiting with several alternatives.

In regards to the first aim, forecasting, Attractive Finland organised two workshops and conducted four study tours (Sweden, Hungary, and Poland twice) to understand the development of human resources in health care, both presently and in the future. The second aim was carried out through four country studies on the nursing workforce, its training and international mobility in the EU. One study was made on Estonia and Hungary, and two were made on Poland. The third aim was implemented by the project actively networking with other European Social Fund (ESF) work that was addressing labour immigration. For instance, Attractive Finland contributed to the project, INSITE.[20]

Lastly, the fourth and fifth aims were met by proposing cooperation with Poland to recruit nurses. This would not be the sole solution for the nursing shortage in Finland but the project strongly recommended actively recruiting from abroad.

Other proposals and suggestions of the project was to make Finland an attractive country for nurse mobility by considering salaries (as the project suggested that salaries in Finland and other EU countries are narrowing so this advantage will not last long), a national strategy to attain and retain foreign nurses in Finland and to dispel prejudices concerning the Finnish language.

The project also ended with suggestions that the 'best way' to operate in the international labour market of health care professionals was to use the services of a recruitment agency. Nonetheless, the actors that contracted the recruitment agency should also participate in the key phases of recruitment.

Furthermore, it was implied that diversity management, good guidance at work, and non-discrimination are important ways of attracting good professionals.

Figure 6.2 is the social world map for year 2008. The social worlds emerge as their practices and commitments change with the collaboration to recruit from abroad.

The social worlds shift in the year 2008. The social worlds of 'education and training', 'third sector', 'private business and corporate', and 'national security and police' move closer together and overlap as new collaborations are formed surrounding the practice of transnational management of nurses. These social worlds and their representatives socially construct authority in the producer-based care networks by producing discourses in talk and text about the recruitment and placement practices of foreign labour. The Finnish national government is still permeating all these social worlds and the municipal and governmental social worlds are still present as the worlds continue to negotiate their positions in the arena of producers through projects such as Polku and Attractive Finland. The 'domestic and labour economy', in which TEM emerges, is outside the producer-based care networks as the mandate is not the integration and organisation of immigrant labour. The mandate solely focuses on domestic workers and the domestic economy. All practices are within the national borders of Finland.

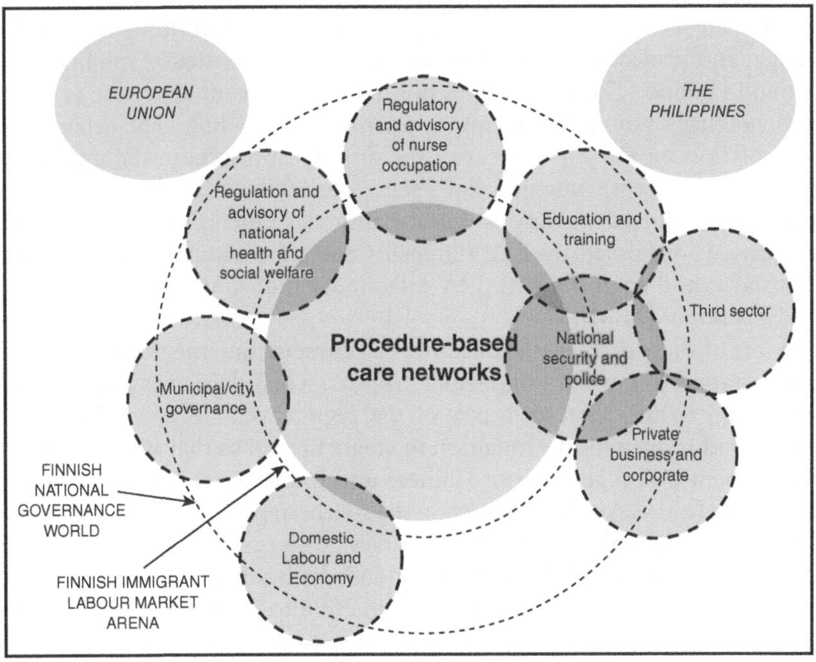

Figure 6.2 Social world map of years 2008–2009

The Legitimisation of Nurse Imports During Economic Recession

At the beginning of 2009, under the Ministry of Interior's direction, two projects were initiated and implemented: ALPO and MATTO. Both projects were funded by the European Social Fund (ESF) and had a projected end date of 2013 (interview #7). The objectives behind the projects were to serve as support structures in developing work-related immigration and integration projects. This support structure would be used to facilitate disseminating information on integration and work-related practices and processes of a foreign workforce. They would also be used to build social networking and a foundation to understanding possible practices for the recruitment and integration of immigrants.[21]

ALPO project focuses specifically on integration. This project was launched by the Ministry of Interior and is used to develop a national model for initial guidance and orientation services such as electronic services for language learning and testing of linguistic skills; initial integration information provided in the most common immigrant languages; nation-wide guidance and orientation services; uniform testing and skills mapping methods; and electronic services in the most common immigrant language.[22]

The MATTO project, on the other hand, is used as a facilitator in different projects around Finland that focus on processes and functions that are associated with labour migration. These processes and functions are recruitment such as selection, training and placement, integration, Finnish language, and projection of what labour is needed in particular municipalities around Finland. The project does not implement or influence the processes and practices but rather serves as an information hub that accumulates information on the experiences of the different projects in the municipalities related to work immigration issues.[23] In 2009 to 2011, there were 30 projects conducted in various municipalities in Finland and most of these projects were funded by ELY (Finnish Centre for economic development, transport, and environment). ELY falls under the Ministry of Employment and Economy (TEM).

Some of these projects included the recruitment and integration of nurses. For instance, in northern municipal projects, when there was a nurse shortage before 2009, representatives of the region went to countries such as China and India with the intention to create networks that would allow the recruitment and placement of Chinese and Indian nurses both at the time and in the future. Another project, in the southern province, Uusimaa, examined what potential countries could nurses be recruited from (interview #7). The project, entitled INSITE, later produced a book on this project as well as various other projects that lasted from 2008 to 2010. This book, entitled 'Avoin Suomi—kuka vastaa? Työperusteisesta maahanmuutosta' (in English 'Open Finland-who is responsible? Employment-based immigration'),[24] describes employment-based immigration issues from different perspectives and concludes with practical solutions for the international recruitment of labour in different stages. Specifically, the book discusses the necessity of labour migration as part of the solution for an ageing Finnish work population, and how Finland can attract, recruit, and receive foreign labour. The book presents examples of projects dealing with labour recruitment of immigrants and discusses possible support structures, networks, and forecasting future labour trends. The book was co-financed by European Social Fund (ESF) and ELY.

The main idea behind MATTO, according to the representative, was not to start from zero each time a municipality needed to recruit health care workers. At the beginning of the MATTO project, actors involved and invested in recruiting nurses were unsure as to how and whom to contact or network with. Coinciding with the project sat a steering committee of various Finnish ministries including the Ministry of Education and Culture, the Ministry of Social Affairs and Health, and the Ministry of Foreign Affairs. Other representatives were derived from Immigration Services, Centre of International Mobility, and Valvira. The Ministry of Employment and Economy (TEM) was also involved in the initial stages of the project but was responsible for the funding not the implementation of the project.

According to the representative of MATTO, MATTO aims to capture employers of immigrant labour and their practices to create a report on whom the actors and practices are (interview #7):

> We started in 2009 and these first two years, we basically—these projects have been active now, these thirty projects of the regions, they have been active now and they are like all the time being [sic] doing their job and now there is more or less like it is time where we can start to make some sort of like, how would I say, like sum up what has been done so far and we can draft it and think what would they look like and what would be included in these guidelines, for example. Finland is full of websites for employers and migrant employees and for employers who plan to recruit from abroad, but I don't think we need another webpage or another guidebook. I think we need to more like think how to make these current ones visible for all the participants who need guidance in this issue.

Although the Finnish trio of companies were not part of the steering committee or providing direct information to the MATTO project, as they were recruiting from outside the European union (EU) and the ESF funding is linked to the EU, the representative of MATTO indicates that MATTO is still very interested and aware of the recruitment of the Filipino nurses by the private organisations. The representative states (interview #7),

> [The recruitment company] has done good work. It is excellent, I must say . . . and we are very interested to hear about their achievements, and

I think [the recruitment company] even invited us to go to the Philippines to study their system there, but so far it has not been realised.

The representative of MATTO also indicates that the relationship with private organisations is important to the recruitment and placement by municipalities because of training in Finnish language. The representative states that even if the municipalities recruit, they may not have the resources to provide language training, and this can be contracted out to private actors (interview #7).

> [A]nd we are very interested to hear about their achievements and I think [the recruitment company] even invited us to go to the Philippines to study their system there, but so far it hasn't been realised. But, these projects [case projects by municipalities in MATTO] are, of course, dealing a lot with private companies because if you think about this . . . if a project goes to Bulgaria and recruits the certain nurses to Finland, they must establish basically like give them language training, give them some training about Finnish working life there. So, these are many often done in cooperation with private companies. It is like, I don't know, like procuring? [outsourcing] Like from these private companies, these services that projects are needed.

In 2009, MATTO and ALPO was being implemented during a time of economic recession, a recession that was discussed in most of the interviews conducted in this research. According to the MATTO representative, this changed the emphasis of the project as different municipalities and projects funding had to re-evaluate their skilled labour needs (interview #7):

> I would say both, but also before we had this economic meltdown 2008 to 2009, there were like regions where, some regions were suffering very badly about this lack of skilled workforce. And, it was like regional like activities, there were somewhere like China or India, and they tried to create like some sort of context there, and create some sort of like network for getting skilled professionals there. So, this regional actors, I don't know, who it was that was responsible there or who it will be now, maybe Helsinki centre or something like this, but we must somehow make some sort of continuation here, that not everybody has to start from the zero every time. When these things start, these other actors, they can be these regional authorities, they can be employers or employees, sorry, they can be basically that is more or less about it, I would say. Ok, some educational institutions, they are also doing a lot of these networking, they are just keeping it very much on themselves. They should make more visible these networks that they have there, and for everybody to take use of them also who need it. So, not that

everybody, when there is lack of skilled workers that 'ok, now we go to Bulgaria to look for nurses', they know next time, 'ok, how do we start this thing now? Is there information, somewhere already existing, this and this are the contact points in Bulgaria and here and here you might find these nurses and this is the—what is the market situation of the nurses in Bulgaria and this is how they might find jobs there and this information should be like somehow concentrated on somewhere.

From the first group in 2008 and from January 2009 to April 2010, the Finnish recruitment company transnationally managed 75 Filipino registered nurses in five groups: three groups for practical nursing (three groups went to the Finnish elderly care company) and one group of 25 registered nurses who went to surgical and operational wards (20 were placed in HUS[25] and 5 were placed in Hatanpää),[26] and one group went to an unknown private elderly care institution. As of December 2008, the Finnish recruitment company started their own language training model in the Philippines with a Finnish instructor. The instructor published a section in EMN's report entitled 'Migration of labour necessary for filling in?' (Maahanmuutto Työvoiman Tarpeen Täyttäjänä?) (2010). In the instructor's section entitled 'Integration education in country of origin as a basis for working in Finland' [*Integrovia lähtömaakoulutus pohjana työskentelylle Suomessa* in Finnish], the instructor discusses experiences teaching in the Philippines on behalf of the Finnish recruitment company and the models created to prepare the nurses to migrate and work in Finland. In an interview with a representative from the Finnish recruitment company, the instructor's work in the Philippines is mentioned and how the recruited registered nurses, in particular, received intensive Finnish language training before departing (interview #3):

Everyone who went into the hospital in the health care sector, all receive that [Finnish language training]—yes. That is important for them because, even though the- I mean the Filipino nursing staff, they have 9 months of quite intensive language training and that language training was linked to the job they were coming to do so there was medical terminology, etc., all involved in that. But, as you know, you land here and then you go into that environment and even then, they probably thought, they were speaking another language. So, there is so much more to learn, so the language training is an ongoing thing that we have with them and, if there was one issue, we ran a number of workshops, so like 'get to know you workshops', once the nurses were here and been working for a couple of weeks. We ran workshops within HUS and Hatanpää in Tampere. We needed to get feedback from both the Finnish mentors and the Filipinos. So, we had them all in one room, we had a morning with half day workshops related to them. Taking them through issues. And, I was pleasantly surprised at that, but what we got from that, they were all actually really open with each other. Even only after 2 weeks. If there was one thing that came out of there, it was from the Finnish perspective, was that we would have liked the language skills more advanced when they got here. Because they do have to write reports even basic stuff. They got to fill forms and it is medical, so you can't sort of, get it wrong. That was a really, I think, big learn for us. And, it was a valid point that you, that we would take into the future. If [the Finnish instructor], I think you may have met [the Finnish instructor] at our office, but [the instructor] runs the language programmes. [The instructor] is very, very good, but it is intense. But, it is hard work. But, of course, the nurses are encouraged to speak only in Finnish which at times can be a challenge for them because they can't express themselves when things are not going right. They can only express themselves in their own language or in English. It is more difficult to express some of your inner emotions in a language that you are still learning, so some of that is taken offline a little bit because the Finnish nurses are expected to only speak Finnish with them.

The intensity of the training in Finnish language seems to increase timewise with the job selection. For instance, recruitment of practical nurses initially did not have the same intense training or mentoring as the registered nurses for the OR and surgical wards of the hospitals. According to two of the recruited Filipino nurses who came in January 2009 to work for the Finnish elderly care company, the recruited nurse received a few days of Finnish language training in the Philippines (interviews #11a and #11c):

11c: I was with [name of other recruited Filipino nurse being interviewed]. We were both selected for the second batch. But actually, the hiring to Finland, under [the Finnish recruitment company], is that, one must have done a Finnish course. That is one of the qualifications. But in our case, we just studied it for two months. Actually, we haven't finished it [as of the time of the interview] but I don't know what is their criteria.

11a: For me, I enrolled for weeks but only studied a couple of days. I only been in a class for five days.

INTERVIEWER: That is funny. Because the recruiters said that the nurses received months of Finnish language training

11c: I think because they promised to the employer that they would have this 19 [nurses] who would speak Finnish [referring to the recruited nurses of the second group that came January 2009] but they lack one [only 18 nurses came]. I don't understand what happened.

In January 2009, the second group of Filipino nurses arrived to work for the Finnish elderly care company after the first eight nurses arrived in 2008.

Although the language training in Finnish was promised to the clients by the Finnish recruitment company, many of the recruited nurses revealed that the language training in the Philippines was limited.

In terms of future recruitment of Filipino nurses after the 75 nurses were placed, representatives from the Finnish recruitment company (interview #1b; interview #3) indicate that although there is a need, and it seems that all eyes (as in other representatives in Finland) are watching to see how the pilot projects function. This comment relates to the idea that the Finnish recruitment company is investing in a new model of recruiting nurses for practical and registered qualifications.

INTERVIEWER: And, what is, I am sure you have answered this, but is there any specific reasons why [the private recruitment company] is hesitating now to recruit [nurses from the Philippines]?

INTERVIEWEE #1b: We're actually not hesitating at all. The economic situation in Finland has led to this situation at—all the eyes are on this pilot project. So, they, the other hospital districts, they want to see how HUS does, how it goes for them, and, of course, now that we have more experience and we have information and data on how they are doing, what they can achieve language wise and professionally. I am sure we will recruit this year. But, then it takes a year for them to study Finnish, so there is always a gap between order and the fact of the date when people are coming to Finland. And, we will recruit both practical nurses and registered nurses for those jobs in Finland.

INTERVIEWER: Have you ever thought or has [the private recruitment company] ever thought about recruiting within Finland like domestically?

INTERVIEWEE #1b: There aren't any people—we do that too and we have temps working in certain cities, fields, and, you know, qualified people in Finland. But, for example, here, we don't have those people anymore. And, if you get one, you can never be certain if he or she will be available next Monday. So, this is the problem for nursing homes and also cities and municipalities and also for hospital district that they can't—

INTERVIEWER: Retain them

INTERVIEWEE #1b: Yeah, HUS didn't have—they had a shortage of 200 nurses in the OR and surgical wards when we started this. The situation got a bit better. People came back, you know, during the recession to work—a husband, perhaps, lost his job so the wife came back to work as a nurse. And, still they don't have enough people. So, that is a fact. But, basically, it is too late, in a way, well, it is not too late, but it is harder to find the resources, of course, for mentoring, for example, which is needed. Well, schedules change the mentors cannot always stay with the [recruited] nurses who are practicing. So, that is a challenge. So, I only wish that more clients saw this, really.

Referring to another interview with the Finnish recruitment company, I asked the representative a question about possible recruitment from the Philippines in the future (interview #3):

INTERVIEWER: And, I asked this question to you and [another representative of the company] too, but do you see more recruitment in the future of these nurses because before there was a lot of media attention about recruiting of thousands and thousands of nurses so far the number has been quite limited.

INTERVIEWEE #3: I am wondering if there is a little bit of 'let's wait and see' from other hospitals. They want to see what is happening here and how that is working. There has been a lot of interest, though, I have to say, regarding that. I couldn't, hand on heart, I couldn't say any more than that but we know that in some areas in Finland, there has been a lot of interest in recruiting or the possibility of recruiting Filipino nurses. But, they will want to see, and they all talk to each other—they are all in the same camp in that respect—and they will be watching and evaluating how things work within Hatanpää and here with HUS. I think they'll be pleasantly surprised at how all that works out, but we are in close, and I know that [name of representative from the recruitment company] is on the team. They keep close contact with other nursing authorities. Because of what we do, we do have the, I suppose we are in the amiable position because we are the only company that has actually done this, embarked on this venture. And, it has been a hard, it is a rocky road, you make mistakes, of course you do. And, but we are learning from that and you continually learn as you go along and I think we are in a very good position both from our point of view and from a business perspective but also in the expertise that we have to offer to other hospitals.

The talk of the Finnish recruitment representatives reveals a local problem of retaining domestic, Finnish nurses, and a hesitant policy strategy to recruit from abroad by local officials. The company's representatives' descriptions of 'let's wait and see' and 'all the eyes are on this pilot project' of the other authorities in Finland asserts the company's 'pioneering' strategies. The local problems of nurse retention also indicates structural issues of a workforce that are undesirable to local Finns unless during times of an economic recession. The talk from the recruitment representative (interview #1b) also denotes the gendered nature of the occupation, in which women return to work as nurses in the Finnish hospitals to compensate for the husband's loss of income.

In May 2014, two Filipino nurses from the third group recruited for the Helsinki hospital filed a complaint based on contractual infringements by the Finnish recruitment company and the hospital to the Philippines Oversea Employment Administration. As a result of this complaint, POEA disqualified both the Helsinki hospital and the Finnish recruitment company from recruiting nurses in the Philippines. The complaints are not listed here, but

Philippine Overseas Employment Administration

Republic of the Philippines
Department of Labor and Employment
BFO Building, Ortigas Avenue cor. EDSA, Mandaluyong City 1501

Website: www.poea.gov.ph E-mail: info@poea.gov.ph
Hotlines: 722-1144, 722-1155

24 June 2014

TRICIA CLELAND SILVA
Doctoral Researcher
Hanken School of Economics
Finland
Tricia.cleland@hanken.fi

Dear Ms. Silva:

We refer to your email inquiring on the status of [redacted] Uusima Hospital relative to the complaints of [redacted] docketed as POEA Case No. [redacted]

Please be informed that on May 12, 2014, this Administration has issued an Order finding [redacted] liable for default on their contractual obligations. As a consequence thereof, they are disqualified from participating in the overseas employment program. However, with the filing of a timely appeal to the Office of the Secretary of Labor and Employment, [redacted] Hospital and [redacted] are yet to be included in the Administration's List of Permanently Disqualified Principals/Foreign Employers. As such, they can participate in the overseas employment program of the government pending the determination of their appeal.

We hope we have addressed your concern.

Truly yours,

[redacted]
Director II
Legal Research Docket and Enforcement Branch

Figure 6.3 Letter from POEA about complaint by recruited nurses about the Finnish organisations

the decision was filed to POEA according to a letter I received in June 2014 after placing an inquiry (Figure 6.3).

Figure 6.4 reveals the social world of municipal/city governance emerging between the private business/corporate social world and national security and police; the third sector is also located further away from the producer-based care arena. These worlds emerge as HUS and Hatanpää become primary representatives in the production of care human capital from the Philippines by

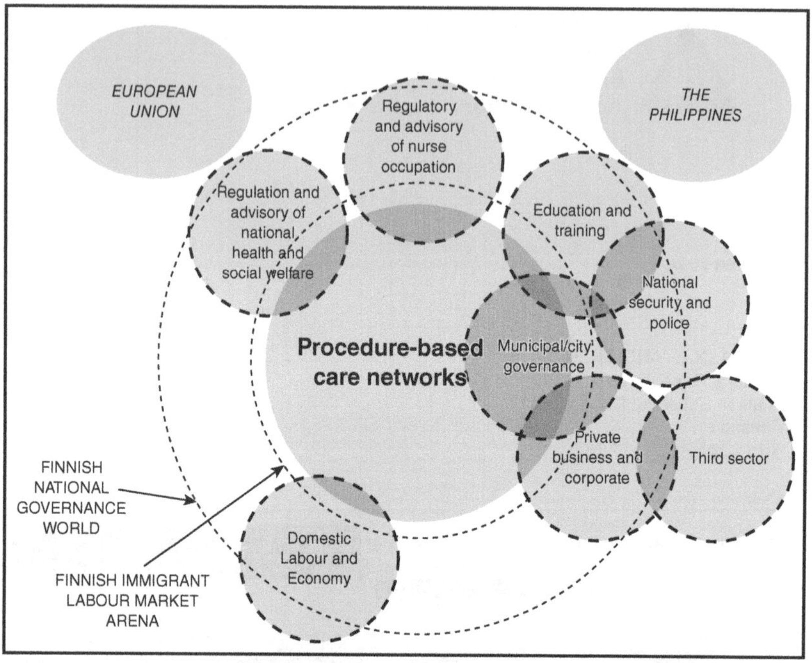

Figure 6.4 Social world map of years 2009 and 2010

recruiting with the Finnish recruitment company and placing a group of Filipinos in the hospital surgical wards. The five worlds—education and training, third sector, private business and corporate, municipal/city governance, and national security and police—interact to create a larger network of producing Filipino nurses and share commitments and practices of recruiting, placing, and training the nurses in accordance to the social worlds.

Situating Transnational Management of Nurses

This chapter sets out to retell a story of a situation with illustrations through social world maps. The situated story revolves around questions that strive to investigate the representatives, organisations, and institutions and their associated social worlds who were interacting and practicing transnational management of nurses. Specifically, the chapter asks

(1) Who are the representatives, organisations, and institutions involved in the recruitment and placement of Filipino nurses in Finland?
(2) What social worlds are they representing?
(3) How do the representatives, organisations, and institutions socially interact and relate?

The story endeavours to capture an arena where representatives and their associated social worlds interact in order to dominate, pacify, or remain silent within the social action of recruitment and placement of nurses from the Philippines. What this reveals is the 'who' of the situation or 'who cares' when it comes to the recruitment and placement of these nurses, as well as the interactions of these representatives within social worlds constructed by the researcher through maps. The story also illustrates gendered and racialised hierarchies in the Finnish nursing occupation that become pronounced in the discourse of how to recruit and place foreign nurses through authoritative claims by the dominant representatives. As argued by Acker (1990, 2006), institutionalised practices and socially constructed criteria of the ideal worker or, in this case, the ideal nurse, reinforces barriers to equality. Transnational feminists have contended that movements of historically gendered and racilialised occupations, such as nursing, have structural and material implications in the way workforces are organised across geographical borders. Reconceptualising the discipline of IHRM to THRM through the lens of transnational feminism facilitates the deeper examination of institutional and organisational representatives, which, in the past, have not been a major focal point of analysis in the management of human resources across national borders. This chapter, with its focus on producer-based care networks, aims to unwrap the representatives transnationally managing nurses and the implications of the discourses and practices from this management that materialises in the Finnish nursing workforce.

To focus on the transnational management of Filipino nurses, the producer-based care networks serve as a platform to capture authoritative claims and pilot practices emerging from the recruitment of five groups of nurses from the Philippines. Within the arena of producer-based care networks, private and public representatives work in their associated social worlds to produce, recruit, relocate, and settle labour transnationally. How the representatives practice the transnationalisation of care is constructed in terms of the organisation's work, commitments (e.g. selling and packaging a product), how the representatives of the organisations practice the work and commitments, and how the organisation and its work are described through discourse. The social worlds maps are illustrative products of these worlds interacting as 'seas of discourses' (Clarke, 2005). The representatives' social worlds interacting in the producer-based care network, in this situated story, are regulatory and advisory of nurse occupation, education and training, national security and police, municipal/city governance, private business and corporate, third sector, domestic labour and economy, and regulation and advisory of national health and social welfare. On the outside of the network were the implicated social worlds of the Philippines and the European Union.

Before the recruitment of the Filipino nurses by the Finnish recruitment company in 2008, there was a space in the producer-based care networks for representatives to assert authority. The responsibilities of regulating and managing immigrant labour within the Finnish ministries remained ambiguous as the central discursive focus and governing practices, before 2006, were on refugees and social integration rather than work-based immigration.

On the other hand, in 2007, the city of Helsinki, through the implementation of the Inkeri project, recruited various social and health workers with Ingrian descent. Through the experience, however, the representatives in the city of Helsinki decided that it was too difficult to recruit transnationally in terms of costs and time and should be left to private businesses to make a case. The Finnish National Institute for Health and Welfare (THL) also reached this conclusion through the 'Attractive Finland' project in which THL recommended that the selection and placement practices of non-Finnish health care labour should be contracted out to the private recruitment companies and that the companies should play an active role in governing practices of the recruitment.

During the years of recruitment of the private companies, the human resource practices and discourses within the government ministries and the city of Helsinki provided a space for business and corporate social worlds and their representatives to assert their authority, both discursively and instrumentally, in providing human capital for health care provisions in Finland. In a recruitment magazine by the Finnish recruitment company, Erik Virtanen, the permanent secretary of the Ministry of Employment and Economy, is quoted as saying that immigration labour policy remains unclear in Finland whereas recruitment of leased labour for private, for-profit purposes operates smoothly.

In 2007, in order to assert dominance in the producer-based care networks, the trio of Finnish companies publically claimed in the media that the companies would collaborate to bring hundreds of practical nurses from the Philippines. To justify this practice of recruiting from the Philippines, the companies invested time and financial capital to make a pilot study of how to transnationally recruit and place nurses into the Finnish health care system both presently and in the future. At the time, this initiative had strong political support as the Finnish government enacted, through legislation, a programme to promote employment-based immigration that would facilitate recruitment from abroad based specifically on the needs of Finnish employers. The government's legislative and policy texts permeated through all the social worlds interacting in the arena of the producer-based care network.

To legitimise their claims to bring nurses from the Philippines, but also to provide models as to how to practice the transnational management of nurses, the trio of companies presented at a Nordic Council (Norden) forum on multiculturalism and health in 2008. This forum had as its audience various governmental officials, executives, and other decision makers. To comply with the forum's theme, the companies assert their expertise on this topic through the 'case of the Philippines' by discursively constructing the companies' roles in recruiting and placing nurses from the Philippines through written text and pictures in their presentations. Discursively, the companies' work commitments were described as action-oriented in which strategies to deal with Finland's lack of practical nurses and ageing population were resolved by recruiting from the Philippines. The Philippines was constructed as an exporter of educated and trained registered nurses ready for export due to overpopulation and unemployment rates. In contrast, the companies were constructed as the producers of selected qualified registered nurses who were trained in the Finnish language. This production of nurses was customised in terms of both the Finnish client(s), those hiring the nurses, and in accordance to Finnish institutionalised regulations and laws. Each company asserted their relationship to regulatory and governing bodies in Finland and how their models, particularly in requalifying the nurses and teaching Finnish language to adults, obeys with local laws, but also was and has been instrumental in integrating the Filipino nurses into workplace.

Within the various texts and talk, the Filipino nurses, the Philippines, the European Union, and the elderly clients remain physically present in body, written texts, and pictures, but those who claim to represent them discursively implicate these representatives. Producing and disseminating socially constructed information on various groups of people (such as an occupation, a country, or a region), if given the space in local and national policy decisions, creates structurally mediating mechanisms for the management of a workforce and a population of people.

Amongst the dominant authoritative voices of Finnish companies, the Filipino nurses are discursively constructed through racialised and gendered representations that reflect traditional and historical pathways of migrants and unequal economic trade and development. The Philippines has exported nurses since the 1950s (Choy, 2003) and one of the main reasons for this exportation was the country's colonial history. Choy (2003) connects the mobility of Filipino nurses to the establishment of US-oriented health and nursing education systems in the Philippines. This system promotes Western ideologies of institutionalised allopathic medicine, and the nurses learn and work in US-American English. From the 1950s to present, the US-American health care system has actively recruited nurses from the Philippines through systematically organised institutional practices, such as visa regulation, and requalifying educational skills. In some cases, the nurses are requested to live on hospital property (Choy, 2003). Within this supply and demand relationship, The Philippine government has established nursing schools and deploys governmental regulations that promote sending migrant nurses abroad. Some reasons for this systematic exportation are to serve Philippine indebtness (Barber, 2000: 399), and remittance payments sent to families by the workers transnationally link government systems and economic exchange (Brown, 1997; UN-INSTRAW, 2007).

In 2008, the Finnish recruitment company selected the first eight Filipino nurses who were recruited based on the Finnish elderly care company's requests. The recruited nurses were to hold a bachelor's degree in nursing science, have experience in working abroad, and speak English. By not requesting recruitment placement fees, the Finnish recruitment company and Finland became competitive amongst other recruitment agencies and countries in which Filipino nurses have historically migrated to, such as Canada, United States, and United Kingdom.

The eight nurses were recruited and flown to Finland to work for the Finnish elderly care company as practical nurses during a period of 'apprenticeship'. This apprenticeship lasted six months and the nurses were expected to live together in a flat provided by the Finnish elderly care company, receive a basic practical nurse salary in accordance to Finnish regulations, and learn Finnish within their workplace as well as weekly classes. The Finnish recruitment company and the Finnish elderly care company also handled the nurses' working resident permits, solely applying for the nurses and not their families. According to Finnish companies, the promise and fulfilment of family reunification would come after the apprenticeship and the initial two-year contract.

The next four groups of nurses, with the exception of the third group of nurses recruited for hospital surgical wards, were expected to be less experienced and younger than the first group. Through the experiences of the first pilot group, 'challenges/problems' arose, and there was a concern about the retention of the nurses. The representatives of the Finnish companies acknowledged the deskilling process of transnational recruitment through regulatory mechanisms of Valvira as well as learning Finnish language, but vocalised and asserted that, through dedication and hard work to the Finnish elderly care company and the Finnish language, the nurses could advance in their careers as well as apply through the immigration police to be reunited with their family.

The socially constructed attributes of the Filipino nurses by the dominant representatives in the producer-based care networks are hard-working, modern heroes (referring to sending money back to the Philippines), warm and caring and embodying a 'cultural bound politeness' to their elders. The nurses are also perceived as entering the nursing occupation not as a career but as a vocation. This construction is legitimised in contrast to the Finnish domestic nursing workforce that is viewed as lower professional quality in terms of compliancy, but also limited in human resource supply as Finnish students are not choosing the nursing occupation and qualified nurses are leaving the profession. However, instead of re-examining the reasons why domestic nurses leave their occupation, the private companies recruit nurses that, through transnational processes of unequal development and regulation, are flexible, complaint, paid the lowest salary, and deskilled to work in elderly care. The producers construct elderly care as heavy, messy, hard, unqualified work that is undesirable to the local Finnish nurses and could be done by anyone.

Representatives disagreed, and conflicts arose in social worlds concerning this construction such as the Finnish nurses' union or Filipino nurses working and living in Finland who were silenced through lack of acknowledgement or dismissal by dominate corporate and business social worlds. At various times, discourses emerged about the hierarchical nature of the nursing occupation in terms of gender, class, and race, as well as the unsustainable practice of treating the Filipino nurses as replaceable, but these discourses were overpowered. The overpowering discourses related to a narrative of worsening labour shortages in Finland as well as the European Union and the urgent need to compete for this much-needed labour as ageing demographics increase within the welfare state. This group of ageing demographics are labelled at various times as 'baby boomers'. The baby boomers are a different generation than pre–World War II as indicated by the Finnish recruitment company. They are healthy and work past retirement and, as Erik Virtanen in the Finnish recruitment company's HR magazine states, want to 'consume hospitality' within the private elderly care sector. This assumption goes beyond basic institutionalised allopathic care of past generations and creates touristic, individualised expectations of the patients when receiving assisted care. These expectations can be purchased and packaged with pre-selected nurses for pre-determined tasks and workplaces where the individual consumer is a resident or being 'hosted' as if on vacation or in a hotel. As the work commitment of the social worlds changed, in terms of recruitment and placement of non-Finnish nurses, so too did the maps which addressed how the social worlds and representatives interacted. What is revealed in the maps, particularly in the last two years of recruitment (2009–2010), was the overlapping of the social worlds around the production of nurse labour (see Figure 6.5). As the third sector was pushed out of the arena, the social worlds of private business and corporate, municipal/city governance, national security and police, and education and training join together which revealed not only collaboration amongst these particular social worlds but also the dominance of a private/business agenda of Filipino nurses through transnational management practices.

By taking for granted the hierarchical nature of the nursing occupation in Finland, particularly in terms of working shifts, salary, and prestige, inequalities continue to be reinforced with the replacement of Filipino workers for a more transient workforce. For instance, as noted by Mackay in 1989 and Davies in the 1990s, the structuring of the nursing occupation in the UK based on the 'disposable workforce ethos—use-once-and-throw-away' (Mackay, 1989: 92–93) in which the ease of young learners replaced more experienced nurses, trivialises the occupation and wastes the potential of the nurses. In Finland, the Filipino nurses are deskilled from registered to practical nurses through transnational processes and easily replace the high turnover of domestic Finnish nurses because of barriers in terms of visa restrictions, Finnish language abilities, and limited contracts associated with mandatory apprenticeships. Kingma (2006) notes that this is a trend in various countries where nurses' skills are devalued and the nurses are treated as an 'extra pair of hands'. This trend has also been empirically documented in

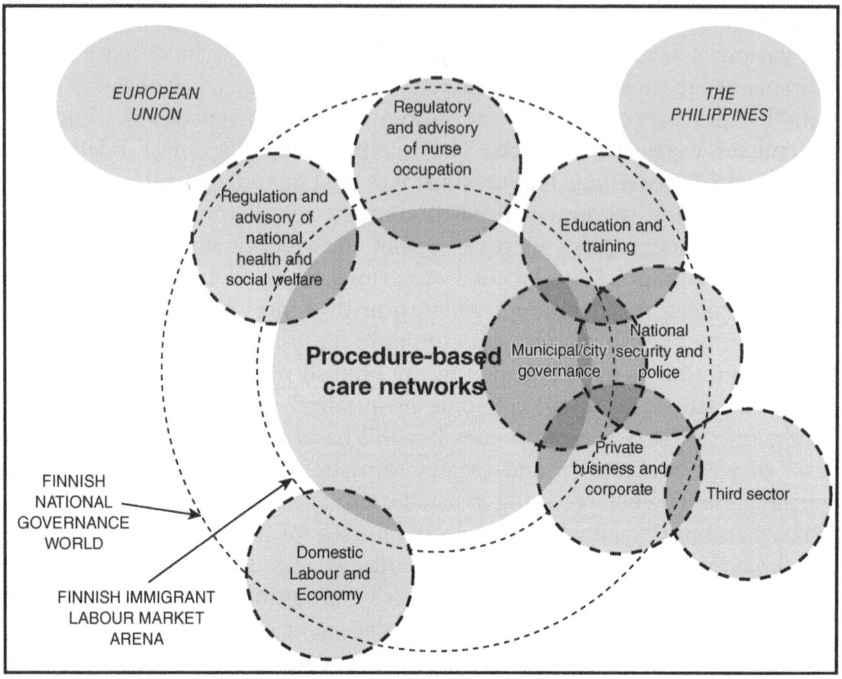

Figure 6.5 Social worlds map in 2009–2010

Portugal (Ribeiro, 2008), Australia (Ho, 2008; McNeil-Walsh, 2008), and Canada (Kelly and D'Addario, 2008).

Through the lens of transnational feminism, the analytical focus on transnational human resource management of nurse labour focuses on situated networks or 'chains' of various representatives, institutions, and organisations who are producing workers that reinforce gendered, racialised and classed hierarchies. This reproduction of unequal hierarchies that are taken for granted in the field of international human resource management reinforces the unequal development of trade and economies as well as divisions of labour that favour production based on monetary profit and competitiveness. The institutionalised ideologies of capitalism and neoliberalism as seemingly rational, business practices that transcend borders and multiple levels of organising naturalise dominant knowledge claims of businesses packaging 'desirable' workers as flexible, disposable, and a commodity that can be imported.

Situating these transnational gendered and racialised processes and practices turns the empirical focus onto representatives and networks that have, in the past, existed and functioned outside the scholarly field of IHRM. Focusing on sites of nurse labour production deconstructs discourses that have material implications for workers' bodies, and highlights the story on how knowledge claims dominate to create particular controlling institutionalised mechanisms at high policy levels of governance, but also within the workplace.

Although the dominant producers of nurse labour, in this book, have collective mandates to make money through financial investment, the THRM practices implemented by the dominant producers have little concern with retention of the workers and sustainability of the future workforce. Reproducing a system of disposability through 'coping management', in other words, not questioning institutionalised practices of regulation and the hierarchical nature of the nursing occupation, designs Finland as a 'stepping stone' for mobile nurses to jump from in terms of other career opportunities in countries that can advance their desired life trajectories. This resonates with the situation of over 35 000 domestic Finnish nurses that choose not to be in their trained professions because of various material grievances such as low salaries, incompatible time work patterns for those with children such as shift work, and lack of status or prestige in comparison to medical doctors. As Mackay writes in 1989, 'what a waste!'

Summary and Concluding Thoughts

This chapter retold a story of the various representatives, institutions, and organisations involved in the recruitment and placement of Filipino nurses into Finnish nursing institutions. This story captured an arena of producer-based care networks of representatives and their associated worlds dominating discursive space and authority in the talk and text surrounding the THRM practices of Filipino nurses. The dominant producers, a trio of private Finnish companies, through pre-selection processes, recruited Filipino nurses based on the needs of Finnish employers. This pre-selection of desirable workers reinforces structural inequalities within the Finnish profession and perpetuates a system of exportation in the Philippines, reflecting colonial histories and uneven economic trade. Using the lens of transnational feminism, this chapter further explores gendered and racialised institutional and organisational practices that reinforce hierarchies amongst nurses in the local Finnish workforce. These hierarchies have material implications for the lives of the migrating nurses and their subsequent career trajectories.

In the next chapter, I examine the discursive positions within the social worlds that arose in the arena of producer-based care networks. The aim of this analysis was to go beyond the discourses of 'knowing subjects' and focus on collective, contested discourses surrounding the social action of transnational recruitment and placement. By focusing on the discursive positions situated in the arena facilitates a close examination of structural barriers to equality for the Filipino nurses in Finland as well as the material consequences of these barriers.

Notes

1 See Context Box 5.1 in Chapter 5.
2 See *Integration Act* (2005) in Context Box 5.1 in Chapter 5.
3 Inkeri Projekti 2007–2011 report. URL: www.hel.fi/wps/wcm/connect/8b5bc780406c9515b487bfdc59c9b43f/Ulkomailta_rekryrtoinnin_hanke_inkeri_projekti_loppuraportti.pdf?MOD=AJPERES&lmod=1489618952
4 The Ingrians are descendants of Finnish speakers who moved to the Eastern shores of the Gulf of Finland after Sweden had annexed this area from Russia in the beginning of the 17th century.
5 All Valvira's licensing guidelines are available on the URL: www.valvira.fi/en/licensing. I was also given, during my interview with the representatives from Valvira, printouts of the website and its licensing guidelines. These printouts were referred to by the actors throughout the interview.
6 Philippines Department of Foreign Affairs (2007) 'President Halonen of Finland accepts invitation to visit the Philippines' *Press Release*. Accessed November 5th, 2008 URL: www.dfa.gov.ph/news/pr/pr2007/sep/pr718.htm
7 Esperi (November 9, 2007) 'Hoiva-alan ammattilaisia rekrytoidaan Filipiineiltä' [Health care professionals to be recruited in the Philippines] *News release*. Accessed October 28th, 2008 URL: www.esperi.fi/ajankohtaista/index.htlm?NewsId=31
8 Sillanpää, S. (January 20, 2008) 'Everyone who wants to go to Finland, raise your hands' *Helsinki Sanomat international edition*. URL: www.hs.fi/english/everyone+who+wants+to+Finland+raise+your +hands (Accessed October 23rd, 2008)
9 Filscandia is a recruitment agency in the Philippines, operated by citizens of the Philippines and registered by POEA (the Philippines Overseas Employment Administration). URL: www.filscandia.com.
10 At the end of 2007, the Finnish recruitment company ended its business relationship with Filscandia over allegations that the company was accepting recruitment fees from the nurses recruited to Finland. Accepting recruitment fees is against Finnish labour laws as well as laws set out by POEA in the Philippines.
11 Amina Mama (2007: 6) argues this point in her work on academic identity and practices. She states that 'our intellectual identities—and the ethics that we adopt to guide our scholarly practices—are informed by our identifications with particular communities and the values they uphold'.
12 In 2015, a Finnish news station, YLE, published an article entitled 'Feeling of not enough' haunts Finland's overworked nurses. The article reads that the nursing professionals in Finland are becoming increasingly dissatisfied with their working conditions as noted by a union survey of 2 500 nurses working in the public sector.
13 TEM's website. Title of page 'History of the Ministry' URL: www.tem.fi/en/ministry/history_of_the_ministry
14 TE and ELY services available in Finnish at URL: www.mol.fi/etusivu/index.htlm. Also, a report with the responsibilities in the ministries as well as TEM's approach to social and health care services labour market is in the report by Laiho, Ul-M, Grönberg, V., Hämäläinen, Stenman, J., and Tykkyläinen, S. entitled 'Yhteiskunnallisen Yrityksen Toimintamallin Kehittäminen' (in English 'Development approach to social enterprise', self translation) (4/11) Helsinki: Ministry of Employment and Economy.
15 English translation from Finnish. Finnish text 'Haluanmme tulla hoiva-alan Nokiaksi' Accessed October 28th, 2008 URL: www.eperi.fi/Esperi/Ajankohtaista/index.html?NewsId=36

16 Niva's forum conference programme. Accessed October 20th, 2008 URL: www.Niva.org/courses
17 Niva's forum conference programme. Accessed October 20th, 2008 URL: www.Niva.org/courses
18 Polku project. URL: www.seure.fi/polku
19 Attractive Finland (2010). The report is published solely in Finnish and is entitled 'Attraktiivinen Suomi'.
20 Presentation by Simo Mannila to explain the INSITE project 'Työvoiman maahanmuuton ennakointiseminaari rekrytointitarpeiden ennakoinnin työkalut ja muuttoliike' (in English 'Labour Migration: anticipation of recruitment needs, forecasting tools, and migration' seminar) 4 March 2010. Information about INSITE and its collaboration with Attractive Finland project is also available in the English summary in the Attractive Finland report published by THL.
21 Ministry of Interior (2009b) 'Developing work-related immigration and integration' Helsinki: Ministry of Interior publication. Also, available information on this project at URL: www.intermin.fi/matto
22 ALPO project. Ministry of Interior. URL: www.tem.fi/alpojulkaisut
23 MATTO project. Ministry of Interior. URL: www.tem.fi/tyo/maahanmuuttajien_kotouttaminen/kotouttamisen_kehittamishankkeet/matto-tukirakenne
24 Äärilä, S. and Huttunen, H-P (2010) *Avoin Suomi: Kuka Vasta? Työperusteisesta maahanmuutosta* Helsinki: Uudenmaan Ely-Keskusksen.
25 The Hospital District of Helsinki and Uusimaa is a Joint Authority formed by 24 municipalities. The aim is to offer patients in all member municipalities a timely and equal access to specialised medical care. This covers a population of approximately 1.5 million.
26 Hatanpää is a district of Tampere city and is a referring to a city hospital that provides services of surgery, neurology, internal medicine, and general practice and geriatrics.

References

Äärilä, S. & Huttunen, H. P. (2010) *Avoin Suomi: Kuka vasta? Työperusteisesta maahanmuutosta*. Helsinki: Uudenmaan Ely-Keskusksen.

Acker, J. (1990) Hierarchies, jobs, bodies: A theory of gendered organizations. *Gender and Society*, 4(2), pp. 139–158.

Acker, J. (2006) Inequality regimes: Gender, class, and race in organizations. *Gender and Society*, 20(4), pp. 441–464.

Asa, R. & Bärlund, R. (2010) *Satisfying labour demand through migration*. Helsinki: European Migration Network.

Asa, R. & Muurinen, H. (2010) *Temporary and circular migration: Empirical evidence, current policy practice, and future options in Finland*. Helsinki: European Migration Network.

Barber, P. (2000) Agency in Philippine women's labour migration and provisional diaspora. *Women's Studies International Forum*, 23(4), pp. 399–411.

Brown, D. A. (1996) *Workforce losses and return migration to the Caribbean: A case study of Jamaican nurses*. Center for Migration Studies special issues, 13(4), pp. 197–223.

Choy, C. (2003) *Empire of care: Nursing and migration in Filipino American history*. Durham: Duke University Press.

Clarke, A. (2005) *Situational analysis: Grounded theory after the postmodern turn.* Thousand Oaks, CA: Sage.

Davies, C. (1995). *Gender and the professional predicament in nursing.* London: McGraw-Hill Education.

Ho, C. (2008) Chinese nurses in Australia: Migration, work, and identity. In J. Connell (ed.) *The international migration of health workers.* New York: Routledge, pp. 147–163.

Kelly, P. F. & D' Addario, S. (2008) Filipinos are very strongly into medical stuff: Labour market segmentation in Toronto, Canada. In J. Connell (ed.) *The international migration of health workers.* London: Routledge, pp. 77–98.

Kingma, M. (2006) *Nurses on the move: Migration and the global health care economy.* London: ILR Press.

Mackay, L. (1989) *Nursing a problem.* New York: McGraw-Hill.

Mama, A. (2007). Is it ethical to study Africa? Preliminary thoughts on scholarship and freedom. *African Studies Review*, 50(1), pp. 1–26.

McNeil-Walsh, C. (2008) Migrant nurses and the experiences of skill: South Africa nurses in UK health care sector. In J. Connell (ed.) *International migration of health care workers.* New York: Routledge, pp. 129–146.

Ministry of Employment and the Economy (TEM) (2011) *Working in Finland.* Helsinki: Ministry of Employment and the Economy.

Ministry of Interior (2009) *History of the ministry.* www.tem.fi/en/ministry/history_of_the_ministry (accessed March 4th, 2013)

Pääministeri Matti Vanhanen hallituksen ohjelma [Government programme of Matti Vanhanen]. (2003) www.valtioneuvosto.fi/hallitus/hallitusohjelma/ohjelma/fi.jsp (accessed February 20th, 2014)

Pääministeri Matti Vanhasen II hallituksen ohjelma [Government programme of Matti Vahanen's second cabinet government]. (2007) www.vn.fi/hallitus/halli tusohjelma/pdf/hallitusohjelma-painoversio-040507.pdf (accessed February 20th, 2014)

Ribeiro, J. Sousa (2008) Gendering migration flows: Physicians and nurses in Portugal. *Equal Opportunities International*, 27(1), pp. 77–87.

Selberg, R. (May 2013) Nursing in times of neoliberal change: An ethnographic study of nurses' experiences of work intensification. *Nordic Journal of Working Life Studies*, 3(2), pp. 9–35.

Strauss, A. L. (1978) A social worlds perspective. *Studies in Symbolic Interaction*, 1, pp. 119–128.

Työvoiman maahanmuuton toimenpideohjelma (The action plan for labour migration) (23, 2009) Helsinki: Ministry of Interior pulications. www.intermin.fi/intermin/biblio.nsf/86C1C347491A1C85C2257665003AACC7/$file/232009.pdf (accessed February 15th, 2014)

United Nations and Training Institute for the Advancement of Women (UN-STRAW) (2007) *Feminisation of migration: Gender, remittances and development.* Geneva: United Nations.

Yeates, N. (2009) *Globalising care economies and migrant workers: Explorations in global care chains.* Basingstoke: Palgrave Macmillan.

Yeates, N. (2011) Going global: The transnationalization of care. *Development and Change*, 42(4), pp. 1109–1130.

7 Discursive Positions and Structural Barriers to Equality in Transnational Human Resource Management

This chapter addresses the discursive positions of the claims in the talk and text of representatives and organisations. Specifically, this chapter asks this question:

> How, through discursive positions in the claims of the produced talk and text, are the representatives and organisations socially constructing the practices of recruitment and placement of Filipino nurses in Finland?

The aim is to illustrate the major contested issues in the discourses amongst representatives transnationally managing Filipino nurses. As argued in Chapter 6, dominant representatives and their associated social worlds emerge into the producer-based care networks through claims to authority in the transnational management of Filipino nurses. These authoritative claims were made in the talk and text of the representatives and their organisations as well as in the social actions to negotiate and legitimise claims to an audience of other representatives and the Finnish public. A focus on the dominant discursive positions of the representatives highlight socially constructed expectations of the implicated Filipino nurses as a recruited group, how the recruited workforce is managed and structurally organised, and what is considered ethical practices within transnational recruitment.

Referring to the ordered map in Chapter 5 and the analysis in Chapter 6, this chapter is divided into categories of discursive positions to discuss the implications of these positions in terms of structural inequality barriers (Acker, 2006). The discursive positions are not from a particular representative or organisation but rather dominating the discourses within the domain of the producer-based care networks. As the talk and text from the trio of private Finnish companies dominant the authoritative space in the producer-based care networks, the organisations gain control on how the transnational management of the Filipino nurses should be practiced and how the Filipino nurses are regarded as working nurses in Finland. I argue that the discursive positions that emerge from the talk and text are in regards to the supply of ideal practical nurse labour from the Philippines for Finland's ageing and under resourced health care system, Finnish-language teaching and standardised work requirements as a practice for the placement of Filipino nurses, and ethical transnational recruitment.

The first discursive position on the Philippines is as an exporting country of nurse human capital as well as the issue of representation of the recruited Filipino nurse. Analysis focuses on how the Philippines is socially constructed by the dominant representatives in the arena of producer-based care networks, and how this serves as a basis for structural inequality in terms of underlying gendered and racialised assumptions and expectations of the Filipino nurse as a worker. The next section looks at the ongoing practices of teaching and requiring Finnish language among the recruited nurses. These practices are textually informed through the trio of Finnish private companies. The analytical approach to these practices is framed with Acker's approach to the practices of managed work as (re)producing inequality regimes. This section tries to highlight how the Finnish-language use and its requirement for work in Finland serves as a legitimate, institutionalised control of the nurses and their work as well as an internalised compliance amongst the recruited and non-Finnish nurses. The third section examines the positions on selecting and recruiting a Filipino registered nurse to work as a practical nurse in Finland, and how these practices are legitimised through the discursive positions on ethical recruitment.

In the discussion, I consider compliance amongst Filipino nurses as a result of these discursive positions and the subsequent ongoing practices and material implications in terms of structural inequality barriers that are transnationally gendered and racialised but also not limited solely to the domestic workplace.

The Philippines as a Source for Nurse Human Capital and the Warm, Optimistic Filipino Nurse

The Philippines is constructed by the representatives of the trio of Finnish private companies as a source for human capital, whereas the Filipino nurse is constructed as an ideal worker to care for Finnish elderly patients through attributes of optimism and warmth. This construction is discursively produced in the talk of the representatives and text of the organisations by comparing Finnish nurses and Finland to Filipino nurses and the Philippines. These discursive constructions, subsequently, inform the practices of how the Filipino nurses should be recruited and placed by the trio of Finnish private companies who dominate the arena of producer-based care networks.

In October 2008, after the first group of recruited Filipino nurses arrived, the CEO of the private elderly care facility presented an action strategy to deal with the labour shortage in the Finnish welfare system at a Nordic Council conference entitled 'Multiculturalism in Health Care'. The CEO legitimised this 'need for action' because of demographic changes in Finland (e.g. population is ageing) and changes in the labour market. The CEO presented the claims in a power point slide where it was written that practical nurse work is heavy and an undesirable profession for Finnish young people.

The representatives' discursive construction of practical nurse work with elderly patients as 'hard' or 'heavy' was illustrated through culturally specific proverbs and metaphors. Representatives from the Finnish private recruitment company used a Tagalog proverb at various times in the data, which was 'walang matiga na tinapay sa mainit na kape' and was translated by the representatives as 'no bread is too hard for warm coffee'. For instance, in interview #3, the representative from the private recruitment company says

> But, the Philippines for us is, I suppose, in some ways, like it is a natural, I don't want to use the word resource—it sounds terrible—but, for us, we would go to the Philippines because one, the training is good there. We know that we are not going to have to search too hard for the nurses there and they are-they have this ability to sell in other countries very quickly, just like the saying that you would be aware of, that Tagalog saying 'there is no bread too hard for warm coffee'. And, that is a wonderful saying from the Filipino point of view that they will go anywhere. Just treat them right, look after them, and they will pay you back tenfold.

This proverbial reference is made in a published text written by the representative quote here and also in a report by the recruitment company's Finnish teacher and coordinator of the language in the Philippines (Huijser, and Huijser, 2011: 82; Asa and Muurinen, 2010: 96). This proverb is associated with adjectives such as optimistic and warm to describe nurses from the Philippines. This discursively captures the Filipino culture and the Filipino nurse as warm coffee that can moisten hard bread or hard work. These attributes and the institutionalised educational training of the Filipino nurse become a natural human resource to be recruited externally.

The Philippines as a source for nurse human capital is constructed in the Finnish recruitment company's representatives through the nurses' cultural attributes, nursing qualifications and English-level proficiency in the Philippines, as well as the institutionalised educational system that is derived from the United States and is set up to export nurses abroad. The following reflections from a representative from a recruitment company (interview #1b) are responses to my question 'why was the Philippines chosen as a country to recruit nurses?':

> There are many things that speak for the Philippines. They value education and the quality of nursing education is good. It was basically planned by the Americans, so it is no wonder that there are so many Filipino nurses in the United States. So the quality of the degree and of course the culturally bound politeness and, when we think of the elderly

> people here [Finland], they [Filipinos] have a natural respect for the elderly which we could learn from actually. And, also, that they speak English and they have studied in English. Even though not everybody speaks as well as earlier because the schooling language can also be the local language in the primary schools and the secondary, I believe. But, the nursing schooling is in English. So, that makes it easier. We have, in a way, a common language then in Finland so we don't need interpreters which is, actually, you couldn't have as a doctor or a nurse within health care or even within elderly care as a practical nurse, you can't have an interpreter with you all the time. And, most Finns speak English somehow. At least. So, it is easier to communicate and make sure that the recruited one and the employer understand one another.

Another representative from the Finnish recruitment company echoes these points (interview #3):

> Philippines has placed a lot of value in the training and development of nurses. I mean there are a lot of nurses in the Philippines. So, they had more nurses that they can ever hope for to look after their own, if you like, national and domestic requirements. And, the Philippines is a country that relies heavily on exporting their skills and talents, so they're big earners, probably the major earner for the Philippines. But, why do we do that from a nursing point of view? They get good training, they speak English, which is—which irrespective of coming here—I think the Philippines in general has a good international record. All of the nurses that come here, have had previous international experience, so we know that they are not coming raw, they haven't been anywhere else. And, a lot of have been to countries where they don't get treated very well, but we won't go any further down that line. But, here they do. And, when I speak to them, I meet them in the supermarkets, Tricia, and they always got a smile on their face and they are very happy, and I just talk to them, and I think that they are surprised at the way that they are treated here and been received here which is nice.

In the discourses of the representatives, Finland, as a country and a culture, is depicted as 'better' than other destination countries for Filipino nurses in terms of treatment and reception of the recruited nurses. 'Here', or Finland, entails work practices of commonality (e.g. English language and US-American model of patient care and medicine), but also fair work practices where the non-Finnish nurse is treated the same as the Finnish nurse by law. This fair treatment is reflected in the smile and happiness of the recruited Filipino nurse going about daily life in the supermarket.

In an interview with a representative whose organisation works on behalf of Finnish private business employers,[1] the representative compares Finland to Saudia Arabia as a better country. The representative states that 'I think for them [Filipino nurses], it is better to work in Finland than some Arab country' (interview #16). This argument is also illustrated in the Finnish recruitment company's HR magazine's, *Optimist*, interview with a recruited Filipino nurse, Ruby. Ruby is said to have reflected on her experience in Saudia Arabia as being culturally different from Finland and Finland not being such an extreme adjustment to daily work and life routine. Because of her experiences in Saudia Arabia, she is not nervous about the move (2008a: 8).

The Finnish recruitment company selected registered nurses from the Philippines to work as practical nurses in Finland because the organisation's client, the private elderly care company, requested particular human resources. A representative from the private Finnish education centre recalls this objective of the two organisations, and reiterates in the talk that the Philippines is chosen because of the country's history of exporting nurses and what is termed a 'culture' that cares for elderly people and family (interview #10a):

> [The private recruitment company] had the customer [private elderly care company] and they talked together and [the private elderly care company] had needs about the new practical nurses and they decided how it is possible to get people from other countries. And, after quite long research, they decided the country should be the Philippines because they had long time experience about exporting the nurses out to say Canada, everywhere. And, that is why. And, the culture. It is really nice. Especially, the nurses. Because they love people. They understand that the elderly are very important. They are keen about other people's feelings and they love the family. And, that is the point. Then they can understand easier when they come here. They have really tight groups and they live together when they get here and they support each other.

When the nurses arrived in Helsinki, they lived together as the private elderly care company rented the flat for groups of nurses (the male nurses lived together and the female nurses lived together). The rent was paid by the nurses to the private elderly care company and all the furniture was also provided by the private elderly care company (source: interview #11). These practical aspects of the recruitment and placement are reminiscent of Choy's (2003) historical account of Filipino nurse migration to the United States in the 1950s and 1960s in which they were placed together in residences near the hospital or their workplaces. The nurses' lives become managed both in the workplace but also privately, at least during the initial six months of their apprenticeship in Finland. The Filipino nurses are constructed in terms of a group, segregated by sex, which is accommodated because of commonalities in culture but also experience with the Finnish organisation.

The construction of the nurses viewing nursing as a calling or vocation rather than a career is illustrated in *Optimist*'s story of Francis who is quoted as saying '[W]hen I started as a nurse, I didn't think about money or moving abroad. This is my calling' (2008a: 9). The calling to the nurse profession has been written about by various scholars as highly gendered through emphasis on the feminine characteristics predominately of women and Asia men, such as caring and warm (see Wrede, 2010: 11; Webster, 1998).

In *Optimist*, the recruited Filipino nurse and the producers are contrasted both within the written and visual text. For instance, in issue #3, the nurses, through their 'stories' are described as hard working, versatile, international, experienced, family oriented, and viewing the nursing occupation as a calling rather than an occupation. The producers, on the other hand, are constructed in terms of 'pioneers', 'action-oriented', 'visionary', 'ethical', and 'bold'. As written by the CEO of Finnish recruitment company in the companies HR magazine *Optimist*:

> [The Finnish recruitment company]'s nurses are an example of a solution looking into the future. The Philippines are struggling with a population explosion, and the country will have skilled workers for all sectors for decades to go. . . . Such a bold way of working will make Finland a model country that can set an example of other European countries.
>
> (2008b: 5)

Figure 7.1 *Optimist*'s covers for issue #3 and issue #4 (2008a, 2008b)

These contrasting constructions of the recruited Filipino nurses and representatives of the recruitment company can be viewed visually with the choice of pictures on the cover of *Optimist* to represent the different groups. The titles are also telling. For the nurses, the titles are 'International workforce and a versatile working community' and 'New heroes of work: Philippinean practical nurses arriving in Finland'. For the representatives of Finnish recruitment company, the title is 'Headed to the Future'. One issue is constructing the Filipino practical nurse workforce; the other is constructing the producers of the future workforce.

The practice of recruitment is foundational to constructing the nurses in terms of their nationality, culture, or ethnicity before they reach Finland. The constructions of the recruited nurses serve to direct the nurses into particular jobs that reconstruct the workforce of practical nurses. The work is constructed as hard and undesirable by local Finns, but instead of restructuring the domestic practices of organising work, the Filipino nurses are constructed and produced by the recruiters to serve the desired workforce or what the Finnish recruitment company calls 'the new heroes of work'.

Using Acker's framework of structural inequality barriers to organisations, the trio of Finnish companies' discursive constructions of the Philippines and the recruited Filipino nurses serve to entrench racial differences between the recruited nurses and the Finnish nurses. This entrenchment of racial differences legitimises hard work or the work not done by the domestic Finnish nurses to be done by the recruited Filipino nurse.

Standardised Work Requirements of Filipino Nurses and the Use of Finnish Language in the Workplace

The use of Finnish language is the most pronounced discursive position in the producer-based care network arena in Finland. Each representative spoke about the use of Finnish language, and in the documents, the practice of recruitment and placement of the nurses are framed in terms of learning the Finnish language. Within the Nordic Council conference (NIVA) presentations of the Finnish companies, the theme of multiculturalism in the workplace centralises around the topic of learning Finnish. In the Finnish recruitment companies HR magazines, the Finnish-language training and models of training the recruited Filipino nurses was central to the issues' themes; and, in each of the 27 interviews conducted for this study, all the actors talk about Finnish-language use. The focal points are on language competence tests, the recruited nurses working in Finnish, and patients receiving care and Finnish nurses working with non-Finnish nurses. The dominant discursive position by the representatives on the use of Finnish language is that the nurses should speak and work at a professional, competent level.

The dominant discursive position on work requirements and the use of the Finnish language systematically, either intentionally or not, creates a high degree of internal segregation in the Finnish nurse occupation for the recruited Filipino nurses. Using Acker's analytical approach to how inequalities in work organisations are produced, the later analysis examines how textually informed practices socially construct differences based on ethnicity, class, and linguistic abilities that maintains systematic disparities between actors in control and implicated actors in compliance. The practices suggested by Acker that I focus on here in terms of Finnish language are (1) organising the general requirements of work, (2) organising class hierarchies, (3) recruitment and hiring, (4) wage setting and supervisory practices, and (5) informal interactions while 'doing the work'.

Organising the General Requirements

The recruited nurses are hired and placed by the Finnish recruitment company based on the customers' needs as well as the regulatory system in Finland for skill regulation. In this situation, this organisation is Valvira. All of the recruited five groups of nurses (with the exception of the third group hired for hospital surgical wards) are hired as practical nurses. The representative from the private Finnish education adult centre reflects that being hired as a practical nurse and not a registered nurse came as a surprise to the Filipino nurses. The surprised reaction became a question about ethics (interview #10b):

INTERVIEW #10b: When we began, it was some kind of ethical question, issue, in Finland. This workplace immigration, this whole thing, it was new. We have to be a little bit careful with and how we train and act. So, everything was like that.

INTERVIEWER: What concerns of ethics did you have?

INTERVIEW #10b: Well, the nurses were already nurses [registered] when they came to Finland and we agreed to [be] practical nurses which is a different profession than a registered nurse. And, there was a little bit of a problem first because a lot of the Philippine nurses, they didn't know, they didn't knew that, they hadn't understand, they hadn't understood that when they came here.

The other representative from the private Finnish education adult centre believes that the surprise about being hired not as a registered nurse but as a practical nurse is because of the Filipino culture, which does not institutionalise elderly care but relies on the family to care for the elderly (interview #10a):

> It is the different culture. They don't, there [the Philippines] they take care of their older people at homes. In Finland, this is very uncommon

at present and we have places where the old people, maybe you know the system, how it works in Finland? It is so big culture difference. We have to learn them [teach them to] understand the system first. Because they are trained for the nurse. They understand that it is care. It is health care. It is not like different type of care. It is like caring for old people in Finland. We help people to do something. It is not only giving medicine . . . it is basic care.

The nurses, although experienced and qualified, are required to requalify themselves to become a certified practical nurse (LPN) in accordance to Finnish regulation and standards. This requires the recruited Filipino nurses to take 120 study credits with the Finnish adult education centre, which takes approximately two years to complete. The time is shortened if the credits are taken parallel to an apprenticeship. In the case of the Filipino nurses, the apprenticeship is six months in the customer's organisation. It is believed that the Filipino nurses worked hard in comparison to other recruited nurses. In the case of Finnish recruitment company, four Chinese nurses were also recruited but did not graduate with the Filipino nurses who started at the same time. The reason for the Chinese nurses not graduating is thought to be because there is no common language between the nurses and the trainer, but also difference in culture. The Filipino nurses are considered hard working but also clever (interviews #10a and #10b):

a: What we have noticed with the training period, with the three groups [recruited Filipino nurses]. We now have four people from China, and it is always different culture and now we understand better that the people that come here start to train as practical nurses. We know that they are already nurse[s]. They must have very good English language or something because we have to start the training in English. That is the language we can both use. More or less. And, little by little, they have to learn Finnish because the customer, the elderly really need Finnish. Some don't speak at all English. Some don't speak Swedish, some speak only Finnish, and that is a little bit of a complication. Depends on the place because what type of people living in the homes [elderly homes]. Some speak [Finnish elderly] very good English, and that is a problem because they start to speak English with the Filipino nurse. And, it means when the elderly speak English, the nurses don't learn at all Finnish.

b: But, the Filipino nurses, they have learned very quickly.

a: Very quickly. They [Filipino nurses] are very clever!

b: But, they worked very hard. We gave them extra, language studies because these language studies which we planned, it wasn't enough. So they studied here in the evening, and we gave them extra studies all the time and support to the workplace to learn them [to teach them] these professional sentences [in Finnish language].

At the same time as the apprenticeship, the nurses are expected to take Finnish lessons and work in Finnish with the elderly patients, although the recruitment and initial training is in English. When the nurses complete their studies, they are expected to continue with Finnish language (representative from the Finnish recruitment company [interview #1b]):

> So basically once they are here and they have accomplished their studies and are ready to work, they still need, all these people, they still need Finnish lessons. So, at that point, at least, I believe, the foreigners can get something.

The organisation of general requirements, which, in this case, are Finnish language as well as Finnish practical nurse qualifications, are institutionalised and enforced practices that exclude nurses that do not meet specific competencies textually set by the trio of private Finnish companies. If the non-Finnish nurse aspires to progress in his or her career or increase his or her wage or schedule his or her hours, for instance, the structure of his or her work and life pattern is subjected to the institutional structures and practices of the Finnish domestic model. The idea of transnational living or non-Finnish worker's rights and needs become barriers to equality in the workplace.

Furthermore, the general requirements requested by the client become a search for nurses who are trained in an institutionalised system that separates elderly care to the home and the responsibility of the family. The conversation in the talk begins to revolve around searching for a culture that is conducive to caring for the elderly as family and not patients and a work ethic of committing to the clients' needs by working as an apprenticeship and studying after working hours. In Finland (or outside of the Philippines), these practices and expectations of the nurses deskill the recruited nurse from a professionally registered nurse to a family-oriented, hard-working, Finnish-speaking practical nurse outside the private home.

Class Hierarchies

The dominant discursive position on language creates structural class hierarchies within the nurse occupation in Finland. If the recruited Filipino nurses are not systematically evaluated as competent in Finnish language use, the recruited nurses cannot aspire to work as qualified registered nurses in Finland as regulated by Valvira. The recruited nurses, however, are hired on the basis of being a qualified registered nurse with experience in the Philippines, so to work as practical nurses in Finland is to be deskilled in the profession.

A representative from the Finnish recruitment company indicates that the recruited nurses have complained about not working as a registered nurse, but once the nurses realise their limitations in Finnish language, they comply with working as a practical nurse (interview #1b):

> They [Filipino nurses] experienced or some of them experienced that well . . . ummm . . . this is something I know I can't, I work as a registered nurse. But, then of course, as soon as they, in practice, they realise—I remember an occasion where a nurse went to a doctor with a client and found it extremely difficult [to communicate in Finnish]. And, after that, he said 'well, now I see why I can't work as a registered nurse yet'.

Working as a recruited Filipino nurse, the organisations pay basic salary. As an apprentice while requalifying and studying Finnish language, recruited nurses do not receive a full salary as a practical nurse; it is 5% less than the average salary. When the recruited nurses are qualified then, by law, the nurses receive 1 700 euros/month. This is legitimised as the same as other Finnish practical nurses, but creates a hierarchy of registered nurses receiving a practical nurse salary because they are educated in the Philippines not Finland and cannot speak fluently the local language of the workplace. Therefore, the salaries between the Finnish nurses and the Filipino nurse are not equivalent.

Recruitment and Hiring

The practice of recruitment and hiring, according to Acker, is about finding the most suitable worker for the particular position. From the start, the Finnish recruitment company researched a country for the nurses requested by the Finnish elderly care company. These nurses would be recognised as practical nurses, work in Finnish, and be required to requalify themselves during a period of apprenticeship that would require lower pay and set hours by the client. In addition, the working visa is applied for by the recruited nurses but, as in legal Finnish practice, the nurses would require a contract with a Finnish employer (in this case, the Finnish elderly care company). In addition, the recruited nurses would come without their families, as set out by Finnish immigration regulation, but these families could be brought at a later date if the recruited nurses continue on a fixed employment contract for two years until a permanent contract is granted. The permanent contract gives the nurses 'A' status in Finland, which allows the nurse to apply for family ties.

Wage Setting and Supervisory Practices

In interviews with Filipino nurses who are educated as registered nurses in Finland and have lived in Finland for over ten years, the nurses speak about 'not being seen' by those in management because of their limits in the Finnish language. The use of the Finnish language becomes not only about being seen but complying with this limitation even though it is viewed as unfair (interview #4a).

INTERVIEWEE #4a: But, I think that is the biggest obstacle, that is the biggest problem for a foreigner. For a foreign nurse to progress here in Finland. Because with our degree, bachelor of science degree, we could be a ward manager already because that is the only requirement, you know. To be a bachelor of science degree in nursing then you could progress to management already. But, we couldn't do that, we couldn't do that, we couldn't even be what they call specialised nurse because of the Finnish language. Because, what will happen is even if you know that you can be a specialised nurse, like an expert, you can have that title like an expert nurse. . .

INTERVIEWER: Like a specialised nurse?

INTERVIEWEE #4a: Yeah, specialised nurse. You know that you can do that, but then you yourself have doubts. Can I, do I have the confidence to do it, whenever there will come a problem or papers to fill in, all in Finnish for you to do this and do that. Can I manage it? And, if I can manage to understand, can I manage to convey to my co-workers or to my subordinates. So that is the most difficult, that is the reason why I think the foreign nurses don't progress here because of that. And, I find that, although the management say that they are hiring foreigners because they are not racist, but somehow, if you will notice it, they might not show it that they are racist . . . like show it . . . like superficially that they are racist. But, there are the hidden racism, you know. Because they could, even though you are capable, they might give you a little bit of leave, like ok, you can do this, we can trust you to do this, but they wouldn't trust you to be an assistant ward manager, for example. They won't trust you to be, probably they would trust you to be a specialised nurse if you had enough Finnish but seldom. For all the 10 years that I have been a nurse in the city of Espoo, I have only seen one foreign nurse who is a specialised nurse that is an African. She can speak very well Finnish. Very well.

INTERVIEWER: So, just to get this point right. You think that the reason why foreigners are not progressing is because of the limits placed upon themselves because of the Finnish language?

INTERVIEWEE #4a: From the employer. You cannot progress. You do the jobs, in my opinion, you do the jobs that their people doesn't want to do. How many young Finnish nurses want to be in a long-term ward or in a nursing home? Few. Very few. Most of the Finnish young nurses who graduated go to the hospitals. If you go to the hospitals, you could find that most of them are Finnish, the young ones. They don't have in the hospitals now foreign nurses, no. You probably heard that they

> are hiring in [HUS (Helsinki Hospital)], in the operating room, these foreigners, but it is in the operating room! Do you speak Finnish in the Operating room? In the post operating room, everybody is sleeping! So if you could just manage a few basic Finnish (speaks basic Finnish . . . mitä kuulu). And so! it is nothing!

Another Filipino nurse educated and living/working in Finland as a practical nurse (interview #4b):

> They don't actually like really trust, 100% trust us because maybe because of the language

This comment is followed with the first nurse saying (interviewee #4a):

> They don't really see us, they don't really see that we are capable to do what the Finns can do. Sometimes, you see, you might think that it could be also culture. They might think that maybe the culture is different because they do things differently then we, for example, Asians do things. Sometimes when we do things in an Asian way, they don't agree, you know. So, they will say, ah that is because we have different culture, and you probably don't understand. And that is the most common explanation

This supervisory practice of limiting the Filipino nurses because of the Finnish language is also expressed by a recruited nurse who views the language as a barrier to career progression, but the recruited nurse views it as temporary circumstances while being trained in the language (interview #11a).

> And, for me also, it is very unfair for us that the other batch [the third group of Filipino nurses recruited for a hospital] because they got [recruited] from the Philippines and hired as to be a nurse here [a registered nurse in Finland]. It is also, how can I express, very unfair for us because we also have the same degree that we got from the Philippines, and how got the other group as a nurse here? Very unfair. They also gave us the option that they can give us, that they will give a chance that we can study to be a nurse here and the same salary as we got right now [referring to study and working solely as a practical nurse]. But, for this moment, maybe it is a bargaining. That I am satisfied in my job right now because of the language barrier is very difficult and it is very risky for us [Filipino nurses].

This last comment sparks agreement in the interview, which consists of two other recruited nurses in the same group who are also working as practical nurses.

In addition, when asked by the interviewer why the recruited nurses decided to come to Finland and if they were aware of the deskilling of their degrees and work experience, most of the recruited nurses state that they wanted to work abroad for the salary. This is one of the main motivations, but nursing, to those recruited, is constructed as registered nursing rather than basic care provided by practical nurses in Finland (interview #11a).

> In the Philippines, I don't think of practical nurse because you always think of the salary. For that, I am not so aware of practical nurse. I think it [being hired] as a practical nurse by [the Finnish recruitment company and the Finnish elderly care company] because I am a registered nurse in the Philippines. I cannot do a broad scope in my professions. Like getting blood, I.V. I can give medications [in the Philippines]. There is no need for that [in Finland] because also the Finnish barrier, the Finnish language barrier. You cannot do anything. You cannot do everything. For now, maybe it is ok if I am practical because of the language; I cannot do as a full nurse because of the language.

The discursive positions of the employers and employed nurses contrast in the discourses on Finnish language use. For representatives employing the Filipino nurses such as the Finnish recruitment company and the Finnish elderly care company, Finnish-language use can be resolved through hard work, requalifying through language and nursing courses with the Finnish adult education centre and taking competency tests through Valvira. For the Filipino nurses, the dominant discursive position on Finnish requirements is impeding their careers chances and segregating them in the workplace amongst their Finnish colleagues.

Informal Interactions While 'Doing Work'

The informal interactions while 'doing work' are pronounced in the talk within the interviews with both the recruited Filipino nurses and migrant nurses originally from the Philippines who obtained a bachelor's in nursing from a Finnish institution and have been working in Finland for over ten years. Informal interactions while doing work, as discursive positions, are captured in the talk of those doing the work. However, the dominating discursive positions of the authoritative representatives, such as the trio of Finnish companies, structure social relations shaped by the organisations' discursive social constructions of the recruited Filipino nurses.

Informal interactions in daily work routines and practices are shaped by gender-, race-, and class-based assumptions (Acker, 2006), and behaviours and expectations amongst the nurses become commonplace or taken for granted. For all the non-Finnish nurses, at the workplace, there is a period of time at the beginning of the job that the nurses do not have the skills or confidence to work in Finnish. They find themselves in situations where they cannot read important 'black and white' documents about the practices in their work or their rights in the workplace. Also, hesitation arises when doing assigned tasks such as answering the telephone in Finnish or asking a colleague for help. Sometimes the nurses find agency and speak in English to clarify their positions and duties, but as one Filipino nurse asserts, limits in communication are compensated by working harder than the Finnish nurses and not making any mistakes. The nurses take on extra work or jobs that their Finnish colleagues do not want as a way to hide discomfort and/or the feelings of inadequacy.

Here is interview #4a, b, and c (a group interview of three non-recruited Filipino nurses who work in a Finnish private elderly care institution). It is an excerpt from of a conversation between three non-recruited Filipino nurses. In the conversation, the nurses discuss the use of Finnish language in the workplace and their Finnish colleagues' interactions during daily work practices.

b: The good side is that they [Finnish managers] appreciate if you are a good worker, they appreciate it, and they will make a feedback about you.
c: Yeah, they forget the language. The language is not the matter anymore. It is how you work, your skill, your knowledge.
a: They can tolerate
c: But the good thing also, I have not made any mistakes at all since I have started, until now. I didn't get any mistake at all in my job including medications and everything, and communication with the doctor. I understood because I am also brave enough to ask the doctor in English if I don't understand. But, my co-workers, they allow me to have a dictionary there, and now, they are also familiarised with the different kinds of foreigners who are working. So, they are now helping the foreign nurses

INTERVIEWER: And, do you find that you work harder than your Finnish colleagues, for instance, or co-workers?

All nurses agree forcefully that the answer is 'yes!'

a: Definitely.
b: I have plenty of experience with that.
a: And, sometimes, you can even feel that they are taking advantage of you.
c: Yeah, that is the negative. There is also a negative side on that matter not only a positive side because even to answering the phone. You are a nurse and they will ask you to answer the phone even though they speak better Finnish then you. But, since you are a nurse, it is your responsibility to answer the phone. So, that is another negative, and if they. . .
b: But it is really like that. Because you are the one responsible for the work
c: But then again, just to pick up the phone . . . or they can give it to you afterwards if they need a nurse or they are just going to ask something. If

they are just going to ask something, do you still need a nurse to answer the phone? And that, and also if they see that you are like easy to be. . .

b: Bullied.

c: Yeah! Like, oh you can do that or ok, I can do that. Because as a Filipino we are like that . . . as long as we can do that, we don't need to ask from our colleagues. We can do that.

b: We don't need initiative.

c: We don't need to give it to another co-worker although we can do that already, so we don't need to pass it on. But, then, as long as they have learned that you are like that, they are not moving anymore. It is all yours.

a: Or sometimes they can do so that, ok, they can leave some work, they knew that you are coming in the afternoon, they are working in the morning, and you should be coming in the afternoon. 'ok, i leave this because so and so is coming in the afternoon, anyway, she will do it'. Just like her (pointing to B), she always do that because in our nursing home we have this 'sauna day' so then nobody in her department do Sauna, except her!

b: It is our responsibility! Because at least two times a week, they should go to sauna. That is like one of their activities that they really love, Finnish people, you know. So, and my co-workers doesn't like, they don't think about it at all. They are like somehow ah she has done this, so maybe she can do it for her.

a: Whereas, in my department, in my ward, I don't allow them to do that because sometimes, they will tell me that 'ok, so and so have to go to sauna' (response) 'well, you can bring her to sauna if you want!'

The nurses then discuss how, as time passes and they become more aware and confident of their positions at the workplace, the Finnish nurses continue to expect the non-Finnish nurses to do work that is not their responsibility or assigned during their work shifts. The workplace dynamics shift and create resistance but also compliance amongst the non-Finnish nurses as they do not want to be troublesome or unfair to the elderly patients. The dynamics at this point seem to socially construct a hierarchy amongst the Finnish and non-Finnish nurses, although the language is no longer seen as a barrier.

c: You know at first, I was like that if they give me a job, I am just doing that responsibility. That was the first because I don't complain, I don't understand, I don't know how to complain, but then again when I knew that this was my responsibilities, I give the limit also that now, you cannot do that anymore with me because now I understand everything and because at first, they were just, you know, telling you everything, you do this, you do that. I cannot complain anymore. Of course, I don't have any choice I just have to do the job. But, then again, when I have more

Finnish words, then I could already explain, I could already say no, I know my limits, so that I could explain. And, they knew that.

b: Actually, for me, it is really difficult to say 'no'. If it is not done, I feel so stressed if it is not done. So, if they don't do it, I will do it. I don't know, is it my personality, maybe, that I feel stressed when the work is not done.

a: But, then, it is true what she says that when you know more about the Finnish language, then you know more your rights because you can read it, you know. Because they have all the papers. The Finns love papers, you see. They put everything, the rules and regulations on paper. In black and white. And, so, when you can read it, and you can understand your rights, then you can fight for your rights. If you just want to fight it but sometimes, it is so troublesome because then you will destroy the working environment because if you insist on your right, you can do so because you have the right to insist because it is in the paper but then you are destroying your relationship with your co-workers then in that way, you are destroying your working environment also. So, then you have to think twice before you . . . if you want to have a fight with them.

c: But, if you want to have a good relationship with them, with your colleagues, on that matter, it is with the schedules also, you know our work schedules are prepare already, one month in advance, 6 weeks ahead, yeah, so my co-workers, they are ok to change the shift with me, but if I am the one that needs to change the shift with them, it is too difficult . . . but on my side, just to have a good relationship with them it is also a part of me that if it is ok, i have nothing to do then, you can . . . but then once you need that it is too difficult to ask from them like can I change my schedule with you so somehow.

The recruited nurses also speak about being recruited as practical nurses and treated differently than their Finnish colleagues. They believe they work harder and receive a salary as Finnish students who are entitled to social benefits from the state (interview #11):

a: Maybe today, I am happy with my salary but I am not happy with my profession because it is not growing. There is no knowledge.

c: There is no challenge.

a: There is no challenge. Because I want more challenge with my imagination, I want to rescue with a helicopter. Like that. (laughs). I want more challenges even though I don't have that good communications. But, maybe I can show my skills, that I can do my own best. I want more challenge to care. Intensive care unit. But, here, I am satisfied with my boss and my colleagues. Finnish people are very nice, calm, supportive, they are not aggressive. But me, it is my professions, not more challenge. It is like some days I am very bored. It is always very routine. Assisting the patient to the toilet. Baking a cake. Giving food to the patient,

> it is like that. And, my five years of experience in the Philippines, half of that is wasted. Because if a patient is having like a heart attack, you don't know the history because it is in Finnish. For my experience and my knowledge, you should know the history of the patient because how can you care. The language is also the barrier. And, the first month in Finland, it is very difficult in me because every day we work in practical nurse, and every Wednesday we go to school and the salary is not good. It is almost 700 euros as a student. But, we were more than a full practical nurse. We overtime like the other [full-time nurses]. But, when we compare some student here, it is different. They are more pampered, but unlike us Filipinos, we receive only that salary.

The discursive positions of the dominant representatives in the transnational human resource management of Filipino nurses in Finland materialise in the actual 'doing of work' of the Filipino nurses, either recruited or not. Preassigned roles are constructed amongst the Finnish colleagues as to who does the heavy work, works undesired shifts, and receives a lower salary.

Discursive Positions on Ethical Recruitment

Within the interviews with the representatives as well as the text of the documents collected, there is a recurring debate on the ethics behind recruiting registered nurses from the Philippines to work as practical nurses in Finland.

According to the text and talk from the Finnish recruitment company, the organisation's recruitment practices are ethical as there are no placement fees, there is cooperation with local authorities, provision of language skills prior and after arrival, adequate information prior to arrival (e.g. expected income, cost of living, working environment, employment legislation), and accommodation with furniture arranged (interviews #1a and #1b).

Discursively, ethical recruitment by Finnish actors is constructed through practices of no placement fees and treating the Filipino nurses equally to Finnish nurses by providing employment contracts as well as the possibility of the nurses bringing their families to Finland. The Finnish practices are considered a model by abiding by both national and transnational rules. In practice, by abiding by bureaucratic rules, the Finnish recruitment company and the Finnish elderly care company work with other social worlds in the producer-based care network such as the national Finnish police and security (e.g. Ministry of Interior and the police issuing work visas) and the regulation and advisory world of Finnish national health and social welfare (e.g. Valvira). In order to recruit transnationally, the two companies must comply with the Finnish national regulations as well as Filipino national laws even though it is discursively constructed as a model of ethical recruitment and benevolence.

Discursively constructing the practices of the dominant organisations of the three Finnish companies as 'ethical recruitment' masks the practices of systematically deskilling the Filipino nurses in the recruitment process to Finland. The nurses do not have to pay placement fees or the logistics for their migration from the Philippines to Helsinki, but once in Finland, their skills as a registered nurse in practice are not recognised. The nurses are hired as practical nurses and work as practical nurses unless the nurses requalify themselves. This ongoing practice is contested by other representatives in the producer-based care network. As stated by a representative from SuPer, the practical nurse union (interview #6),

INTERVIEW #6: But, I know that some of the Filipino nurses, they are here working as practical nurses which is not equivalent to their training in the Philippines.

INTERVIEWER: Because they have been trained as registered nurses.

INTERVIEW #6: And, that is why we don't find it ethical. We think it would be ethical if a nurse would be employed as a nurse and a doctor would be employed as a doctor. Not a cleaner. That is our aim. That is also our common aim with the PSI [Public Services International] which is—we have, it is not a union, but a collaboration with nine public sector trade unions. We have made our own ethical rules that we want to encourage. So, this is one of the main points that we have been discussing with the recruitment agencies that if they bring someone/somebody, we want it to be ethical. And, it means that a nurse should be working here as a nurse. And, what has happened is that they don't always do it like that but they do something else.

In an interview with the registered nurse union, TeHy, the representative discusses how the term 'ethical recruitment' became part of the dialogue in the media as well as among recruitment agency because of the work done by TeHy to make the topic relevant in Finland. She notes that recruitment agencies work with TeHy and other unions because of the concern that the union will create problems for them. She also advocates against the recruitment companies asking for placement fees as it is against Finnish law and the unions reinforce this practice (interview #5):

INTERVIEW #5: What we are trying to do, the trade unions in Finland, we brought this term ethical recruitment to Finland. Nobody talked about it like a couple of years ago. But, we organised several seminars and we organised press conferences and so on about ethical recruitment and it has been, there has been a lot of discussion about that in the media. So these recruitment companies, they noticed it and now many of them tell in their webpages, you know, we have this ethical processes and ethical recruitment things, and they want to come and tell us that they work in an ethical way.

INTERVIEWER: Right

INTERVIEW #5: Yeah, so I think in that sense we have done a good job because people realise that there can be problems and these recruitment companies, they want to prevent the situation that when problems arise, you

> know, they are going to get difficulties with the trade unions, so they want to work with us. And, that why we were being in touch with them.

Within the interviews with the recruited Filipino nurses (interviews #11a, b, c, #12 and #13), the common argument surrounding the reason to come to Finland is not based on placement fees, but rather a desire for a larger salary and to go abroad. In all of the interviews with the recruited Filipino nurses, the nurses recall that they have applied to various countries including Finland, and it was because the Finnish recruitment company called first and interviewed the nurses before other recruitment agencies that the nurses migrated to Finland. According to one recruited nurse (interview #11a),

> My idea in the Philippines is I want to go abroad even if I pay a placement fee, but I want to go abroad. It's like if you go abroad, your future is secure. It is like that. And, the Filipino culture, if you go abroad and work there, you are rich. And, that is the main point because my parents are also, I am thankful for them, they are very supportive. They don't want me to go abroad but if it is my decision, they will support me. I paid 50,000 [pesos] to an agency to go to Canada, but Finland called me first, and I withdrew the 50,000 and paid it back. A whole 50,000, then I come here.

Another recruited nurse in the same interview says that she went to Finland because it was abroad and to go abroad was a dream. The nurse reflects (interview #11b):

> I came here [Finland] for the salary but it is also my dream to go abroad, and we said let's try. Before, we don't know Finland that well; it's like ok that's right, once we are here.

Another recruited nurse states that she stopped working as a nurse in the Philippines to study for entrance exams in order to be recruited to the United States. Because she was still waiting for an American social security, she decided to have an interview with the Finnish recruitment company at the same place she was taking Finnish classes. She recalls (interview #11c),

> And between these times, I took some Finnish language lessons, and on that place where I took that language lessons, I didn't know that there is also this recruitment agency. And, since they were reviewing the files of the students doing the lessons, so I was, I think, somebody asked me if I like to come to Finland and work. And, since I know it is taking a long time for the US to do the social security, although I do have the exams passed already, so I say why not.

When I asked the nurse why she decided to take the Finnish lessons in the first place, she explains (interview #12),

> Just because they were available. It was my sister, she has some friends who were taking the Finnish language test. I mean, for Finnish, they were already having a test. She was saying would you like to go there because you are not doing anything and I said why not.

The contested discursive positions in the producer-based care networks in Helsinki create structured exclusions in the Finnish nurse workforce through the evaluation of the Filipino nurses' qualification and competence in accordance to Finnish institutionalised rules. These processes are being constructed as ethical as the Finnish recruitment company is abiding by national and transnational rules. However, how the registered nurses are constructed in the Philippines differs from the construction of the Finnish recruiter and employers. And as argued by Davies in the 1990s about the gendered structuring of the nurse profession that makes it impossible for female nurses to demonstrate and enhance the value of their work, the practice of recruiting overly qualified registered nurses for practical nursing positions in Finland not only devalues the recruited nurse's skills but also creates a workforce that is disposable, transient, and ethnicised.

Furthermore, the focus on ethical recruitment, whether or not the Finnish recruitment company is practicing this with the Filipino nurses, legitimises the inequalities between the Filipino recruited nurse and the Finnish nurse by arguing that there are no placement fees and the recruited nurses are treated the same as Finnish nurses. The Finnish recruitment company as well as other dominant representatives in the producer-based care networks do not view themselves in a position of privilege to define the practices and discourses on how the recruited nurses live and work in Finland, and this creates a social construction of the Filipino nurses' skills as less than valuable as the Finnish registered nurse. It also enforces inequality barriers through direct (e.g. bureaucratic rules) and unobtrusive controls (e.g. selecting powerless workers in terms of the Filipino nurses not controlling their own recruitment and placement).

Structural Inequality Barriers Through Transnational Human Resource Practices

In Chapter 6, dominant representatives emerged into the producer-based care networks through authoritative discourses surrounding the practices of recruitment and placement of Filipino nurses.

The dominant discursive positions on the practices of recruitment and placement of the Filipino nurses not only shaped transnational processes but also the institutionalised ways in which the recruited nurses were subsequently managed in the workplace and treated by their Finnish colleagues. Dominant discursive positions structured the daily work lives of the recruited and non-Finnish nurses that reflect not only gendered assumptions of the nursing occupation but also racialised and domestic ideas on how daily life and work was done and managed.

To examine the structural inequalities materialising from the collective discursive positions within the claims of the talk and text, this chapter has framed the discussion on transnational management of nurses in terms of Acker's inequality regimes (2006). Inequality regimes are 'loosely interrelated practices, processes, actions, and meanings that result in and maintain class, gender, racial inequalities in particular organisations' (2006: 443). According to Acker, inequality regimes are sustained through six inequality barriers: (1) bases of inequality, (2) degree and shape of inequality, (3) organising processes, (4) invisibility of inequality, (5) legitimacy of inequality, and (6) control and compliance. To conceptualise inequality regimes and barriers in terms of transnational processes, the analysis focuses not only on subsequent organising practices in the workplace of the recruited and non-recruited Filipino nurses, as Acker does in her work, but also on the claims surrounding the transnational human resources practices taking place in the Philippines and Finland of the 75 Filipino nurses.

The analysis of the structured inequality regimes was grounded in the ordered situational map constructed in Chapter 5 (see Table 5.2), as well as the discussion on the dominant representatives in the producer-based care networks in Chapter 6. Various social elements in the situation were considered, but as the focus is on discursive positions, the major contested issues in the talk and text were central to the analysis in this chapter. Through saturation in the analysis, the collective discursive positions of the representatives emerged in terms of the Philippines as a source country for nurse human capital and the Filipino nurse as the desirable worker, standardised work requirements and the use of Finnish in the workplace, and ethical recruitment.

Discursive positions on the Philippines as an ideal source country of human capital were based on the dominant representatives' collective claims that, in the Philippines, there is an oversupply of trained nurses who speak English and are educated in an US-American model of medicine. The Filipino nurse was selected from this supply because of personalised attributes such as being hard working, well educated and experienced, caring and respectful to the elderly, English speaking, and family/community oriented. Through the naturalisation of these dominant discursive positions, the structural mechanisms of control, such as the Philippines systematically educating nurses with US-Americanised training specifically for export, remained unmentioned. And, the dominant social construction of the Filipino nurses in the claims created a collective discursive position amongst the representatives of which nurses should be selected for recruitment, and the expectations of how the general work requirements of the nurses should be organised once the nurses begin work in the Finnish workplace.

Ongoing transnational practices of recruiting Filipino nurses on the basis of employers' needs and requests manages the Filipino nurses in terms of gendered, classed, and racialised assumptions that produce inequality barriers, both formally and informally, as work processes are carried out, as captured in Acker's inequality regimes. For instance, both recruited and non-recruited Filipino nurses said that they work harder than domestic Finnish nurses, get paid less, and cannot advance in their careers because of their limited Finnish-language abilities and the under recognition of their nursing degrees from the Philippines. They also point out that even as their Finnish abilities improve, their colleagues still demand and expect that the Filipino nurses do the tasks that are not assigned in their job description. Designing ongoing work and managerial practices of the nurse occupation in terms of who speaks Finnish and those who do not speak Finnish 'well enough' not only segregates, in terms of class and race hierarchies (with very material/tangible consequences such as wages and working hours), but also internalises compliance amongst the nurses, both the non-Finns and the Finns. As mentioned by both the recruited Filipino nurses and the producers, the recruited nurses comply with their workplace status and wage because of their limited abilities in Finnish. As one recruited nurse indicates, 'it is like a bargaining' to stay in a lower-status position while improving in Finnish' (interview #11a). The standardised hierarchies becomes taken for granted and the foreign and recruited nurses become deskilled. Subsequently, the workplace as well as the Finnish labour market becomes flexible and compliant to the producers' social construction of the nurses and nurse labour.

In addition, through the discursive positions of ethical recruitment, the low wages and status of the recruited Filipino nurses becomes legitimised as taken for granted, reinforcing racial and class assumptions that the Filipino nurses will comply as they are coming from a country that has high unemployment, an oversupply of nurses, and lower salaries. The discursive positions that no placement fee equates to ethical recruitment masks a hierarchy of nurses but also imposes managerial controls as benevolent before the nurses arrive in Finland. The emphasis on fees also creates a competitive advantage for the Finnish producers as they stand out from other traditional destination countries of migrating workers such as Canada, the United Kingdom, Australia, and the United States, which are countries that do ask for large recruitment placement fees. As mentioned by the recruited Filipino nurses, there is a strong desire amongst Filipino nurses to work abroad and the recruited Filipino nurses interviewed for this book had already applied to the United States and Canada and paid the fees (interviews #11a, b, c, and #12). It was not until the Finnish recruitment company contacted them first that they decided to move to Finland and not another destination. This reveals that placement fees are not a determining factor as to which country the nurses would choose, but rather the chance to go abroad is the alluring factor to migrate.

By focusing on a meso level of structuring inequalities through discursive positions by producers on transnational management broadens the dialogue on global care chains, nurse care chains, and the transnationalisation of care. Hochschild's (2000) concept on global care chains creates links between service-providers and service-recipients, and these global linkages are textured within wider socio-economic inequalities that reinforce hierarchies of nation-states, genders, and ethnic groups. Hochschild's analysis, as well as those of many other scholars who employ this concept empirically, examines the familial level of transnational linkages. For instance, within the global care economy research, Hochschild looks at unpaid domestic work such as nannies. She argues that, through the migration of these service-providers of domestic reproductive care, networks are made between the migrating nannies' families in their home countries and the service-recipient families in the destination countries (usually a Western country). By focusing on these linkages, she reveals the distributive nature of these global transfers of reproductive care labour. Within sending countries, (re)distributive features can be viewed in terms of the social division of gender, absence of men in the distributive process, as well as racial hierarchies in terms of who is working in place of the absence of the migrating women. In the receiving country, the migrant women nannies replace the working mothers that hide structural gendered divisions of reproductive labour already systematically entrenched.

In 2009, Yeates argued that global care chain analysis should be extended beyond unpaid reproductive labourers to include skilled care professionals such as nurses. Through this extension of the chain analysis, Yeates' conceptualisation of 'global nurse care chains' points to the regulation and organisation of highly skilled and specialised workers in institutional settings by a variety of public agents, provisions, and interests. These meso-level actors and institutions are transnational in terms of geographical space and porous borders of organising. As in global commodity analysis, meso-level actors are considered to be producers and consumers of commodities and/or packages that move along transnational chains or nodes that are nationally and internationally governed and regulated. Institutions that become part of this analysis could be nursing institutions (whether hospital or nursing homes), educational institutions both in the source and host countries, recruitment agencies, training companies, trade unions, nation-states' governance, and international agreements, particularly on ethical recruitment.

This chapter and this book, as a whole, have endeavoured to capture this transnational network of producers and providers of a service, nurse labour, through the management of Filipino nurses for Finnish nursing institutions. Discursively, to investigate and map discourses that are long-range interests (Alvesson and Karreman, 2000) and distal contexts (Wetherell and Potter, 1992) of gender and racialised assumptions and hierarchies would be problematic, as the analysis would be likely to ignore the situational elements of the recruitment and placement practices. This investigation emphasised empirically the discursive positions of Finnish representatives on their practices of recruitment and placement of Filipino nurses during a time of political support and when the producers dominated the space to define how these nurses would be organised. These practices, subsequently, materialised in the workplaces where the recruited nurses were placed and have the potential to structurally control how the future non-Finnish nurses are treated in terms of inclusions and exclusions in workplace practices. Complicity to transnational human resource management practices outside of the traditional empirical divide of 'global integration' and 'local centralization' in the field of IHRM (Ståhl et al., 2012) recasts patriarchies and imperialism in the division of care labour and other unequal power relations that are systematically divided and historically produced. Transnational flows of unequal power relations, specifically in terms of control of the producers and compliance of workers, within practices and discursive positions by dominant producers re(produce) gendered and racialised negotiations that are institutionally embedded in regulatory practices, normative expectations, and rules and behaviours both within and outside the workplace. This embedded and taken-for-granted quality of transnational power relations makes the analysis of the transnational producers of human capital even more important. Conceptualising and empiricialising transnational human resource management stresses a shift in the IHRM field of discipline from a monolithic, centralised conceptualisation of borders and levels of organising to a complex web of various actors, organisations and institutions working with, around, and amongst transnational, multi-linear flows of people and capital.

Summary and Concluding Thoughts

The chapter has attempted to advocate a meso-level analysis of the producers of transnational nurses' labour and how, at this situated level of organising, structural implications in terms of inequality barriers to the local workplace transpire. Specifically, the examined data and discussion on dominant discursive positions within the claims of the representatives' talk and text illustrates a chain or linkage of transnational processes and practices of organising nurse human capital. The transnational process and practices of this organising has the potential to be deconstructed in terms of taken-for-granted or prescribed practices of the dominant representatives. These discursive positions of unequal power relations, in terms of control of the employers or producers and compliance of the recruited workers through historical and colonial institutional mechanisms, socially construct the Filipino nurse as an available raw resource. When materialised, the discourses recast migration pathways into the domestic workforce that are hierarchical in terms of race, gender, and class (mis)representations as well as makes invisible the inequalities amongst the workers organised in a transnational capitalistic economy.

Note

1 Private employment agency association (HPL): union and legal service association for private business employers.

References

Acker, J. (2006) Inequality regimes: Gender, class, and race in organizations. *Gender and Society*, 20(4), pp. 441–464.

Alvesson, M. & Karreman, D. (2000) Varieties of discourse: On the study of organizations through discourse analysis. *Human Relations*, 53(9), pp. 1125–1149.

Asa, R. & Muurinen, H. (2010) *Temporary and circular migration: Empirical evidence, current policy practice, and future options in Finland*. Helsinki: European Migration Network.

Choy, C. (2003) *Empire of care: Nursing and migration in Filipino American history*. Durham: Duke University Press.

Hochschild, A. (2000) Global care chains and emotional surplus value. In W. Hutton & A. Giddens (eds.) *On the edge: Living with global capitalism*. London: Jonathan Cape, pp. 130–146.

Huijser, M. & Huijser, D. (2011) *Managing mindsets*. The Netherlands: Model of Freedom.

Opteam (2008a) *Optimist*. Issue 3. Helsinki: Opteam.

Opteam (2008b) *Optimist*. Issue 4. Helsinki: Opteam.

Ståhl, G. B., Björkman, I. & Morris, S. (eds.) (2012) *Handbook of research in international human resource management*. Cheltenhuam: Edward Elgar Publishing.

Webster, W. (2005). *Imagining home: Gender, race and national identity, 1945–1964*. UK: Routledge.

Wetherell, M. & Potter, J. (1992) *Mapping the language of racism: Discourse and the legitimation of exploitation*. New York: Harvester.

Wrede, S. (2010) How country matters: Studying health policy in a comparative perspective. In I. D. Bourgeault (ed.) *The Sage handbook of qualitative methods in health research*. London: Sage, pp. 88–105.

Yeates, N. (2009) *Globalising care economies and migrant workers: Explorations in global care chains*. Basingstoke: Palgrave Macmillan.

8 Conclusions

This book began as a journey with research questions and ended as a retelling of that journey's story and its situational elements. The premise of the journey and the situated story were based on a research questions that led to a deeper investigation to examine a second research question. The first research questions were (1) Who are the representatives, organisations, and institutions involved in the recruitment and placement of Filipino nurses in Finland?; (2) What social worlds are they representing?; and (3) How do the representatives, organisations, and institutions socially interact and relate?

In September 2008, after presenting my PhD research interests on the international migration of health care workers, it was suggested at a course on postcolonial feminism in Denmark by a fellow Finnish colleague that I should investigate the recent active recruitment of eight Filipino nurses by Finnish private companies. She mentioned that this recruitment had made national and local news in Helsinki, and it would be an interesting empirical case. I came home from the course and decided to enter the field to know more about this case by conducting websearches and reading the local media. I also started to try to make contact with the companies to conduct an ethnographic study on the placement of the Filipino nurses within the elderly care company. I was yet to make sense of the recruitment and placement situation so I wanted a 'theoretical sample' to make notes and reflections of possible data and the data implications. Through the demands of course work, as well as the Finnish companies not answering my postal letters, emails, and phone calls about my research interests, the data collection beyond websearches and media did not begin until January 2010 with my first interview with the Finnish recruitment company (interview #1a).

After the initial access to an interview with Finnish recruitment company, I was emailed a month later by the interviewed representative that the recruitment company was not interested in granting research access because of concerns that information about their practices may be leaked to their competitors. That autumn, the HR director of the recruitment company, presented at the European Migration Network's (EMN) themed conference on the migration of skilled labour. Through my participation at this conference, I observed the presentations of the 'experts' on this migration, and

I received a document with all the participants and their emails. Through this conference, I gained more research access as I emailed some of the participants including the recruitment company. This juncture was crucial as I was able to make myself visible in the discussion as well as more knowledgeable of the field.

From the end of year 2010 to August 2011, I conducted various interviews with participants from the EMN's conference list and through the recommendations of those participants on who else could provide information on my research interests. During this time, I was also invited to participate in some of the informal meetings of both recruited and non-recruited Filipino nurses working in Finland. Through these meetings, I conducted interviews after the meetings or during an arranged time with the nurses.

As I conducted the interviews and collected documents either through participating in events, meetings, or formally arranged interviews, I made notes and tables of the interview data and received documents. Through these notes and tables of the data, representatives began to emerge as central to my analysis of transnational management of nurses. To illustrate the emergence of these representatives recruiting and placing Filipino nurses into Finnish nursing institutions, I created situational maps, both messy and ordered, which became by-products of the story's journey to guide the investigation. Through these maps, I was able to create social world maps informed by the data. In the social world maps, the focal points were an arena or, as Strauss metaphorically calls, a 'battle field'. Through work-oriented social worlds constructed by me with the other maps, the representatives in their associated social worlds enter into an arena where negotiations surrounding the practices of recruitment and placement of Filipino nurses took place. By entering the arena, the representatives produced knowledge claims on how to recruit and place nurses, and the dominant representatives, the trio of Finnish companies in this story, were able to legitimise their dominant roles in the management of non-Finnish nurses in Finland. Through these social actions and negotiations of the representatives, dominant and implicated representatives and social worlds emerged, and the arena became conceptualised to be a 'producer-based care network' (Yeates, 2009). The producer-based care network not only conceptualised the social actions and interactions of the recruitment but also metaphorically described the arena where the nurses are being produced. In this case, the dominant representatives produced 75 Filipino registered nurses through a pre-selection of the nurses on the basis of Finnish customer needs through transnational management of the nurses.

Mapping the Social Worlds of Transnational Human Resource Management

Much like a commodity is linked through a supply chain, migrant nurses who are recruited for selected destinations intersect with transnational processes and practices. This mobility and physical organising allows nurses to be recruited, relocated, and resettled in other areas of the world. Nurses are human capital and are interlinked at various levels of social organising through, for instance, individuality and families. Subsequently, the transnationalisation of care links people, institutions, nation-states, and places across politically and socially defined borders.

To illustrate the various links in the transnationalisation of care, Hochschild (2000) developed the concept of 'global care chains' to examine connections within the transnationalisation of reproductive care labour such as private child care. With the use of 'global care chains', Hochschild's analysis focuses on the familial/micro levels of various people (mostly women) migrating from poorer to wealthier economies to work in paid domestic care. These chains serve to highlight the links between the service-providers (the migrant care workers and their families) and the service-recipients (the private employers and their families). As the concept of GCCs derives from global commodity analysis (GCommC), this analysis also considers the mechanisms of production and exchange of care labour, the creation of value and distribution of care labour within the chains, and the emotional as well as material inputs into the transnationalisation of care. This analysis situates the chains in wider social-economic inequalities deriving from hierarchies of nation-states, classes, genders, ethnic groups, and families. The conceptualisation of the chain is also a metaphor that derives from global commodity analysis, which constructs links through the movements of industrialised commodities not human labour.

Yeates (2009, 2011) extends Hoshchild's GCCs to include skilled migrants such as nurses with her concept 'Global Nurse Care Chains' (GNCCs). Global Nurse Care Chains consider migrant nurses as highly skilled professionals with qualifications that can be regulated in institutional settings by a variety of public and private agents, provisions, and interests. GNCCs consist of many actors and institutions such as nursing institutions (e.g. elderly care facilities and hospitals), educational institutions in the sending and receiving countries of the nurse labour, recruitment agencies, training companies, governance (state ministries and regulatory bodies), and international agreements. Other groups that influence the chains are trade unions, NGOs, advocacy groups, as well as friends, families, and colleagues that facilitate the entry into the chains either through financial or emotional support. These actors and institutions like GCCs form a global value chain and are considered to be producers, service-providers, and consumers (e.g. patients) that are regulated and governed, and yet the chains are far from linear in directional force.

Visually and to provide a deeper understanding of the practices of transnational human resource management, I strove to map the representatives of organisations claiming authority on and about the recruitment and placement of the Filipino nurses from 2007 to 2010. The representatives, within the talk and text, legitimised and negotiated their work roles, commitments, and mandates to enter the domain of producing nurses for the local labour market, whether or not their organisations were directly involved with the Filipino nurse recruitment.

Transnational Human Resource Management: A Theoretical Contribution

International human resource management (IHRM), as a discipline and field of study, has been subjected to critique by management and organisational scholars for a lack of engagement with the discipline's dominant epistemological stance of 'functionalist-positivism' (Jack et al., 2008). The epistemological stance has favoured prescribed and instrumental theories and methods of understanding the management of people in various geographical contexts through multinational corporations (MNCs), multinational enterprises (MNEs), and/or transnational corporations (TNCs). The people being managed within these organisations are working either in headquarters or subsidiaries and are often conceptualised as expats or locals. These dual geographical divisions of management across nation-state borders are viewed in terms of centralisation (global integration) versus decentralisation (local responsivess) and organised around the production of global capital (Ståhl et al., 2012).

Many scholars have argued that the IHRM field's narrow focus prompts an inefficient examination of the research's inclusions, exclusions, and its effects such as the reproduction of universalist assumptions that marginalise voices and decontextualise practices (Westwood, 2006; Nkomo, 1992; Jack et al., 2008). The discipline's managerial and functionalist approach to the field, as argued by Delbridge et al. (2011), also limits the scope of examining social and structural questions such as the production of knowledge and power amongst various actors through negotiations and networks, the situatedness of managing people, and the economic and political institutions and structures regulating borders in which practice and people cross. This narrow scope to the examination of the management of human resources may also explain why the field privileges MNCs, MNEs, and TCs as empirical entry points to the field as these examinations spend little focus on other levels of organising. Other levels of organising are, for example, meso levels of nation-state governance where representatives are interacting and networking to produce, manage, and gain profit from the human resources from more regulated sectors of health and social service sectors.

In this book, I have wanted to engage with the discipline of international human resource management (IHRM) by empirically highlighting actors, organisations, and institutions that are practicing human resource management (for instance, recruitment and placement of human capital) across national borders through complex networks of historically and socially situated practices and processes. These private actors are not recognised in the conventional analysis of MNCs producing global capital that gain financial profit from the production of reproductive care labour in the sectors of health and social services. These services are highly regulated by nation-states, and the sectors are predominately made up of female employees.

Socially situating the management of human resources locally and at a meso level questions prescribed models and practices that control people in socially constructed ways that are historically gendered, racialised, and classed. Occupations within the health care sector have been empirically analysed as hierarchical in terms of gender (Davies, 1992; Mackay, 1989), and class (Apesoa-Varano and Varano, 2004). When health care workers migrate abroad, either through their own initiatives or through the active recruitment of an agency, the intersectionalities of gender, class, and race impact the transnational practices of the various representatives interacting in networks to move human resources from a source country to a receiving country. Scholars have revealed that gendered, racialised, and classed transnational practices of migrating health care workers, particularly nurses, have led the workers into career trajectories of downward mobility in terms of occupational seniority and overall financial status through a lack of education recognition (Ho, 2008; McNeil-Walsh, 2008). Furthermore, as pointed out in Ribeiro's study (2008), institutional conditions and regulatory control mechanisms of the nursing occupation have created both female migratory tracks towards low-status professional segments and new intra-professional divisions that reflect the status of citizenship and place of graduation of the migrant nurses.

In this book, I suggested a transnational feminist framework (transnational + feminist). The transnational conceptualisation is critical of the concept 'international', which suggests rigid borders between nation-states and within processes of connectivity between people, ideas, and organising. The feminist lens deconstructs social constructions of organising workers and questions issues of representations particularly in terms of exclusion, inclusion, and organising control within institutionalised practices. These focal points of transnational feminisms are discussed in terms of real material implications on worker's bodies and lives. Reconceptualising IHRM as transnational human resource management (THRM) situates HRM practices in terms of geography, structures, economies, and societal and ideological histories that intersect with gender, race, and class. Transnational intersections of structures, identities, and practices interact in networks within the transnationalisation of care labour providing space for an empirical examination of dominant discourses and practices that have material implications on domestic and transnational workforces of care labour.

Transnational feminists' works, which I discussed in Chapter 3, framed my theoretical understanding of transnational feminisms and my subsequent data analysis in terms of the intersections of gender, race, and class. These socially constructed intersections recast the transnational organisational control of workers' lives, particularly women, with material and structural implications. These material and structural implications not only impact the physical and social lives of nurses (e.g. salaries, occupation status, family reunification, where the workers live), but also the future institutionalised pathways of other recruited non-Finnish nurses or workers.

Transnational Human Resource Management of Nurses: An Empirical Contribution

This book examined the transnationalisation of care through value chains of nurse work like Global Nurse Care Chains. Specifically, the book strived to understand the representatives, organisations, and institutions involved in the recruitment and placement of Filipino nurses into Finnish nursing institutions (elderly care facilities and surgical wards in hospitals). Between the years of 2008 and 2010, a Finnish recruitment company recruited 75 Filipino nurses in five groups for Finnish nursing institutions. The first, second, and fourth group of Filipino nurses were placed in a private elderly care company and the third group were place in the Hospital District of Helsinki and Ussimaa (HUS) and Tampere University Hospital [TAUH].

In 2007, a trio of Finnish companies publically announced in the local media that the organisations would collaborate to bring hundreds of Filipino nurses to Finland. Although the organisations invested time and money into the social action of recruiting, placing, and training the Filipino nurses for work in Finland, a deeper analysis of the situation reveals various Finnish private and public representatives, organisations, and institutions working within the production of the recruited Filipino nurses for Finnish customers.

The Finnish representatives and their organisations conduct their work (in this case the recruitment and placement of Filipino nurses) within social worlds. The social worlds reflected the representatives and organisation's work objectives and roles as well as the deeper commitments to the work in the social world. This commitment to a social world reflects what the representatives consider meaningful, and the representatives maintain their commitment to the social world through negotiations, maintaining boundaries, and gaining social legitimisation for the world itself.

The first research questions asked:

1) Who are the representatives, organisations, and institutions involved in the recruitment and placement of Filipino nurses in Finland?
2) What social worlds are they representing?
3) How do the representatives, organisations, and institutions socially interact and relate?

I explained that although there are various private and public actors negotiating within the arena of producer-based care networks, the trio of Finnish companies, through various discursive resources, dominate the arena and discursively legitimise themselves as experts. This dominance created an authoritative voice for the three organisations on how and by whom the recruitment of Filipino nurses is conducted within the discursive positions.

As the book addressed the practices of recruitment and placement of Filipino nurses by various representatives and their respective social worlds, the second research question examined the discursive positions about the practices amongst the representatives interacting and working in social worlds. The second research question asked:

> How, through discursive positions in the claims of the produced talk and text, are the representatives and organisations socially constructing the practices of recruitment and placement of Filipino nurses in Finland?

Through the analysis of the collective discursive positions amongst the representatives, social constructions of the Filipino nurse as warm and caring and the Philippines as a supply country of nurse human capital becomes legitimised and naturalised amongst the other representatives. Other discursive positions on practices such retraining the Filipino registered nurses to work as practical nurses and testing the levels of Finnish language abilities through regulatory mechanisms materialise in the nurses' workplace through deskilling, low salaries, and long working hours during a six-month apprenticeship. These practices, which create hierarchies amongst the nurses in terms of ethnicity, nationality, and linguistic use, were justified through the discursive position of cultural differences between the employers and the recruited nurses and ethical recruitment in which the representative comply to domestic and international regulations and laws.

To map the social worlds in which the representatives interact and negotiate through various discourses and discursive resources, this book used the method of situational analysis. Situational analysis provides cartographic approaches to various elements in the situation and asks the question 'what are the conditions in the situation?' As discussed through the conceptualisation of Global Nurse Care Chains, investigating empirically the networks of various private and public actors, organisations, and institutions that work and negotiate in transnational processes of care labour requires deep exploration. By situating the empirical study, the study examined the different actors in the chains and the nuances of practices within the transnationalisation of care.

Mapping Social Worlds in the Arena of Producer-Based Care Networks: A Methodological Contribution

In the book, I have created cartographic maps of seven social worlds: (1) advocacy and advisory of nurse occupation, (2) education and training, (3) third sector, (4) private business and corporate, (5) national security and police, (6) municipal/city governance, and (7) regulation and advisory of national health and social welfare. These categories of social worlds in the maps derived from the interviews with the representatives and the documents functioning in the work organisations. The worlds were based on the collective social action reflected in actions such as work responsibilities of the representatives, vision and mandates of the organisations, and the organisation's goals, such as to make profit or sell products or services to clients.

The arena that the social worlds emerged onto was entitled 'producer-based care networks'. This concept developed by Yeates (2011) captures the network of various public and private actors, organisations, and institutions recruiting, placing, and settling labour transnationally. In other words, the producers of labour negotiate practices and discourses within the transnationalisation of care. Production of the transnationalisation of care takes structural and material forms through practices and discourses of the producers, which have various implications on the recruited nurse's life such as how and where the nurse works, what the nurse is paid, and how the nurse is constructed as employees in the workplace.

As discussed in Chapter 6, the dominant representatives emerging in the producer-based care networks were the trio of Finnish companies and their associated social worlds with the social action of transnational management of Filipino nurses. The collective discourses of these representatives and social worlds were constructed as private business and corporate, third sector, and education and training. As these social worlds dominated the arena, the agenda of making profit and packaging nurses in compliance with the needs of the Finnish customers (in this case private elderly care institutions and public hospitals) became a legitimate practice. Subsequently, structural barriers to inequality within the domestic workforce in terms of language, recognised qualifications, race, and gender became silenced as a legitimate discourse in the recruitment of the nurses. The recruited nurses were socially implicated to fit the needs and goals of the producers. The structural barriers led to the control of the recruited workforce, but also these practices materialised in the interviews with the recruited and non-recruited nurses through talked-about behaviours of compliance with Finnish language as the language restriction was perceived as a temporary limitation until the language was acquired. And, yet, after the language was fluent, the Filipino nurses still talked about feeling they were being ignored and facing limited career mobility.

Strauss (1978) and Clarke (1991) methodologically examine social worlds and representatives of those worlds at situated national and local levels. The scholars functioned in the disciplinary fields of sociology and health sciences, and through empirical investigation, the scholars mapped social worlds based on 'conditions within the situation' as influenced by grounded theory. Strauss and his colleagues empirically investigated institutional settings such as mental health hospitals, and Clarke's work centralised on reproductive medicine and techniques (e.g. Clarke and Montini, 1993).

In this book, the 'conditions of the situation' were institutionally situated in Finnish nursing institutions but also moved across national boundaries (Hearn, 2004) through transnational process and practices of organising nurse human capital. This book builds on Strauss' and Clarke's social world maps by adding a transnational dimension that not only extended the situational boundaries, but also problematised these boundaries. The critical extension of these boundaries also aimed to explore other actors and institutions that are producing nurse capital and may be unrecognised in the investigation of managing and organising nurse human capital from outside national borders.

Policy Implications

In this book, structural mechanisms, particularly in terms of institutional, national, and international policy and law regulations, have been addressed in terms of THRM practices as well as discursive positions dominated by representatives in the producer-based care network.

Before 2006, discourses and practices concerning the migration of people to Finland were organised and viewed largely in terms of refugees and family ties. Work-based immigration was, statistically, low, particularly in comparison to other European countries. Because of this immigrant demographic, national and municipal policies and practices centralised on 'social integration' (learning Finnish language and receiving state social financial benefits) instead of work or economic-related integration. In 2006, the former government of Matti Vanhanen introduced, for the first time in Finland, an immigration programme and ministerial action plan with the intention to promote employment-based immigration or make Finland more 'attractive' to migrating professionals. As the action plan was to increase professional immigration to Finland, it was suggested, through recommendations of governmental projects, that private companies should be contracted for active recruitment from abroad and that the recruitment should be based on Finnish employer's needs. A space of opportunity was opened for private companies in the arena of the producer-based care network because of political support and political directives.

Through the domination of private and corporate social worlds within the producer-based care network, future national and municipal policies were influenced with the work agenda of the dominant social world. In this case, the private and corporate social world, in which the trio of Finnish companies function, is oriented to private financial investment for a return in financial profits. They recruited and packaged 75 Filipino nurses, through a transnationally regulated process of deskilling, for the Finnish elderly care company who requested practical nurses, without their families, willing to learn Finnish and work for a basic salary while requalifying and completing an apprenticeship. In terms of immigrant integration such as language training, education recognition, state benefits, family reunification, workplace salaries, and professional status, these social constructions of the Filipino nurses and the Philippines as an ideal exporter of pre-selected packages reinforce transnational hierarchies and institutionalised these practices through knowledge claims on how to recruit future nurses.

Not the End of the Journey: Future Research Possibilities

This is not the end of this journey's story. In this book, a situated case study of the recruitment and placement of 75 Filipino nurses by Finnish private companies served to highlight a more complex phenomenon of transnational human resource management.

These transnational human resource management practices organised nurses who work in an occupation that has been empirically documented as socially and historically gendered, racialised, and classed. Through transnational flows of migrants, individualised 'push' and 'pull' factors that have been widely used by the World Health Organisation, as well as other international authorities on global health, do not encompass the multi-linear and multi-linked transnational flows of actors, organisations, processes, and practices that define and redefine transnational patterns of care workers' migration.

Ignoring and complicity enacting transnational practices of managing nurses that reproduce what Acker entitles 'inequality regimes' (2006) may comply with the demands of the Finnish private employers and recruiters for a flexible, transient workforce. Nonetheless, this workforce may become unsustainable for not only the producers, non-Finnish and Finnish nurses, but also the Finnish Nordic welfare state as the migrating nurses view Finland not as a country to lay down roots but as a 'stepping stone' to more desirable countries in terms of pay, professional trajectories, and equal opportunities.

Building from this case, future research could investigate other groups of recruited nurses by Nordic private actors (e.g. recruitment agencies and private elderly care facilities) as well as public actors (such as hospitals) from countries within and outside the European Union. Examination of transnational conditions (e.g. actors, institutions, networks) may be mapped to investigate further emerging conditions and provide more information and insight on HRM practices of inclusion and exclusion.

Furthermore, deeper investigation of the transnationalisation of care beyond macro and micro levels that centralise on statistically generated patterns of migration as well as the nurses' experiences and subjectivities can shed light on power relations of institutionalised control and compliance at the meso level, which potentially perpetuates an uneven development of transnational health care systems. Working towards an integrated agenda that recognises conditional and situated organisation of care transnationalisation questions wider developmental impacts of social and economic restructuring within Nordic welfare states and the other countries.

References

Acker, J. (2006) Inequality regimes: Gender, class, and race in organizations. *Gender and Society*, 20(4), pp. 441–464.
Apesoa-Varano, E. C. & Varano, C. S. (2004) Nurse and labour activism in the United States: The role of class, gender, and ideology. *Social Justice*, 31(3), pp. 77–104.
Clarke, A. (1991) Social worlds/arena theory as organizational theory. In D. R. Maines (ed.) *Social organization and social process*. New York: Aldine de Gruyter, pp. 119–158.
Clarke, A. (2005) *Situational analysis: Grounded theory after the postmodern turn*. Thousand Oaks: Sage.
Clarke, A. & Montini, T. (1993) The many faces of RU486: Tales of situated knowledges and technological contestations. *Science, Technology, and Human Values*, 18(1), pp. 42–78.
Davies, C. (1992) *Gender and the professional predicament in nursing*. Buckingham, UK: Open University Press.
Delbridge, R., Hauptmeier, M. & Sengupta, S. (2011) Beyond the enterprise: Broadening the horizons of international HRM. *Human Relations*, 64(4), pp. 483–505.
Hearn, J. (2004) Tracking "the transnational": Studying transnational organizations and managements, and the management of cohesion. *Culture and Organization*, 10(4), pp. 273–290.
Ho, C. (2008) Chinese nurses in Australia: Migration, work, and identity. In J. Connell (ed.) *The international migration of health workers*. New York: Routledge, pp. 147–163.
Hochschild, A. (2000) Global care chains and emotional surplus value. In W. Hutton & A. Giddens (eds.) *On the edge: Living with global capitalism*. London: Jonathan Cape, pp. 130–146.
Jack, G., Calás, M. B., Nkomo, S. M. & Peltonen, T. (2008) Critique and international management: An uneasy relationship. *Academy of Management Review*, 33(4), pp. 870–884.
Mackay, L. (1989) *Nursing a problem*. New York: McGraw-Hill.
McNeil-Walsh, C. (2008) Migrant nurses and the experiences of skill: South Africa nurses in UK health care sector. In J. Connell (ed.) *International migration of health care workers*. New York: Routledge, pp. 129–146.
Nkomo, S. M. (1992) The emperor has no clothes: Rewriting "race in organizations". *Academy of Management Review*, 17(3), pp. 487–513.
Ribeiro, J. Sousa (2008) Gendering migration flows: Physicians and nurses in Portugal. *Equal Opportunities International*, 27(1), pp. 77–87.
Ståhl, G. B., Björkman, I. & Morris, S. (eds.) (2012) *Handbook of research in international human resource management*. Cheltenhuam: Edward Elgar Publishing.
Strauss, A. L. (1978) A social worlds perspective. *Studies in Symbolic Interaction*, 1, pp. 119–128.
Westwood, R. (2006) International business and management studies as an orientalist discourse: A postcolonial critique. *Critical Perspectives on International Business*, 2(2), pp. 91–113.
Yeates, N. (2009) *Globalising care economies and migrant workers: Explorations in global care chains*. Basingstoke: Palgrave Macmillan.
Yeates, N. (2011) Going global: The transnationalization of care. *Development and Change*, 42(4), pp. 1109–1130.

Appendix

Table of Interviews

Interview number with representative	*Year of Interview*	*Social World*	*Affiliated work organisation*
Interview #1a and b	2010; 2011	Private Business and Corporate	Private recruitment company in Finland
Interview #2	2010	Nurse occupation and the Philippines	Finnish elderly care institutions
Interview #3	2010	Private Business and Corporate	Private recruitment company in Finland
Interview #4a	2011	Nurse occupation and the Philippines	Finnish elderly care institutions
Interview #4b	2011	Nurse occupation and the Philippines	Finnish elderly care institutions
Interview #4c	2011	Nurse occupation and the Philippines	Finnish elderly care institutions
Interview #5	2011	Advocacy and advisory of nurse occupation	The Union of Health and Social Care Professionals in Finland (TeHy)
Interview #6	2011	Advocacy and advisory of nurse occupation	Practical nurse union in Finland (SuPer)
Interview #7	2011	National security, police, and the European Union	Ministry of Interior (Intermin) and European Social Fund(ESF) (ALPO and MATTO project)

Interview number with representative	*Year of Interview*	*Social World*	*Affiliated work organisation*
Interview #8a	2011	Regulation and advisory of national health and social welfare	The National Supervisory authority for welfare and health (Valvira)
Interview #8b	2011	Regulation and advisory of national health and social welfare	The National Supervisory authority for welfare and health (Valvira)
Interview #9a	2011	Municipal/city governance	City of Helsinki
Interview #9b	2011	Municipal/city governance	City of Helsinki
Interview #10a	2011	Private Business and Corporate	Private adult education centre in Finland
Interview #10b	2011	Private Business and Corporate	Private adult education centre in Finland
Interview #11a	2011	Nurse occupation and the Philippines	Finnish elderly care institutions
Interview #11b	2011	Nurse occupation and the Philippines	Finnish elderly care institutions
Interview #11c	2011	Nurse occupation and the Philippines	Finnish elderly care institutions
Interview #12	2011	National security and polices	The Finnish Ministry of Interior (Intermin)
Interview #13	2011	Nurse occupation and the Philippines	Finnish elderly care institutions
Interview #14	2011	National security, police, and the European Union	The Finnish Migration Services (MIGRI)
Interview #15a	2011	Nurse occupation and the Philippines	Finnish elderly care institutions
Interview #15b	2011	Nurse occupation and the Philippines	Finnish elderly care institutions

(*Continued*)

Interview number with representative	*Year of Interview*	*Social World*	*Affiliated work organisation*
Interview #16	2011	Private Business and Corporate	Private employment agency association (HPL): Union and legal service association for private business employers
Interview #17	2011	Labour and Economy in Finland	Ministry of Employment and Economy (TEM)
Interview #18	2011	Private Business and Corporate	The Finnish elderly care services company

Index

Note: Page numbers in *italics* indicate figures and in **bold** indicate tables on the corresponding pages.